Treasures Of
Darkness

By Miriam Ruth Malachi

Published by BAC Printers
9 Kallang Place #04-09
Singapore 339154
Tel: (65) 62912525 • Fax: (65) 62965588

Copyright © 2002 by Miriam Ruth Malachi
Second Edition 2005
Third Edition 2008

Printed in Singapore

ISBN 981-04-6633-1

Bible translations taken from the New American Standard,
New King James, and New International Versions
(All emphasis in bold or italics by Miriam Ruth Malachi)

Table of Contents

Preface

"And I will give you
The **treasures of darkness**,
Riches stored in **secret places**,
So that you may know
That it is I, The Lord, the God of Israel,
Who calls you by name."
(Isaiah 45:3)

Darkness is covering the earth, even thick darkness, but there are _treasures_ hidden in the shadows, _spiritual riches_ in secret places. The Lord had been giving me Isaiah 45:1-4 for years, and I always believed it referred to supernatural provision for the fulfillment of His Kingdom purposes in my life. It wasn't until I moved to Jerusalem that I came to realize that, while it may also be referring to hidden wealth in the natural, the promise was speaking primarily and particularly about the Ultra-Orthodox. Even as I write these words, an excitement is swelling in my heart that the _mountains will be leveled_, and _the gates of bronze and bars of iron will one day break open!_

This guide is designed for intercessors that have a burden for the Ultra-Orthodox, particularly the Chasidim, in the hope that it will provide greater understanding of this community, insight into what the enemy has planted that needs to be uprooted in prayer, and suggested ways to pray.

While searching for materials describing the lifestyle of the Ultra-Orthodox, the owner of a religious bookstore told me quite frankly, "Why would anyone want to write a book about the Ultra-Orthodox? If you're on the inside, then you already know what's going on. If you're on the outside, you only think you know what's going on, but

5

no one's going to tell you what's really happening." Because the Ultra-Orthodox system is a *closed system*, this writing will not be an exhaustive treatment by any means. I have learned what I will be sharing primarily from general sources, public literature written by Chasidic authors, observations in the neighborhood on numerous prayerwalks, asking questions whenever I can, learning from those who are still in the system, but secretly believe in Messiah, and those who have come out and are open believers. Our journey into the Ultra-Orthodox world is for the purpose of *heart focus to inspire prayer.*

While the book is separated by chapter headings, there is a degree of overlapping as these issues are deeply intertwined both in the Scripture and in Jewish history. The hope is to gain an appreciation of how the enemy has spun a web of deception that overlaps and builds upon itself unto the present day so that our prayers may be most effective in setting the captives free. As such, this is not a scholarly work, nor is it intended for academic pursuit, head knowledge, or to wet the appetite of readers to traverse the mystical universe of the Ultra-Orthodox.

> *"But solid food is for the mature,*
> *Who by constant use*
> *Have trained themselves*
> *To distinguish good from evil."*
> *(Hebrews 5:14)*

Discerning truth from error is a hallmark of our maturity in Messiah Jesus. The grace to rightly divide the Word of God is a weapon of our warfare and a safeguard against deception. To the degree that we are abiding in the Branch, we come under the wings of His protection, we bear fruit that lasts, showing that we are His disciples, and are able to teach others, advancing His Kingdom for future generations. This guide to understanding and praying for the Ultra-Orthodox is dedicated to Jesus (Yeshua), my precious Lord and to the remnant of Israel that will come to know their Messiah because of the intercession it seeks to inspire. *Jesus literally saved my life.* He is the lover of my soul, my Savior, and Husband. I am a lover of Zion and called to

Jerusalem, but Jerusalem is not the love of my life. *Jesus is the love of my life* and, by the grace of God, as I keep my eyes fixed on Him, and purpose to exalt Him as my first love, He will keep me in perfect peace, balanced in doctrine, of sound mind, and protected from the seducing spirits of these latter days.

My Testimony

"Praise be to the Lord,
For He showed His wonderful love towards me
When I was in a besieged city."
(Psalm 31:21)

The angel of death was at my door. It was getting dark and in roughly sixty minutes I would leave my dormitory room and retreat to a wooded area of the university campus and quietly end my misery. I had given myself two weeks to build up the nerve to go through with the plan and now I was equipped with the necessary courage and an assortment of uppers and downers reminiscent of the hippie era. In this driven frame of mind, the unexpected knock on my door was disturbing. Two college girls were standing in the hallway, with glowing faces expressing concern. "We live upstairs and we were praying and God told us to come to *this room* because there's someone here in trouble." *Wow!* I should have been grateful for this miracle, and the friendly gesture of these young ladies, but the truth is, I wasn't happy to see them. Instead of falling on my knees and giving my life to God, I tried to discredit them with a sweet mocking tone, "Really? There's nobody here in trouble, but thanks for coming," and I started to close the door.

I am alive to write these words because these young intercessors were so confident they heard from God. They placed their hands on the door and persisted in a very gentle manner. "No, no, we're sure. It's *this* room. There's a *crisis* in *this room.* Could we come in for just a moment and talk?" In an effort to get rid of them, I agreed that, if it would make them feel better, they could come in and say what they had to say, but to make it snappy because I didn't have much time. As they stepped from the hallway into my room, just taking that one step, they brought in a *presence* I never felt before in my life and it *filled* the room. I wouldn't have known to call it *holiness,* but it was pure, clean, full of love, and radically different from the hell raging in my tiny prison of hopelessness. "God *loves* you," their voices beamed with enthusiasm, "You're *precious* to Him, and there's something He wants to do with your life He can't do through anyone else. He has a special *purpose* for you."

Although I was raised Catholic, I had never really heard that God loved me or cared about me in a personal way. Then the girls asked if they could *"pray"* for me. Well, all I knew about prayer was the "Our Father," "Hail Mary," and other 'pre-arranged' petitions. For me, prayer was a meaningless exercise, but there was nothing "canned" about their words. They were fresh manna from heaven. These two sisters laid their hands on me and prayed *powerful, personal, prophetic* prayers. They talked to God like they *knew* Him and what really impressed me was that they spoke to Him as if He was a *kind and gentle Person.* They *prayed from the heart* and I had never heard anything like this before. As they were praying over me, the wall in my heart of fear, anger, and rebellion began to crack. Through the tears, I confided, "Alright, you don't know what I was about to do. If *God* loves me, I'll take *God. But I don't want Jesus.* I don't want that morbid, creepy, spooky dead guy on the cross." You see, that's the only Jesus I knew, and, in that moment, without realizing it, I was thinking very much like a Jewish person. I know what it's like to want the *Father*, but not want the *Son*, because the image of the Son you've been given is so mangled and distorted, it's nothing like who Jesus really is.

In that moment, there was a battle for my soul. If the enemy can't destroy us before we find the Lord, he will try to derail us into religion without Jesus, or even religion with another Jesus. That night, the girls contended against the lies of the enemy, assuring me, "The Person we prayed to, the Person who sent us to this room, the Person who loves you, is Jesus, and He's not dead, He's alive!" They invited me to attend a campus meeting later that weekend and promised there would be no strings attached and that they wouldn't even be there. And they weren't. I never saw these two precious ladies again. *They could have been angels.* All I know is that the speaker at this meeting gave the most thrilling, profound teaching about the resurrection I ever heard and it opened my eyes to see the Bible wasn't just fairy tales. It was *history!*

I was born again and started reading the Scriptures for the first time. I didn't know the first thing about a burden, a vision, or a calling. I only wanted to know *who this God was* that took the trouble to save my life. People commit suicide every day. Why did He stop *me*? I was ravenous for Him and devouring His Word like a sponge. In pursuing Him so fervently, I stumbled upon a precious truth — simply that when we seek God purely for Himself, when we're not asking Him for anything, only desiring to know Him more deeply, *He begins talking.* I soaked in the Scriptures, literally falling in love with Him at the turning of each new page. After several readings, I came to the Book of Ezekiel, Chapters 2 and 3, and experienced an encounter with the Lord I will never forget. All of sudden, the words of these chapters were lifted off the page, they became living, breathing words. I wasn't reading them. They were being *imparted* to me. I found myself on my face weeping from the depths of a well in my spirit I didn't know existed and God was pouring into me His love for Israel. He was flooding me with waves of revelation and saying two things simultaneously, " I love My people like a husband loves a wife. I am passionate and jealous for her and, oh, how I long to capture and draw her to Myself, surround her with my love and bless her." I could feel the holy desire of God, His burning passion to pursue the beloved, His firstborn, His inheritance, His wife.

The tears were welling up from the *unbearable grief* in the heart of God, the *agony of rejection*: "I love My people so much, but I can't get their love. *My wife has left Me.* They turn away from Me and don't know who I Am." The God of Israel was literally weeping through me, travailing for His lost children. This was not an expression of anger, but the groanings of a *broken heart*. As this visitation progressed, the Lord spoke to me personally. It was the first time I ever heard His voice and I haven't heard it on this level of intensity very many times since. It was based on the Ezekiel passages and very clear, "I'm sending you to the House of Israel." From that moment, my heart has burned for the salvation of the Jewish people, with a particular burden for the Ultra-Orthodox.

"So I went down to the potter's house,
and I saw him working at the wheel.
But the pot he was shaping from the clay
*Was **marred** in his hands;*
So the potter formed it into another pot,
Shaping it as seemed best to him.
(Jeremiah 18:2-4)

The heart of God is to bless and fulfill His purposes for our lives. But first He must *break us* of any sense that we are a *good* person, that we *deserve* anything from Him, or even that we could fulfill His destiny for our lives *in our own strength,* leaning on our *spiritual gifts,* or *natural talents.* He must bring us to the threshing floor and winnow the chaff so the *wheat* can be used for His Kingdom and glory. Whether He accomplishes this purging through a prolonged illness, a personal failure, the death of a loved one, or the loss of a business, His purpose is to *shape us into another vessel, fit for the Master's use.*

Many years later, I was married and divorced. Divorce is a personal and spiritual *failure.* The enemy of my soul had convinced me it was the *worst* failure, that God was now finished with me, and I came to believe I would never fulfill the call upon my life concerning the House of Israel. I gave up on myself, along with a few others, and even backslid for a season. When I most needed the *grace* of God, I didn't know how to grab hold of it. Praise the Lord, the Good Shepherd did not give up on me. He sought me out, gently draped me on His shoulders like a little lamb and led me to a congregation where I would go through a season of *deep repentance, inner healing,* and *deliverance.* I was to discover the *beauty* and *power* of genuine repentance, which begins with the recognition and acknowledgement of our *absolute spiritual bankruptcy.* To my utter amazement, during these years of humbling myself before the Almighty, He would not only wipe away my sins as far as the east is from the west, but would re-commission me and literally send me to the nation of Israel!

"for the gifts and calling of God
are irrevocable."
(Romans 11:29)

I can give testimony to the blessed truth of these words. Only later would I begin to appreciate that when God is building a prophetic intercessor, He may actually permit us to *experience the thing we will be praying for* because He doesn't want us praying from some lofty, self-righteous perch of condescension or condemnation. God is going to give Israel a new heart. I know what it is like to have a *hard heart.* Israel *failed to live up to her calling.* I have experienced the suffering and heartache to the Father of failing to remain faithful to my calling for a season. Like Israel, I know what it is to *profane the name of the Lord* among the nations, so to speak. And yet, wonderfully, because the gifts and calling of God are *irrevocable* (Hallelujah!), He mercifully brings us through and never gives up on the good work He began in us. If God is faithful to restore *a grafted-in one* like me, *how much more* will He delight in fulfilling all His good promises to His chosen people Israel!

Preparing For Battle

"And when they began singing and praising,
The Lord set ambushes against the
Sons of Ammon, Moab, and Mount Seir,
Who had come against Judah; so they were routed."
(II Chronicles 20:22)

Let Judah go up first! Jehoshaphat sent worshippers in *holy attire* to lead the army of Judah into battle against Moab and the Ammonites. The Lord graciously responded by *setting ambushes* and *routing the enemy. Worship is our heartfelt expression of love to God, but it is also warfare.* We enter His gates with thanksgiving, bow before His Throne, pour out our adoration, exalt the mighty Name of Jesus, and praise Him for what He will do as if He has already done it. *As we lift Yeshua up, the enemies of His Kingdom fall down.*

As we pray for the Ultra-Orthodox, we need to keep a few essentials in mind. First, the Father is *seeking worshippers* who will worship Him in Spirit and in truth (John 4:23-24). Second, Jesus came to *set the captives free* (Luke 4:17-19).

Yeshua gave His life so that captives could be transformed into worshippers. Love of God and love of truth must kiss each other if our worship and warfare is to be pleasing and effective.

Our spirits must soar up to heaven while our feet remain rooted and grounded in the truth of God's Word.

"And I searched for a man among them
Who should build up the wall
And stand in the gap before Me

For the land, that I should not have to destroy it;
But I found no one."
(Ezekiel 22:30)

As in the days of Ezekiel, God is *searching* for intercessors who will faithfully stand in the gap so that He can pour out *mercy,* so that His Kingdom, manifested in the *fruit* of the Spirit, along with signs and wonders in the *power* of the Spirit, can bring hope, deliverance, and salvation to a person or a nation in distress. Intercession is *praying beyond yourself*, standing in the place of prayer between life and death, whether spiritual or physical. The two young ladies who came to my dormitory in 1974 prevented me from taking my life. My mother was praying for me in those dark days. Her prayers touched the heart of God and paved the way for His mercy to flow into my life.

When we stand in the gap for a person or nation, we position ourselves in the breach that is *between God's perfect will* and *the place where they are spiritually at this moment.* This gap is the place of *judgment.* In the place of wrath, we plead for mercy because of the *righteousness of Messiah*, not our own righteousness. We appeal to God on the basis of the *Blood of the Lamb* that was shed for the forgiveness of sin and the fountain of mercy that flows from this sacrifice.

"Now if you obey Me fully
And keep my covenant,
Then out of all the nations
You will be My treasured possession.
Although the whole earth is mine,
You will be for me
*A **kingdom of priests** and a **holy nation**."*
(Exodus 19:5-6)

As intercessors, we stand before God as *priests* who minister first *unto Him* and then *on behalf of others.* Although the entire nation of Israel was called to be a *holy nation*, under the Old Covenant, it was the *tribe of Levi* and the descendants of Aaron that were chosen as the *priestly family.* The Levites ministered before the Lord in the duties of the temple, but only the High Priest was privileged to enter the Holy of Holies once a year to present the atoning sacrifice for the nation. The priests were to be *separated unto God* and *a walk of holiness* to define their lives. Even their garments were to be sacred and undefiled. God commanded that Aaron and his sons be *washed, consecrated,* and *anointed* for service. An animal was sacrificed for personal sin and then some of the blood was placed on their right *earlobe*, right *thumb*, and right *big toe*. This symbolized the privilege of the priests to hear the voice of God and dedicate all they hear to the service of God, that the work of their hands would be devoted to God, and that their personal walk would follow the path of holiness. These same areas were then touched with the sacred *anointing oil* following the *application of the blood*.

The Holy Spirit will manifest His power and anointing only upon the life of a person who has been first *washed in the Blood of the Lamb*. Just as the sons of Aaron were *born into* their calling to serve as priests, we are *born into* the kingdom of priests by *new birth* in Messiah. Effective intercession prays with *faith* that God hears our prayers and will answer exceedingly, abundantly, beyond what we could ask or think and is fueled by the *power of the Holy Spirit*. The Spirit lifts our prayers to heaven just as the wings of a 747 lift it off the runway, gives utterance when we know not how to pray, and imparts discernment and revelation in the midst of prayer.

The dual strategies of prayer for the priestly army can be seen as a double-edged sword: *intercession and spiritual warfare*. Generally speaking, intercession is <u>*addressing God*</u> and appealing for mercy on behalf of a person or nation, and spiritual warfare is <u>*addressing the enemy*</u> and taking authority in the Name of Jesus over the works of darkness in the territory where we have been assigned to pray. Both are the privilege of every believer. You may feel your gifting is stronger in one or the other and I encourage you to pray where your strengths and gifts lie. Intercession *cultivates a friendship with God* and moves upon His heart, while spiritual warfare *exposes and confronts strongholds*. In later chapters, we will be investigating three strongholds in the Ultra-Orthodox community: the *rabbinic spirit*, the *religious spirit*, and *Kabbalah*. Declaring God's Word, prophetic acts (as the Spirit leads), and fasting are also vital components of spiritual warfare.

Intercession

> *"But Moses sought the favor*
> *Of the Lord his God...*
> *'Turn from your fierce anger;*
> *Relent and do not bring*
> *Disaster on Your people.'"*
> *(Exodus 32:11a, 12b)*

Moses served as a faithful intercessor for the nation of Israel. He was a *friend of God* and pleaded with Him to spare the people after they built the golden calf in the wilderness (Exodus 32:7-14). God was angry enough to destroy Israel and make Moses a great nation, but Moses interceded and God relented. Often, the traditional church is ready to take God up on His offer, positioning themselves in the place of Moses. "Israel failed in their calling. Make of us a great nation!"

Moses is a shining example of the intercessor's heart that pleads for mercy and desires to see the promises of God fulfilled, for the sake of His holy Name. Intercession is the "If I have found favor in Thy sight" type of prayer.

Nehemiah wept and fasted over the devastation of Jerusalem after the Babylonian captivity, repented for the sins of the nations, and reminded God of His promises to restore and rebuild the city (Nehemiah 1:4-10). *Abigail* and *Esther* were also "types" of the intercessor. Abigail entreated David not to destroy all the males of the house of Nabal (I Samuel 25:4-35), and Esther sought the favor of the King and was able to spare the entire nation from destruction (Esther 4:15-16).

> *"Oh, that my head were waters,*
> *And my eyes a fountain of tears,*
> *That I might weep day and night*

For the slain of the
Daughter of my people."
(Jeremiah 9:1)

Jeremiah has been called the *weeping prophet*. His soul ached for the restoration of faithfulness and spiritual purity all the days of his prophetic ministry. *Daniel* is also a classic model of intercessory prayer. He confessed *his sins* and *the sins of the nation*. He prayed from a position of *identification*. Our prayers for the Ultra-Orthodox must be fueled by *love* and *humility*, acknowledging that we were all saved, by grace, *out of* whatever form of deception we were trapped in as unbelievers. We may have a holy hatred for the sin that engulfs the beloved, but we pray from a heart of *compassion* against every high thing exalting itself against the knowledge of God. As we daily present ourselves before the Lord to search us, know us, and cleanse us from any impure motives, or anything in our lives that is partnering or has partnered with the demonic realm, our prayers will have power in heaven. Daniel *prayed the Scriptures* and reminded God of His promises and this is perhaps the purest form of prayer we can pray.

Spiritual Warfare

"For we do not wrestle against flesh and blood,
But against principalities, against powers,
Against the rulers of the darkness of this age,
Against spiritual hosts of wickedness
In heavenly places."
(Ephesians 6:12)

Intercession needs to be *combined* with spiritual warfare. The Bible clearly teaches that believers in Jesus are in a *war*. Whether we engage in this heavenly battle is our choice, but the forces of hell will attack us regardless of our decision. Scripture warns us to *be on the alert* because our enemy is prowling around like a roaring lion seeking whom he may devour. We are commanded to *resist him* (I Peter 5: 8-9). During a ministry trip to Kenya in 1999, I had the awesome privilege of experiencing a safari and observing lions in their natural habitat. The females do all the hunting. To behold an elegant lioness sprawled out on a comfortable mound in the wild with her adorable cubs nestling up to her is any photographers' dream. From a distance, she appears gentle, content, harmless as a kitten. The male lions, with their glorious flowing manes, are stunning in appearance, attractive to the eye, and fascinating to watch. It is a strategy of the enemy *to transform himself* into an angel of light, to *appear as gentle as a lamb, yet be ravenous as a lion.* When visiting the Lion Park in South Africa, I heard of a tourist that was lured from his car to get a better picture. He was tragically devoured. While our warfare is *not* against flesh and blood, we would do well to keep in mind that the enemy may use willing vessels, even in the Body, just as the Lord anoints those whose hearts are surrendered to Him.

Spiritual warfare confronts the powers of darkness with the victory of Calvary, the Word of God, faith, and passion for God's Kingdom and Holy Name, fueled by His love for the lost.

David facing Goliath (I Samuel 17:41-46), *Elijah* challenging the prophets of Baal (I Kings 18:21-24), *Jesus* casting out demons (Mark 1:21-25) are classic examples: "This day the Lord will hand you over to me and I will strike you down and cut off your head" type of prayer.

> *"For as I walked around and looked carefully*
> *at your objects of worship,*
> *I even found an altar with this inscription:*
> *TO AN UNKNOWN GOD.*
> *Now what you worship as something unknown*
> *I am going to proclaim to you."*
> *(Acts 17:23)*

Effective prayed is also *informed prayer.* As intercessor priests, we need to be walking closely with God in *holy attire*, and we also need to *know what the devil is doing in our assigned field.* While the *Apostle Paul* was waiting for Silas and Timothy to join him in Athens, he *observed the city* and was distressed to see that it was full of idols. He challenged the men in the Areopagus to turn from their pagan idols and unknown gods to the living God. What has become known in recent years as *spiritual mapping* can be used in *spiritual warfare* as well as *intercession* and *evangelism.* If we want to pray effectively for our cities, we may want to research the history of the city and ask the Lord to reveal what the *ruling spirit* is and *where* this spirit is most strongly manifesting itself. Then we *press in with prayer* until we see a breakthrough.

> *"See, today, I appoint you*
> *Over nations and kingdoms*
> *To uproot and tear down,*
> *To destroy and overthrow,*
> *To build and to plant."*
> *(Jeremiah 1:10)*

If you live in any African nation thriving with wildlife, I was assured the last thing you want to see in your neighborhood is an elephant. An angry elephant can easily rip off the roof of a house, tear down a fence, pick up or turn over a vehicle, or uproot a tree with its powerful trunk. Elephants destroy and uproot, but they never build or plant anything. God is not calling us to be spiritual elephants who trample and trumpet in spiritual warfare with soulish anger or mere displays of aggression. As sons and daughters of the King, *we war in the love and victory of Messiah.* I am unspeakably grateful to the Lord for surrounding me with seasoned warriors whose hearts burn with the love of Messiah for His Jewish people. *Love* (that never fails) and *Truth* (the Sword of the Spirit) are two powerful weapons we have been given to advance the Kingdom of God.

The sole purpose for *uprooting* something in the spirit realm is so that something can be *planted* in its place. We do not simply trample and leave behind destruction, nor do we come to the battlefield wearing garments of self-righteousness, pride, or anger. As ambassadors of the King, we clothe ourselves in His righteousness, in love and humility, yet advancing with holy passion to usher in the Kingdom of God in the field we have been assigned.

> *"When He had **disarmed***
> *The rulers and authorities,,*
> *He made a public display of them,*
> *Triumphing over them through the cross."*
> *(Colossians 2:15)*

As we pray, let us be encouraged that *Jesus is the Ultimate Intercessor and Spiritual Warrior.* He *disarmed* the enemy on Calvary. We fight from a position of victory! We follow His lead, approach the Throne of Grace in His Name, and engage the enemy by His power. Yeshua triumphed over every principality, power, and dominion *and* He ever lives to intercede for us (Hebrews 7:25). He is seated at the right hand of the Father and Ephesians 2:4-6 says we are seated there with Him, Hallelujah! Even as Jesus prays for His Body of believers, we can be sure He is also praying for His brothers who are descendants of Abraham, Isaac, and Jacob.

Although we fight from a position of victory, spiritual warfare is, nevertheless, *WAR* and requires careful inspection of the troops to avoid casualties. The lions we will be encountering as we progress through the following pages are *ancient, hateful,* and *harmful*, which is not to inspire fear, but *holiness* and *humility*. Jesus has already won the battle and goes before us as the Captain of the Host. Nevertheless, we must ensure that we are properly dressed in all the armor of God as we go into battle. I invite you to pray the following prayer with me (or something similar) as we prepare our hearts to stand in the gap for the Ultra-Orthodox.

Father God, we present ourselves before You. Search us and know us. Cleanse our hearts, renew our minds, and increase our faith as we intercede and confront the forces of darkness on behalf of the Ultra-Orthodox. We humble ourselves before You. Fill our hearts with love, a jealous love for your people, a holy love that tells the truth, a courageous love that risks its life. As intercessors and prayer warriors, we ask you to bind us together and give us one heart as we stand against the wiles of the devil, the real enemy of your people, the serpent who has hated them from the Garden, even from the pronouncement of judgment that, through the Seed of a woman (Yeshua), his head would be crushed (Genesis 3:15). Purify our hearts, O God. We cover ourselves, our families, and all that is near and dear to us with the precious Blood of Jesus. We ask for angelic protection and a fresh wind of your Spirit over our prayers, and we cancel every assignment of hell against us as we co-labor with You to set the captives free. In the name of Yeshua we pray, Amen.

As we go into battle, we must know the enemy and also *know ourselves.* We must be willing to bring any weaknesses, areas of bondage, or ungodly attitudes to the Lord for healing. There are two dangers currently facing the Church. Both are unscriptural and unhealthy *extremes.* One is *Replacement Theology,* the belief that, since the Jewish leadership rejected Jesus as Messiah, God has rejected Israel and all the promises for Israel now apply only to the Church. Not surprisingly, those who hold this position generally apply only the *blessings* for Israel to the Church, interpreting all the *judgments* as still applying to Israel. This dangerous theology *breeds Anti-Semitism.* Many of us who love Israel are deeply grieved and have participated in some form of *identification repentance* for the sins of the vast majority of Church history relating to Israel. Believers who are not physical descendants of Abraham, Isaac, and Jacob are *grafted in* to an olive tree, the roots of which are *Hebraic.* In these last days, we must seek the *heart of God* and the vision of His *prophetic destiny* for Israel. *Because of Jesus,* we are connected to the chosen nation. Furthermore, the command to *pray for the peace of Jerusalem* in Psalm 122:6 is for everyone who reads it. This scripture verse is the only place in the Bible that promises if you will pray for a certain city, God will bless you.

> *"For I am jealous for you with a godly jealousy;*
> *For I betrothed you to one husband,*
> *That to Christ I might present you as a pure virgin.*
> *But I am afraid, lest as the serpent*
> *Deceived Eve by his craftiness,*
> *Your minds should be led astray from the simplicity*
> *And pure devotion to Messiah.*
> *(II Corinthians 11:2-3)*

The other extreme, perhaps the more subtle danger, is *idolatry of Israel.*

As intercessors for the Ultra-Orthodox, we must take caution that our love for Israel does not turn into worship of Israel, a romantic fascination blinding us to the spiritual issues that must be confronted in prayer.

Intercessors and prayer warriors are like *spiritual firefighters*. If we were trapped in a burning building, we wouldn't want the firefighters to stand on the sidewalk speaking blessings over us and discussing whether the fire is hot enough to consume us, debating whether there are any people in this building who really want to be rescued, or pondering if maybe there is "one like the Son of Man" walking around in the flames. We can be sure we would want them to commission every weapon of fighting fires at their disposal, break through every barrier, hack their way through doors, walls, and windows, and get us out of there! Perfect love, the passionate love of God that casts out fear, risks its life to rescue the lives of others.

Father God, we come before you in the Name of Jesus and ask you to search our hearts for any trace of replacement theology, Anti-Semitism, or idolatry of Israel. If any of these are hidden in our hearts, we repent before you now and renounce them. We love your people, stand with them in their trials and afflictions and present ourselves to You as vessels of intercession, but we devote our worship to <u>You alone</u>. We rejoice with Israel in all the blessings You will pour out according to your prophetic promises. Holy Spirit, cleanse us now from any unholy or unhealthy attitudes or beliefs imparted to us through our families, churches, friends, school systems, teachings or from any other source.

My Beloved

"I remember the devotion of your youth,
How as a bride you loved me
And followed Me through the desert,
Through a land not sown.
Israel was holy to the Lord,
The first fruits of His harvest;
All who devoured her were held guilty
And disaster overtook them."
(Jeremiah 2:2-3)

The God of Israel created romance and intimacy in marriage as an image of His desire for a deeply personal relationship with His creation. In these last days, the passion of God for His bride is being stirred up and He is calling Her back to Himself. His heart aches to re-ignite the *intimate fellowship* He once enjoyed with His beloved. Israel was created to be His *wife*, and also a *witness* and a *light* to the nations, to spiritually impart a revelation of the one true God. There was an *anointing* (given selectively at first) which *remained* on those whose hearts were fully devoted to Him. For a season, Israel loved her God as a Husband in the wilderness, but gradually her love became *mixed* with idolatry. Eventually, she rejected Him as Husband and King and demanded a human ruler so she could become *like the nations* (I Samuel 8). The nations had *kings*. They also had *pagan gods. .*

"Did you present Me with
Sacrifices and grain offerings
In the wilderness for forty years,
O house of Israel?
*You also carried along **Sikkuth** your king*
*And **Kiyyun**, your images,*

The star of your gods
Which you made for yourselves."
(Amos 5:25-26)

God told the prophet Samuel that Israel had forsaken Him and served other gods *which they had made for themselves* even from the day He brought them out of Egypt (I Samuel 8:8). Similarly, when we come to salvation, we may ignorantly bring into this new love relationship our *kings, images,* and *stars of our gods* from our former life. We love the Lord, but we love our idols too. If we are to be vessels fit for the Master's use, our walk must embrace *discipleship* and *deliverance* from the idols we bring into our new relationship with Jesus.

"And the Lord told him (Samuel),
'Listen to all that the people
Are saying to you;
It is not you they have rejected,
But they have rejected Me
As their king.'"
(I Samuel 8:7)

Avinu Malkenu, Our Father, Our King. These precious words abound in the Siddur, the Jewish prayer book, and liturgy for Sabbath and festival services. Every Jewish person has spoken them at some time in their life. It is a declaration that God (Adonai Eloheinu) is Father and King over Israel.

How it must have crushed the heart of the Father to be shoved aside in favor of an earthly ruler. He had led them with His Presence, a cloud by day and pillar of fire by night, opened the Red Sea before them, rained down manna from heaven, given their children an inheritance in a land flowing with milk and honey, and rescued them from their enemies time and again. Most recently, He had *thundered with a loud thunder* against the Philistines, throwing them into a panic and routing them before Israel (I Samuel 7:10). Who else could thunder, whistle for the flies, or command the hornet like the God of Jacob?

***Right at the beginning of Israel's history a precedent of rejection
was set which continues to the present day. You see, rejecting the
Son (Yeshua) as Messiah was simply a byproduct of rejecting the
Father (Yahveh) as Husband and King.***

Once we understand this, the words Yeshua spoke to the Pharisees
and the scribes jump off the page with fresh meaning.

> *"And so they were saying to Him,
> 'Where is Your Father?'
> Jesus answered,
> 'You know neither Me, nor My Father;
> If you knew Me, you would
> Know My Father."*
> *(John 8:19)*

When Israel asked for a king, they *opened a door* to Satan. Their
request for a king *changed the system of government* from a theocracy
(ruled by God) to a monarchy (ruled by man) and gave the enemy
legal access to *all the earthly systems* of the people of Israel that
would later develop. It is extremely important to see that, *in the spirit
realm*, this decision to ask for a king became a *seed* that would later
bear deadly fruit. When a door is opened to the enemy, it stays open
until someone *repents, renounces the spirit behind the sin, and closes
the door.* Then, blessing, healing, and restoration can occur.

Let's try and *think like the devil* for a moment. Now that the door is
open, what strategy would he use to come in and steal the *intimacy*,
the *calling*, and the *anointing* from the people of Israel? Wouldn't he
try everything in his power to lure them away from their simple
devotion, their covenant relationship, their purpose for being created
as a nation, draw them into idolatry and invent some *religion* to keep
them *busy* and *estranged* from God? As we will see, this is precisely
what the enemy did.

> "And what comes into your mind
> *Will not come about, when you say:*
> *'We will be like the nations,*

Like the tribes of the lands,
Serving wood and stone.'"
(Ezekiel 20:32)

Israel's desire to *be like the nations* eventually grew into national apostasy. Ezekiel Chapter 20:1-32 details a panoramic history of the nation from the time of their miraculous exodus from the hands of Pharaoh. We can hear the broken heart of God lamenting the rejection and rebellion of His people *in Egypt* (20:8), *in the wilderness* (20:13), and *in the Land* (20:21). Time and again, the anger of the Lord was so aroused that he determined to pour out His wrath, but *for the sake of His holy Name*, He showed mercy. Eventually, He was forced to scatter His beloved to the nations.

"Therefore, behold, I will allure her,
Bring her into the wilderness,
*And **speak tenderly** to her."*
(Hosea 2:14)

We are living in the days of Hosea. God is leading Israel into the *wilderness*. Anyone who has visited the Sinai Peninsula can testify to its awesome beauty. The Sinai is a spectacular sight and unforgettable experience if you are visiting it on a day trip under the protection of a guide and returning to "civilization" in the evening. But the wilderness of the Sinai becomes a *hostile environment* if you are traveling alone, camping along the way. The heat of the day, cold by night, and sand storms can be dangerous enemies. What can you expect to encounter in the wilderness? Perhaps snakes and wild beasts. You might pray that you encounter a well. Scenery aside, the wilderness is a place where you are *completely isolated and dependent upon God for your very survival.* God is leading His beloved Israel into such a place and in this intimate place, at a time when the only words she will be hearing are words of hatred, rejection, and condemnation, He will *speak tenderly* to her.

"Then I will give her her
Vineyards from there,
And the valley of Achor as a door of hope.
And she will sing there

As in the days of her youth,
As in the day when she came
Up from the land of Egypt."
(Hosea 2:15)

In this barren desert, this valley of trouble, this life-threatening environment, the Bible says that Israel will *sing!* She will sing because in this dry, desolate place there will be a *door of hope!* In the natural, we might be inclined to think this door is a *thing,* some sort of escape hatch. But Someone in the Bible once said that *He is the Door* (John 10:9-10). When Yeshua spoke these words He also affirmed that He came to *give life abundantly.* Vineyards are a symbol of abundance, as well as an outpouring of the Spirit. God is positioning Israel for blessing and new wine. When no one else cares for her, the Door of Hope will gather her into His arms and restore her vineyards!

"And it will come about in that day,"
Declares the Lord,
'That you will call me Ishi
And will no longer call me Baali.
*For I will **remove the names of the Baals***
From her mouth, so that they
Will be mentioned by their names no more.
"In that day I will also make
A covenant for them
With the beasts of the field,
The birds of the sky,
And the creeping things of the ground.
I will abolish the bow,
The sword, and war from the land,
And will make them lie down in safety.
"And I will betroth you to Me forever;
Yes, I will betroth you to Me
In righteousness and in justice,
In lovingkindness and compassion,
And I will betroth you in faithfulness.
Then you will know the Lord."
(Hosea 2:16-20)

What thrilling promises! While the fig tree is blossoming and more Jewish people believe in Jesus as their Messiah than at any time since the first century, for the most part, Israel *does not know the Lord,* and precious few of those who believe have come from an Ultra-Orthodox background. But in the days of the wilderness, God will transform the hostile environment *in the field, in the sky, and on the ground.* He will remove war and terrorism from the Land and cause His people to lie down in safety. We can hardly imagine this with today's headlines and yet Scripture says it shall be so.

As we pray for the Ultra-Orthodox, our heartcry must be for God to restore the intimate bridal relationship with Him that is their spiritual destiny, but also to deal with their taste buds.

The Baals that the prophet Hosea is referring to *have names* and these names must first become *distasteful,* so that the Name of Yeshua can be proclaimed as the Name above all Names. God told Ezekiel to *eat a scroll* of His Words (Ezekiel 3:1-4), because whatever you put in your mouth as *spiritual food* is what will come out of your heart. Whatever *bread* you are feeding on, whatever the *source* of your spiritual springs, you will esteem and adore. If the *Word of God* is your fountain of truth, then you will quote the Scriptures and the prophets, you will quote Yeshua (if you are Messianic). But if your source is *extra-biblical,* you will quote the names of these sources. *In the wilderness,* God will expose the futility, the powerlessness, the hopelessness of every other name but the Name of Jesus and, in that day, His Name alone will be exalted. Israel will *know Yeshua* and He will become her *Spouse,* her *Security,* and the *Source* of blessing.

God is a romantic and He wants His wife back. He's coming after the unfaithful wife of Hosea, which is *not the Church.* He is pursuing His Beloved, the yet to-be-saved remnant of Israel. He is also coming for the Bride of Messiah (the One New Man). There is fire in His eyes and a sword of victory in His hand, the fire of His *love* for Israel and the Bride of Christ. In the desert, God had a devoted wife. Granted, her love was mixed with idolatry, but she did not yet have a heart of stone. There was *relationship.* Hardness of heart came after the *seed of rejection* fully blossomed. Once God captures our *hearts,* then He can give us the *mind* of Messiah, not the other way around.

This is a *love relationship* first and last. In these last days, an army of intercessors and spiritual warriors are being gathered from the four corners of the earth to *pray the wife back to her husband*!

<u>Our role as intercessors and prayer warriors for the Ultra-Orthodox is to stand in the gap, entreat the Lord for mercy, and do battle on their behalf so that the process of blessing, healing, and restoration can begin</u>.

There is a further issue that must also be addressed before intimacy with God can be restored. There is a *deep wound* in the heart of the Jewish people because of the Holocaust. I have heard it said in Israel, "If God didn't come for us in Germany, why should He come for us now? If this is the God of the Bible, we don't want this kind of God. We can take care of ourselves." These are honest words of distress and disillusionment. God is dealing with His people at this very moment and causing them to ask hard questions which will eventually lead to repentance, deliverance, and restored intimacy.

Repentance begins in the house of God. When we look at Israel, we are really looking into a mirror. If we are honest, we would have to confess that at some time in our lives we also *rejected God*. Our prayers for Israel need to begin by repenting for any rejection of God in our own lives for who He *really is*, for creating a comfortable illusion of what we would like Him to be because it's more pleasant to our souls. We also need to repent for any *idolatry* in our lives. If we ask Him, the Holy Spirit will shine His Light on any hidden areas that need to be cleansed. Since this is a prayer guide specifically for the Ultra-Orthodox, if you are a Jewish believer, I invite you to repent on behalf of the generations of Israel going all the way back to Samuel, who rejected God as Father and King and the grafted-in believers will stand with you in agreement.

Avinu Malkenu, Our Father, Our King. We thank You for Your faithfulness and precious promise to betroth Your people to Yourself once again. O Lord, woo and allure them into the wilderness and speak tenderly to them according to Your word. We pray they would be satisfied and fulfilled by your love and that you would remove the sword, the bow, and war from the Land. Lavish Your affection upon Your beloved who has suffered so tragically and relentlessly at the hands of the enemy. Father we pray, in the Name of Yeshua, that you would heal the wound in the heart of Your people and restore them to Your love.

Our Precious Father, how Your heart must break when we reject You for the ways of the nations. We repent for pushing You away in any area of our lives and re-defining you, not according to Your Word, but according to our flesh. We repent of exalting ANYTHING in our lives made with the hands of man. We repent of all generational idolatry and rejection of You by our ancestors going all the way back to Adam who passed down to us man-made religions of any form. We desire only a personal, intimate relationship, a covenant relationship, with the Living God of Israel. We repent for opening the door to the god of this world, for giving him legal access to our various cultures, identities, and social structures, and, in Yeshua's Name, we proclaim that You alone are Father, King, and Husband over our lives and over Israel. We renounce rejection of God and idolatry in all of its manifestations. We declare that ALL our springs are in You. And we repent, along with our Jewish brothers and sisters, for the generational sin of rejecting You as Father and King going all the way back to Egypt, and most particularly to the elders of Israel in the days of Samuel who demanded an earthly king. We renounce man-made political and religious systems, and every Satanic-inspired form of worship.

In the Name of Jesus, we take back all legal ground that was given to the enemy to steal intimacy from Israel, to kill the Jewish people, and destroy the nation of Israel. We re-claim all the blessings the enemy has stolen from Israel, the apple of Your eye, most particularly the bridal relationship. In the Name of Jesus, we bind the spirit of rejection of God and idolatry away from our personal lives, away from the lives of our unsaved relatives, and away from the people of Israel. Capture our hearts, O God, and capture the hearts of the Ultra-Orthodox, so that we may take captive every thought to the obedience of Messiah. In Yeshua's Name we pray, Amen.

Who Are the Ultra-Orthodox?

"So then, all Jews know my manner
Of life from my youth up,…
That I lived as a Pharisee, according
*To the **strictest sect** of our religion."*
(Acts 26:4a, 5b)

I have had a personal burden for the Ultra-Orthodox ever since the Lord touched me with His heart for Israel in 1975. If Saul of Tarsus lived in our day, he would be *Ultra-Orthodox.* After his Damascus Road encounter with Messiah, the great apostle later described himself as having lived according to the strictest sect of the Pharisees, meaning 'I was as religious as you can get.'

The Ultra-Orthodox are the modern-day Pharisees who practice Rabbinic Judaism (and beyond) according to the strictest standards of religious observance. They are generally recognized by their black hats and coats, full beards, and payess (sidecurls), appearing to have literally stepped out of the Middle Ages into the contemporary world.

Distinguished from Modern and Traditional Orthodox, many Ultra-Orthodox do not recognize the State of Israel. Yes, you read that correctly! They believe the *Land* is holy, but the *State* is not, and that only Messiah can establish the true Israel. Many believers can say "Amen" to this separating of the holy from the profane, recognizing that the current State of Israel is very much the "dry bones" of Ezekiel awaiting the breath of God to raise it to spiritual life. The world of Orthodox Judaism is quite broad in its spectrum of observance. *Modern Orthodox* Jews differ from *Traditional Orthodox*, who yet differ from the *Ultra-Orthodox* and it is unlikely that any definitive description can be reached this side of heaven. However, I will attempt to give a brief overview of the groups within Orthodox Judaism.

Several months before moving to Israel, while still living in the States, the Lord led me to tear out the listing in the Yellow Pages for all the temples and synagogues in my neighborhood. There were many and every Friday evening and Saturday morning, I would visit a different *shul* (Sabbath service) and silently intercede. One of my favorite synagogues was *Modern Orthodox*. The men were separated from the women, however, the *mechitzah* (divider) was low enough so that everyone could see the Rabbi, the Torah Table, and each other. Each group was permitted to touch the Torah as it was paraded through the sanctuary, not only in the Men's Section. What's more, some of the members apparently lived too far away to walk and drove to the synagogue. I know this because they were parking on the same side street that I was. While this is extremely rare even in Modern Orthodoxy, it is a phenomenon that would lead to stoning in an Ultra-Orthodox neighborhood. The women wore fashionable dresses, cosmetics, and jewelry. Their Orthodoxy was designed to observe the essentials, while embracing the realities of a modern world and exhibiting a high degree of tolerance for other branches of Judaism, with the exception of Messianic Judaism. Modern Orthodox Jews are *Zionists*, but not radical Zionists. They support the State of Israel and love the Land, but are quite willing to share it for the promise of peace.

For the sake of clarification, all who believe that God has promised Israel an inheritance within the defined borders of Scripture are, in a sense, Zionists. This does not mean we necessarily support every action of the State, and while the State is secular at present, its existence, nevertheless, fulfills prophecy and believers are urged to pray for the peace of Jerusalem (Psalm 122:6) and to stand as watchmen on her walls (Isaiah 62:6-7) until all the purposes of God for her are fulfilled.

The *Traditional Orthodox* could be described as the more zealous Zionists. These are the Jews who wear multi-colored knit kippahs (skullcaps) as opposed to the black velvet of the Ultra-Orthodox, establish themselves in the settlements (Jewish communities), such as Hebron, and would fight to their last drop of blood for the survival of the State of Israel. They believe in the biblical boundaries of the Land promised to the patriarchs and resist the giving of any portions of it to the Palestinians, or anyone else, under any circumstances. Many Christian Zionists who pray for Israel identify most closely with the Traditional Orthodox.

__The psychological structure of Ultra-Orthodoxy reveals it is a cultic system, however unpleasant this may be to acknowledge. The strategy is to create dependence on the community, shelter the inhabitants from the outside world, keep them ignorant of literature outside the boundaries of "Torah" and instill fear of punishment or ostracism for any slight disobedience of rabbinic decrees or attempts to break away from strict conformity to the system.__

> *"For I say to you,*
> *You shall not see Me again*
> *Until you say,*
> *'Blessed is He who comes*
> *In the Name of the Lord!'"*
> *(Matthew 23:39)*

Why target the Ultra-Orthodox specifically for prayer? As we focus in on *who* Jesus is speaking to when He says these words, the question is easily answered. At the beginning of Chapter 23, Yeshua is addressing the multitudes, His disciples, and anyone in the vicinity who can hear His voice. But in verse 13, He begins to *zero in* on the scribes, the Pharisees, and teachers of the law and ends His discourse with the promising challenge, *"When you (the religious) say to Me*

(Jesus), 'Blessed is He who comes in the name of the Lord,' I will come!" The multitudes had already proclaimed these words, leading Jesus on a colt down the Mount of Olives, welcoming Him with palm branches and spreading their prayer shawls (tallit) on the road a week before His death on the cross. Generally speaking, the multitudes loved Jesus, but the Pharisees *rebuked them* (Luke 19:39) and rejected their Messianic declarations of "Hosanna to the King."

The primary reason for focused prayer for the Ultra-Orthodox is that they are a strategic key to the return of Messiah and end-time evangelism. Of all the streams within Judaism, the Ultra-Orthodox are the most zealous for Messiah. They may be confused and deceived as to His identity, but they, more than any other Orthodox group, embrace a concept of Messiah and fervently await His coming.

> *"But woe to you, scribes and Pharisees, hypocrites,*
> *Because you shut off the kingdom of heaven from men;*
> *For you do not enter in yourselves,*
> *Not do you allow those who are entering to go in."*
> *(Matthew 23:13)*

Matthew 23 is the famous chapter of "woes" and I had often wondered why Yeshua was so hard on the Pharisees. His judgments appear scathing and merciless. One day, He drew me to verse 13. *Those in positions of spiritual authority have the power to shut the door of the kingdom of heaven to their disciples.* They hold in their hands the souls of men. Jesus didn't speak this way to the prostitutes or the tax collectors. They were sinners and knew it. But the Pharisees were self-righteous and controlled the spiritual climate that ultimately led to the rejection of the Messiah. But this is not the end of the story. Prophetically speaking, just as the Pharisees of the first century were used by the enemy to persuade the nation away from Yeshua, God will use the end-time Pharisees to persuade the remnant of the nation back to Yeshua. These are exciting times to be alive in Jesus!

> *"For though we walk in the flesh,*
> *We do not war according to the flesh.*
> *For the weapons of our warfare*
> Are not carnal, but **mighty in God**

For pulling down strongholds,
Casting down arguments
And every high thing that exalts itself
Against the knowledge of God."
(II Corinthians 10:3-5a)

The Lord is stirring up His zeal for the salvation of His people, imparting discernment to His intercessors, and giving us tools that will assist us to effectively partner with Him in prayer so that His beloved may see and embrace the King of Kings and Lord of Lords. Our warfare is not against flesh and blood. If you are reading this book, you likely already have a love for the religious community in your heart and are praying for their salvation.

Our burden for the Ultra-Orthodox will increase, our compassion grow, and our understanding of their fanatic and often unpredictable behavior sharpen as we discover how the enemy has trapped them into mysticism and is controlling them through it.

Later we will be exploring Chasidism, a major movement within Ultra-Orthodoxy. Our purpose for investigating Chasidic concepts is not to gain head knowledge, to criticize or judge, but to expose the works of darkness, identify the pillars of deception, and neutralize, *through prayer,* every high thing that is exalting itself against the knowledge of God. Our supreme joy is to witness the day when the modern-day Pharisees, the Ultra-Orthodox, will greet Yeshua with the Messianic welcome, "Baruch haba B'shem Adonai!"

Father God, perhaps the greatest prayer we could pray for the Ultra-Orthodox is that you would cause the words "Blessed is He who comes in the Name of the Lord" to rise from their lips, however you accomplish this miracle. We thank You that You know the beginning from the end and that all things come to pass in the fullness of time. We praise You that in these last days you are preparing the hearts of the Ultra-Orthodox, the ultimate symbol of religious leadership, to greet and welcome Messiah Yeshua. We present ourselves as priests to intercede on their behalf and we pray that you would anoint and give wings to our prayers that they would rise to heaven and accomplish Your purpose for these end times. In the mighty name of Jesus we pray, Amen.

Mea Shearim

"Isaac planted crops in that land
And the same year reaped a hundredfold."
(Genesis 26:12)

The focus of intercession and spiritual warfare for this prayer guide is Mea Shearim, the Ultra-Orthodox Chasidic *stronghold* in the heart of Jerusalem. Mea Shearim literally means *"100 gates,"* however, the more accurate translation would be *"one hundredfold."* Prayerwalking through the community one day, we asked an Ultra-Orthodox woman who sells Jewish marriage certificates (ketubot) what the gates meant. She told us it is taken from the Torah passage where God blessed the crops of Isaac a hundredfold. When the foundation was being laid for this walled-in, gated community, the weekly Torah portion reading was *Toledot*, which included Genesis 26:12. The name was chosen as a prophetic declaration of blessing for the new neighborhood. While a young bride-to-be was searching through the shops' vast selection of beautifully hand-designed marriage licenses, we had our Bibles out on the counter, the Orthodox woman reading in Hebrew and we in English looking at this passage of Scripture. She said the gates are gates of blessing!

Praise the Lord! Let us ask God to bless Mea Shearim a hundredfold! Pray that He will draw them into a personal relationship with Himself through Messiah Yeshua, the one and only Gate of blessing. As Mea Shearim literally means "100 gates," pray that every gate in the spirit realm which has been unwittingly opened to the demonic realm will be CLOSED and SEALED OFF by the Blood of Jesus and that YESHUA, the one and only Gate, will be the sole entry point of salvation, knowledge, light, truth, wisdom, revelation, and heavenly secrets.

"Now the king and his men went to Jerusalem
Against the Jebusites, the inhabitants of the land,
And they said to David,
'You shall not come in here, but the blind and lame
Shall turn you away,'; thinking,
'David cannot enter here.'
Nevertheless, David captured the stronghold of Zion,
That is, the city of David."
(II Samuel 5:6-7)

King David reigned in Hebron for seven and a half years. When he set out to establish his kingdom in Jerusalem, he needed to first conquer the *Jebusites* and capture the Fortress of Zion. David's Citadel in the Old City is a symbol of this historic conquest that established Jerusalem as the capital and spiritual heart of Israel for all time. In his victory, David illustrated a spiritual principle. If we want to advance the Kingdom of God in a city, we must first confront the *spiritual Jebusites* and capture the stronghold in that city.

Mea Shearim is the religious stronghold in Jerusalem and capturing this spiritual fortress is to capture the city for Messiah.

*"I will give you a **new heart***
*And put a **new spirit** in you;*
I will remove the heart of stone
And give you a heart of flesh."
(Ezekiel 36:26)

God has promised to give Israel a new heart and new spirit. I rejoice in this blessed prophecy. Jerusalem is the heart of Israel and Mea Shearim is the religious heart of Jerusalem. If God is going to give Israel a new heart, then He must deal with Mea Shearim!

Mea Shearim was designed by German architect, Conrad Schick, in 1874. It was modeled after the Old City, meaning it was walled-in and gated for security, as the Turkish Empire ruled Jerusalem at that time. Interestingly, Christian experts were employed in the early stages of construction because there were no qualified Jewish professionals for this type of project. We can praise the Lord that, even as the groundwork was being laid for what would become a *stronghold of mysticism*, the hands of believers were also present.

The guiding principle of the founders, primarily Jewish families from the Old City living on the donations of wealthier Jews in the Diaspora (*halukkah*), was to enable anyone wishing to build a home to do so on easy terms with low payments spread over a long period of time. By 1882 all the houses, 140 buildings in all, including a large yeshiva (rabbinical seminary), a synagogue, bakery, public kitchen, guest house, and ritual bath were completed and Mea Shearim became the *hub* around which a whole complex of neighborhoods would be built. Mea Shearim was the city center of the new developing Jerusalem outside the Old City

The *Yeshiva & Talmud Torah of Mea Shearim* is the root and foundation of the community, established in 1883, the oldest yeshiva ever built outside the old city walls of Jerusalem. What a thrill to discover that this yeshiva is on a street named Yeshuat Ya'akov ("Salvation of Jacob"), a prophetic picture of the purposes of God and His wonderful sense of humor, which abounds in the neighborhood.

At the junction of Shivtei Israel ("Tribes of Israel") and Mea Shearim Street, an entryway and main artery of the community, stands my favorite building. I call it the "Yeshua Building" because the facade of the upper level has the name of Jesus written on it in Hebrew! What's more, a yeshiva we pray for on the street named after the founder of Chasidism is named *Or Pney Yehoshua,* meaning "Light in the Face of Joshua." Joshua is the same Hebrew word as Yeshua!

Pray that salvation and revival would begin on Yeshuat Ya'akov Street. Pray that the love of God and the convicting power of the Holy Spirit would be poured out in this dark place and that everything the enemy has stolen from the Ultra-Orthodox, through history, loss of life, tradition, religion, deception, and exile would be restored. Pray that the name of Yeshua would leap off the "Yeshua Building" and grab the attention of residents. Praise the Lord that His Name is already high and lifted up and that He is watching over Mea Shearim even if the community is unaware of His presence. Pray for revelation LIGHT to shine upon the face of Messiah Yeshua and draw the remnant to Himself.

By 1915, the tiny walled-in city of Mea Shearim became so crowded that the community was forced to spread far beyond its borders into the vast area we now pray for. The four main entry gates were opened and remain so to this day. This area we pray for encompasses several surrounding neighborhoods and, within these borders, there are not only Ashkenazi *Jews (*from Eastern Europe), but also *Sephardic Jews* (from Spain and Morocco). There are *Russian Jews, and Bucharian Jews* (from Uzbekistan in the former Soviet Union), who are Orthodox, but not Ultra-Orthodox. The Bucharian Jews have their own lively neighborhood and shuk (open market) in the midst of the Ultra-Orthodox community. And there are *Persian* Jews (from Iraq and Iran).

"Pass through, pass through the gates!
Prepare the way for the people.
Build up, build up the highway!
Remove the stones.
Raise a banner for the nations."
(Isaiah 62:10)

The Jerusalem Gate

Beit David Gate

Beit David Gate is my favorite of the four original gates. It was so named because it faced the first house ever built outside the Old City of Jerusalem in 1873, a year before the founding of Mea Shearim. This house became known as Beit David and, after the establishment of the Chief Rabbinate in 1922, Rabbi Kook moved into it and lived in the house until his death in 1935. Beit David became a complex of ten homes constructed primarily for the poor, along with a water cistern and small synagogue. Today, the preserved home of Rabbi Kook is the Museum of Psalms.

Virtually every prayerwalker has experienced the *great spiritual darkness* surrounding the other three gates. But David's Gate has a special sweetness, a charm, even an anointing that is perhaps prophetic. David was a man after God's own heart, devoted to heartfelt prayer and worship, intimate with the Almighty, inquiring of Him in every battle campaign, humble, and full of the anointing of the Holy Spirit. Jesus the Messiah is the son of David, the eternal Lamp that God promised would be kept burning for David's throne in Jerusalem *forever.*

> *"Then Samuel took the horn of oil*
> *and anointed him in the midst of his brothers;*
> *and the Spirit of the Lord*
> *came mightily upon David from that day forward."*
> *(I Samuel 16:13)*

Pray for the anointing of David and the restoration of the fallen tabernacle of David in Mea Shearim. God invites us as co-laborers in prayer to "pass through the gates," to enter, engage the enemy, and take territory for His Kingdom. Pray that the growing network of intercessors around the world will be for Mea Shearim a flask of oil poured out in prayer, a horn of anointing poured upon the remnant in the midst of their brothers. Pray that when this horn has been emptied and the oil drenching the heads of the remnant, that the Spirit of the Lord will come upon them MIGHTILY from that day forward as it came upon David. Pray that they will walk in power and boldness of faith, declare Yeshua to be the Messiah, and welcome the Son of David to enter the gates of their community.

Sha'ar Lifta (Gate Lifta)

Sha'ar Lifta (Gate Lifta) was named after the Arab village of Lifta because it faced this village when Mea Shearim was originally built in 1874. The community eventually bought up the property of Lifta to expand their neighborhood beyond the gates. Today, it is strictly forbidden under threat of death for an Arab to sell land to an Israeli, just to give a perspective of how drastically things have changed.

A remarkable answer to prayer occurred in 1999 surrounding Gate Lifta. I have led many individuals and small groups through the gates of Mea Shearim. Entering through Sha'ar Lifta, we would be immediately struck by the thick oppression in the narrow, tunnel-like passageway, crowded on either side with stacks of old, worn-out, dusty books almost piled to the ceiling. No doubt, many of these books were not written by the inspiration of the Holy Spirit. The spiritual greeting to this entryway was like being hit in the head with a two-by-four and on nearly every prayerwalk, we would stop, rebuke the evil spirits, speak the Name of Yeshua, and pray that the Lord would remove whatever was the source of this staggering heaviness. Some months later, I noticed some of the books had been taken away, creating a somewhat lighter atmosphere. Then, suddenly, ***nearly all the books disappeared***! I cannot describe the world of difference this has made! From just a few months before, it is like breathing fresh alpine air. This passageway has remained relatively uncluttered ever since, Hallelujah!

Praise the Lord that the darkness over Sha'ar Lifta has significantly decreased. Pray for the oppression to be completely lifted and welcome Yeshua into this gate as the only way to salvation. Although Gate Lifta currently faces a solidly Jewish area, I believe the Lord would also have us take a moment to pray for the salvation of the Arabs living in Jerusalem as well as for the remnant of Israel. Jesus loves all peoples and died for the salvation of the world. Jerusalem will eventually be a house of prayer for all nations. As the Palestinians cry "Death to Israelis" and the Israelis (even the Ultra-Orthodox) shout "Death to Arabs" let us proclaim "Life in Messiah!"

The Mill Gate

The **Mill Gate** faced a Flour Mill and is the only entrance to the walled-in city on Mea Shearim Street, the major artery of the community, stretching from Shabbat Square to Shivtei Israel. The Mill Gate is perhaps the least favored gate of entry on prayerwalks, simply because Mea Shearim Street is extremely narrow and traffic-ridden, lacking adequate sidewalks, thus crowding, even crushing, pedestrians against shops and buildings to avoid oncoming buses. It is nearly impossible for intercessors to walk side-by-side along this narrow street. The Mill Gate has a unique appearance from the other three gates and is also spiritually oppressive. Nevertheless, there is a praise report of answered prayer surrounding the Mill Gate. Near the end of the dark walkway just beyond the entry, there was a tiny shop consisting of all manner of amulets, hamsas (a hand with a large eye in the center for "warding off the evil eye") and magic charms. You could feel the *suffocating demonic power* pulsating from this storefront long before you arrived at its doorway. Several times in 1999, intercessors agreed with me in prayer that the Lord would remove this business. Within six months, the shop closed and has rarely been opened since!

Pray for a revelation of Yeshua, the Bread of Life, the Living Manna, and the only source of healthy spiritual food for our souls. His Body and His Blood are the New Covenant. It was during a Passover Seder (the "Last Supper") that Jesus proclaimed this New Covenant in fulfillment of Jeremiah 31:31-32. Pray for a visitation of the Messiah upon the Ultra-Orthodox throughout the year, but especially during the Passover season. Pray that the tiny amulet shop would become a flower shop, fruit juice stand, or some other sort of bright, pleasant business, pleasing to the Lord and that He would PROSPER it.

The *Jerusalem Gate* faced the Old City and is closest to Damascus Gate. Just opposite the Jerusalem Gate is one of the larger yeshivas, Chasidei Breslov, housing the famous chair of Rabbi Nachman (1772-1811), the great-grandson of Israel b. Eliezer Ba'al Shem Tov, the founder of Chasidism. This chair was dismantled and carefully transported piece by piece to Jerusalem after the rabbi's death. There are several Chasidic sects in Mea Shearim, but three prominent groups are *Toldot Aharon* (originating in Hungary), *Chabad* (founded in 1788 by Rabbi Shneur Zalman, a Chasidic leader in Belorussia), and the *Breslov Hasidim*. Breslov is the name of a town in the Ukraine where Rabbi Nachman, the founder of the group, spent the last eight years of his life. The Breslovers are one of the most mystical Chasidic groups.

The spiritual destiny of Jerusalem is to be the praise of the earth and a house of prayer for all nations. Pray that the Ultra-Orthodox will rise to their calling to be worshippers in Spirit and in truth of the one true God of Israel and His Son Yeshua and that they will be free from the bondage of individual sects to come together in unity in Messiah. We may well also pray for the already existing Body of

Messiah in Jerusalem to be free of sectarianism and come together in love and unity.

> *"Violence will not be heard again*
> *In your land,*
> *Nor devastation within your borders;*
> *But you will call your **walls** salvation,*
> *And your **gates** praise,"*
> *(Isaiah 60:18)*

Praise the Lord that, as the network of intercessors has been asking God to bless and protect Mea Shearim, He has answered prayer mightily. Early in 2001, within a sixty-day period, there were three terrorist bombing attempts that were miraculously prevented. God may answer our prayers for revival among the Ultra-Orthodox in unexpected ways, but we can praise Him that, so far, He is shaking the community *mercifully*. As the conflict over Jerusalem increases, it is timely that we have been praying over the gates and also for specific streets, yeshivas and synagogues.

Even as you pray for the gates of Mea Shearim, declare the promise of Isaiah 60 —that violence will no longer be heard in her borders, and that her walls will be called Yeshua (salvation) and her gates Baruch (praise)!

It is fascinating to discover city records revealing that Mea Shearim was envisioned to be an attractive neighborhood, that decorative trees and bushes were to be planted inside the walls and that raising sheep and cattle would be prohibited so as to preserve its cleanliness and beauty. Today, the first thing prayerwalkers will notice in the original city is that there are no trees, no bushes, and it is anything but clean and decorative. In fact, it is the most neglected and disheveled district of the surrounding Ultra-Orthodox community. The disorganized and often chaotic appearance of the neighborhood may be somewhat attributed to the fact that, for many years, Mea Shearim was a *closed and self-sufficient township*. Every aspect of life in the neighborhood was handled primarily by local administration, by residents whose first priority was not paving, repairing, and cleaning streets, building stores and markets, repairing water cisterns, ritual baths and public restrooms, and basically ensuring peace and tranquility, but rather *Torah study.*

Prayerwalkers frequently observe the phenomena that the Ultra-Orthodox are in a world of their own, seemingly oblivious to their surroundings, except that they always notice strangers and are generally discomfited by their presence.

There is a distinct *spirit of isolation and poverty* hovering over the community confirmed in city records documenting its inception. According to the record, Mea Shearim is described as having a character all its own. Those who built the neighborhood came from Eastern Europe. They purposely and deliberately built themselves a copy of the old shtetl, a real ghetto, closed off to the outside world and far removed from the main arteries of communication, completely self-isolated so that it should not become desecrated through contact with others. The walls were intended to protect them, body and soul. Although Mea Shearim could not remain strictly isolated for long, and the neighborhood expanded far beyond its original borders, the spirit of isolation remains strong.

> *"The spiritual did not come first,*
> *But the natural,*
> *And after that the spiritual."*
> *(I Corinthians 15:46)*

There is a *kingdom principle* here, even though Paul was referring to the resurrection of the dead and the promise of a spiritual body. What is first sown in the natural produces a spiritual harvest. The prayers of the saints are literally pushing back the weight of heaviness and light is peeking through the clouds of oppression.

I have been prayerwalking Mea Shearim for over eight years, thus cultivating an ever-growing familiarity with the community. It is, therefore, natural to observe the changing physical conditions of the neighborhood over time and also to gauge the *"spiritual temperature"* as hundreds of intercessors from around the world have taken assignments to pray for streets, yeshivas, and synagogues, and prayerwalks have grown to embrace intercessory groups, even pastors.

An ongoing cry of the heart on each walk has been, "Oh Lord, cleanse the neighborhood, inside and out! Purify the hearts and sweep the debris from the streets. Restore the buildings and crush the spirit of poverty. Defeat the ghetto mentality. You came to give us *life* and that *abundantly.*" Praise the Lord, we are seeing a burst of *renovation* and *new construction* in Mea Shearim, particularly since the Year 2000. The community is undergoing a facelift in the natural, but the revival of the spirit will surely follow!

Pray for a cleansing and purifying of Mea Shearim in the natural and in the Spirit. Praise the Lord for the prayers He is already answering in the neighborhood. Pray that the life of Messiah would be planted in Mea Shearim, along with decorative trees, flowers, and lush green plants that will delights the eye and inspire the soul. Pray that the Ultra-Orthodox will be set free from the spirit of poverty and isolation so that they can be a blessing in Messiah to Israel and to all the nations of the earth.

"Moreover, I will make your
*Battlements of **rubies**,
Your gates of crystal,
And your entire wall of precious stones.*"
(Isaiah 54:12)

In the Bible, the names of people, places, and even objects, such as wells, were very prophetic and symbolic. As it turns out, the land that was purchased for Mea Shearim, consisting of approximately eight acres, was originally owned by Arab peasants. This property on the northern outskirts of the Old City was considerably less costly than near the main thoroughfare of Jaffa Road. But this too was of the Lord because the ground the community purchased was called *Kerem Kadkod.* This word "kadkod" only appears twice in the whole Bible, once in Isaiah 54:12 and then again in Ezekiel 27:16, and is translated *"with rubies"* (meaning "bright red"). This means that the original walled-in neighborhood of Mea Shearim was called (in English) *"Ruby Vineyard!"*

When the Lord says that He will make their battlements (or protecting ramparts on top of a fortress) *ruby red*, what can this mean? The color red has always symbolized the Blood of the Lamb. The vineyard is a symbol of Israel (Isaiah 5:1-7), new wine (Amos 9:13-14), and the intimate bridal relationship with the Lord (Song of Songs 2:15, 7:12, Hosea 2:14-17). It is thrilling to realize that the name of this ground is a prophetic picture and promise that, within these walls, there will grow a flourishing vineyard, that when the Lord comes looking for fruit, He will find luscious, deep red grapes that will yield sweet, new wine!

I invite you to pray prophetically into this revelation. Pray and proclaim that the original walled-in city gated community of Mea Shearim will, even now, begin to produce a fruitful harvest, a vineyard of worshippers washed in the Blood of the Lamb. Pray that new wine will be poured into new wineskins. Pray that the Lord will catch and destroy "the little foxes" that would try to spoil the vineyards that are in bloom. Pray that their surrounding walls (battlements) will be protected, in the Spirit, by the Blood of the Lamb, just like the pillar of fire stood between the Israelites and the Egyptians in the wilderness, and that any attempt to hinder or crush the harvest will be shielded by the fire of God.

In 1997, the Lord led me to begin prayerwalking Mea Shearim. Most of the streets are named after prophets or rabbis, but others have intriguing names. Pri Chadash means *"a new fruit,"* Ein Ya'akov means *"Spring of Jacob,"* Ben Amram translates *"Son of Exalted People,"* and Sde Khemed means *"Field of Grace."* The term "prayerwalking" has been used several times and a brief definition may be helpful for those who have never been on a prayerwalk.

A prayerwalk is praying on site, claiming the assigned territory for the Kingdom of God, praying for the city or neighborhood to open up to the gospel, and engaging in spiritual warfare against the principalities and powers that are currently controlling the region.

I encourage intercessors to pray aloud, but not loudly, and to pray any Scriptures or prophetic words the Lord may quicken to their spirit. Declarations, proclamations, words of praise, soft singing, and even anointing with oil can be included in the walk, as the Spirit leads, depending on the situation. *The objective is to pray through the area without disturbing the lives of the residents or attracting notice.* We are always open to and pray for "divine appointments" but we do not solicit or distribute literature. A key to prayerwalking in Mea Shearim without drawing attention is observing the strict dress code, mostly affecting women, the rules of which are clearly posted at every possible entrance to the community.

TO ALL WOMEN WHO PASS THROUGH NEIGHBORHOOD:
Passing through our neighborhood in immodest dress disturbs the holy atmosphere which prevails here and interferes with our way of life and the values we strive to imbue in our children. **Therefore we ask you please:**
DO NOT ENTER OUR NEIGHBORHOOD IN
IMMODEST DRESS
WHICH MEANS: WOMEN'S APPAREL **MUST** BE NON-TRANSPARENT, CLOSED AT THE **NECKLINE**, SLEEVES COVERING THE **ELBOWS** AND ...S COVERING THE **KNEES.** WOMEN'S **PANTS** (TROUSERS) ...) ANY **TIGHT-FITTING** CLOTHING IS **NOT** ACCEPTABLE.
...spect our feelings in our neighborhood and do not disturb ...sanctity of the area and the education of our children.
We thank you and wish you only good things.
The Council of Local Residents

<u>**Women must wear long, loose-fitting skirts to the ankle, blouses with sleeves reaching at least below the elbow, and have their chest area fully covered. It is not necessary to wear a hat and sandals are permitted.**</u>

One day, the Lord showed favor during a prayerwalk where trouble developed. I was walking with a couple in the tiny walled-in city. A sizeable tour group (perhaps 30 people) with cameras hanging from their necks came in with a foreign-speaking tour guide and about half the women wearing slacks, strictly prohibited in this community. It was all the wrong combinations and before long, there was angry shouting and a gathering crowd. We stepped off to the side so as not to be identified with the group. Ultimately, they were forced to turn back and leave the area. After the dust settled and we walked on, an elderly Ultra-Orthodox man approached and began speaking to us in Hebrew. When he realized we spoke English, he said, "We have some crazy people here." While others were being chased out, we were receiving an apology for the disruption (which is truly amazing because rarely will anyone speak to you in this neighborhood).

Nearly all the yeshivas and synagogues that the network prays for were discovered during prayerwalks. Some large buildings house a small synagogue along with apartment dwellings and one synagogue had the following words written on the doorway in Hebrew: "This house will never be sold until the Messiah comes!"

It really touched my heart the way the Lord led us to find a particularly hidden yeshiva. I had recently met a new believer who was formerly Ultra-Orthodox and whose family still lives in Mea Shearim. Her father is the Chief Rabbi of a yeshiva, although the name she gave didn't sound familiar. I didn't have it on my list, yet it is on a street we pray for. After carefully traversing the street with a prayer partner and experiencing no success in finding it, we began to cautiously ask residents if they knew where this yeshiva was. This is always risky business because it may arouse suspicions why two women are looking for a yeshiva. I approached a woman standing in a doorway. She said she didn't know and then proceeded to yell down the street to a young Ultra-Orthodox man standing next to a car (which is precisely what we didn't want, but it turned out to be the Lord.) This young man was a New Yorker, very friendly, and he took us around to the back of a yeshiva we were already praying for to show us where this smaller yeshiva was. Since it was unmarked (a yeshiva within a yeshiva), there is no way we would have found it without his help. It was a precious confirmation that the Lord desires there be prayer for EVERY yeshiva in this neighborhood.

Pray for the salvation of the rabbis in all the yeshivas in Mea Shearim. There is a remnant chosen by grace. Pray also for the salvation of the young Ultra-Orthodox man we met. The Lord knows his name. He was unusually friendly in taking the time to show us around. He even took us inside the smaller yeshiva. Pray that he will be used of the Lord to bring the good news of Messiah to Mea Shearim!

> *"Elijah was a man with a nature like ours,*
> *And he prayed **earnestly** that it might not rain;*

*And it did not rain on the earth
For three years and six months.
And he prayed again, and the sky poured rain,
And the earth produced its fruit.
(James 5:17)*

Mighty man of God and prophet that Elijah was, he, nevertheless, needed to pray fervent, sustained prayers before the sky poured out rain. If we are serious about pressing through in prayer to a visitation of God in Mea Shearim, there is a price in the spirit. Like Elijah, we must be willing to *pray earnestly again and again.*

I have always prayerwalked with a prayer partner or small group of intercessors for two reasons: the prayer of agreement is a powerful prayer and there is a greater dimension of protection and covering when two or more are gathered in His Name. The first year, the Lord was faithful to select a precious sister in the Lord who lived in Jerusalem and had a similar burden for the Ultra-Orthodox. She walked with me every week until she returned to the States.

As we prayed through the 140 streets in the area designated by the Lord, we clearly sensed that many of these streets away from the main tourist center had never been walked before. We were becoming aware of a great resistance in the spirit. One day, as we were walking streets, we turned the corner onto a certain street, and the spiritual atmosphere changed drastically, swift as the snap of a finger. We both stopped simultaneously and began pleading the Blood of Jesus over ourselves, requesting "angelic protection" and binding hindering spirits. I praise the Lord for the assurance of His Presence and reminder that no weapon formed against us will stand!

Early in my prayerwalking experiences in Mea Shearim, there were days when I would return from a walk and need to rest for hours. That initial breaking through was worth all the exhaustion. One day, as I was waiting for my prayer partner on a busy Mea Shearim Street, the Lord showed me a brief vision in the spirit. I saw smiles, laughter, joy, dancing, singing, and davening (bowing) to Yeshua in this place. I saw a deep love and tenderness towards Him. It so encouraged me that it really *will* happen. They will kiss the Son of God just as they daily kiss the mezzuzah on their doorposts and hold Him close to their hearts. Then, the curtain closed and it was as if the Lord said, "Now you know what you're praying for. Keep going!" That vision really encouraged me.

I cannot overstress the spiritual heaviness and oppression hovering over Mea Shearim. The call to pray and the love of God in our hearts compels us into enemy territory. Nevertheless, there is a backlash to every encounter and it is spiritually, emotionally, and physically demanding.

We engage in battle from the position of victory purchased by Yeshua, yet it is extremely important to guard our daily walk with the Lord, put on the full armor, and learn how to pray over ourselves so that the enemy will not overcome us.

Father God, I present myself before you today to search me and know me, to reveal any hidden sin in my heart, that I would confess it, repent of it, and receive forgiveness with thanksgiving. I cover myself with the precious Blood of Jesus and ask the Holy Spirit to breathe upon and empower all my prayers. I put on the full armor of God in Ephesians chapter 6 (in word and also in lifestyle). I ask for a hedge of protection and plead the Blood of Yeshua over my family (marriage, children, parents), my health, finances, possessions, and ministry (or profession), and I bind and rebuke any retaliating spirits that would come against me or anyone close to me. Father, I praise you and thank you that you surround me and all who are near and dear to me with your ministering angels. In Jesus' Name I pray, Amen.

*"**No one** can come to me*
*unless the Father who sent me **draws him***
and I will raise him up at the last day."
(John 6:44)

The Lord has burned this simple truth into my heart as a key prayer point for Mea Shearim. Yeshua said no one could come to Him *unless the Father draws him*. No one means *no one*. None of us came to the Lord through our own efforts or intellect. The Father sought each of us out and drew us to His Son.

Pray that the Father (the God of Abraham, Isaac and Jacob) will DRAW the Ultra-Orthodox in Mea Shearim to His Son, Yeshua, the Messiah of Israel. Pray especially that He would draw the rabbis and teachers in the yeshivas, who have a tremendous influence on the local community and Ultra-Orthodoxy around the world.

As we entreat the Father to move upon the hearts of the Ultra-Orthodox in Mea Shearim and draw them to Yeshua, we want to especially ask Him to touch those who are key leaders in the community.

Pray for the mercy of the Lord to touch the hearts of those in positions of leadership. Pray for the salvation of the heads of yeshivas, the heads of synagogues, heads of rabbinical courts, all influential Torah scholars, leaders of the Shas Party, United Torah Judaism, and the United Religious Party. Pray especially for the salvation of the leadership of Yad L'Achim, the prominent anti-missionary organization and all who engage in anti-missionary activities. Pray for Damascus Road experiences for all these leaders and ask Yeshua to reveal Himself in dreams, visions and personal visitations. Pray that the Lord will lead those who may already be secret believers to other secret believers so they might encourage one another, pray together, and grow in their faith and their desire to courageously declare their beliefs openly.

> *"I tell you the truth," Jesus replied,*
> *''No one who has left home or brothers or sisters*
> *Or mother or father or children or fields*
> **For me and the gospel**
> *Will fail to receive a hundred times as much*
> *In this present age...and with them persecutions,*
> *And in the age to come, eternal life."*
> *(Mark 10:29-30)*

There is no advancing the Kingdom of God without a degree of suffering. An incident in Mea Shearim graphically depicts the degree of suffering which may be involved in reaching out to the Ultra-Orthodox with the love of Messiah.

I had the privilege of meeting three Swiss ladies whose apartment was completely destroyed in the Fall of 1998. Although this event was well-publicized in the media, for security purposes, their names will remain anonymous. Needless to say, these precious sisters were thrilled to hear that hundreds of intercessors from all over the world are praying for Mea Shearim. Their hearts ache that they were torn from this neighborhood they love so much, yet they have completely forgiven everyone who participated in the rampage and continue to pray for Mea Shearim, even though they now minister in another region of the city. We agreed that there was a definite connection between what was happening in the heavenlies through our intercessory prayer (and the prayers of others we are unaware of) and what later took place on the ground.

During the three years they lived in Mea Shearim, they were able to befriend some of the Ultra-Orthodox women and the exciting news is that, for the most part, these women are *hungry for truth*, simply because they are more in touch with their suffering than the men, who are kept busy with the demands of Torah study and other religious activities. I will highlight only one of their fascinating stories.

As one of these sisters was driving home one day and stopped at a busy intersection in downtown Mea Shearim, an Ultra-Orthodox woman opened the front door of the passenger seat and jumped in. Just then, the light turned green and off they went. The woman explained that she had gotten some cleaning solution in her eyes and needed to be taken somewhere. While she was giving directions, they started up a conversation and the woman quickly invited her to visit at a certain time and place as she ran from the car upon their arrival. Because the time the Orthodox woman gave conflicted with the driver's schedule, she sent one of the other ladies to visit the woman and they soon became friends.

This next part is truly incredible. I have always encouraged the intercessors on prayerwalks in Mea Shearim to be "aware of the physical appearance of the neighborhood" because it is often a reflection of the condition of the soul. The Orthodox woman described her hopelessly cluttered, dusty, mice-infested apartment, saying "You see this? This place is how I am on the inside!" She exclaimed that her husband (who was never home during their visits) is "severely emotionally disturbed," abusive, and she cannot motivate herself to cook or clean and is always depressed. Our sister prayed with her many times and, on one occasion when she was visiting, shared about the Messiah and how the Tenach speaks of Him in the 53rd chapter of Isaiah. Interested in what she was hearing, the Orthodox woman carefully searched through the many volumes of books covering the walls of the house, but could not find the Book of Isaiah so that she could read for herself that this is also in the Jewish Scriptures and not only in the "Christian Bible."

It is likely that the woman asked her husband where the Isaiah book was and, next thing you know, she is tearfully telling her friend that she is forbidden to see her anymore, but that she really loves her and feels good around her, but can't continue the friendship. The Swiss sister also felt that someone may have noticed her visits, perhaps followed to see where she lived, and this may also have served as a catalyst to the break-in.

I have also experienced divine appointments, but for reasons of security and privacy, I cannot share the details.

Pray for the salvation of the Ultra-Orthodox lady our sister witnessed to who was hungry for more than religion and curious about the gospel. The Lord knows who she is and that she is hurting, searching and very lonely for friends. Pray that He will bring a new believing friend into her life to water the seed that was planted and pray that she will continue searching for the Book of Isaiah until she reads Chapter 53 in her own Bible. Ask the Lord to confirm the truth that was spoken to her and reveal Himself to her. Pray for the salvation of the men who destroyed the flat of the Swiss ladies. Pray also for the protection of these sisters, that they may be permitted to remain in Israel as long as it is the Lord's will for them to be here.

"Who has ascended into
Heaven and descended?
Who has gathered the wind
In His fists?
Who has wrapped the waters

In His garment?
Who has established all
The ends of the earth?
What is His name or His son's name?
Surely you know."
(Proverbs 30:4)

I have always felt in my spirit that when the marvelous mystery of this riddle is suddenly revealed to the Ultra-Orthodox, sparking revival, it will "blow their hats off." The God of Israel is a God of epic drama - the Flood, the plagues of Egypt, parting the Red Sea, bringing down the walls of Jericho, taking Elijah in a fiery chariot, the Resurrection. I can't wait to see how the drama of salvation unfolds in Mea Shearim. I was especially blessed and encouraged by a vision sent to me by an intercessor in the network:

"As I was praying, I saw a picture of an Orthodox man (black coat, black beard, curls and black hat). He had thick glasses and a troublesome look on his face. He walked in a narrow street with his head low, but all of a sudden light began to shine in this narrow street and slowly the shadows of the buildings alongside this road disappeared until there was no shadow left. There was only this immense bright light and this light changed into wind, first slowly, but more and more strongly this wind began to blow in this narrow street as if it was an open field.

When the shadows began to disappear (before the wind started to blow), this Orthodox man noticed the difference and lifted up his head in surprise about the light entering the narrow street. But then, as he stood there, the wind started to blow. First, HIS HAT WAS BLOWN OFF (Hallelujah - my Hallelujah!), then his thick glasses fell off and this troublesome look on his face could not stay. All of a sudden, he looked immensely young. He tried to continue to walk as he did before and bowed his head to go against the wind, but he couldn't. Then he started smiling in surprise at the strong wind. There he stood for awhile, leaning against the wind, then finally, in surrender, he fell on his knees and bowed his head as to acknowledge that the wind was stronger than his manpower to resist. He didn't look like a man who had failed. He looked like a man totally caught up in praise on his knees, with a wonderful peace glowing from his face."

Praise the Lord for this powerful vision! I would ask you to pray that if this vision relates to a real person, that very soon his spiritual hat would be blown off by the power of the Holy Spirit! Pray that Yeshua would visit Mea Shearim as a glorious brilliant light, and that the Holy Spirit would come like a mighty rushing wind causing every effort to resist Him to fail, bringing the Chasidim to their knees so that the PEACE OF GOD can glow from their faces. Pray that this wind will blow away the darkness and the deception and that the light will so overpower the darkness that it can have no place in their lives.

> *"And the angel of the Lord*
> *Appeared to him (Gideon)*
> *And said to him,*
> *'The Lord is with you, O valiant warrior.'"*
> *(Judges 6:12)*

To be perfectly honest, it is a wonder that God sent me to pioneer prayer for Mea Shearim. I praise the Lord that He has been known to use *unlikely characters* to fulfill His purposes. Gideon is perhaps the best example (Judges 6 & 7). He was fearful, hiding in the winepress, his tribe was the weakest in Manasseh, he was the least within his family, and his faith was not exactly exuberant when the angel of the Lord visited him. He felt unqualified, unworthy, and overwhelmed, emotions I can relate to. Yet, God chose Gideon to deliver Israel from the Midianites. David was the youngest of Jesse's sons and his father didn't consider him worth presenting to Samuel as a candidate for king. Yet this young shepherd boy was God's choice over his older, taller, more attractive brothers (I Samuel 16:1-13). Amos was a herdsmen, tending sycamore fig trees when God called him to prophesy at Israel's royal sanctuary in Bethel during the reign of King Jeroboam II and Amaziah the priest. He was not a seasoned or recognized prophet (Amos 7:14-15).

Pray that God will commission His chosen vessels, even the most unlikely men (and women) in far-off lands, to accomplish His plans and purposes for the Ultra-Orthodox in these last days.

As the prayer network for the Ultra-Orthodox spread around the world and prayerwalks in Mea Shearim intensified, the Lord began to heighten my awareness of the two major rival Ultra-Orthodox groups: the *Chasidim* and the *Mitnagidim.*

The Chasidim

*"For by **grace** you have been saved*
Through faith, and that not of yourselves;
*It is the **gift of God,** not of works,*
Lest anyone should boast."
(Ephesians 2:8-9)

The vast majority of Ultra-Orthodox in Mea Shearim are Chasidim, a secretive, mystical, even cultic community, and there are precious few writings that describe their inner world. Generally speaking, the term *Chasid* refers to pious Jews who maintain the highest standard of observing the religious and moral commandments, or who exhibit exemplary behavior in some aspect of life. They go beyond the letter of the law. Interestingly, the word *Chasidim* means "saints" and comes from the Hebrew word *chesed*, meaning *grace*, literally *saints living by grace!* I was excited to discover this and find it wonderfully prophetic and yet another manifestation of God's marvelous sense of humor. The Book of Zechariah (4:6-7) speaks of bringing forth the capstone with shouts of "Grace! Grace to it!"

Let us speak "grace" over the Chasidim. Pray that the Lord will them give a profound revelation of this amazing gift of God, that He will open their eyes to see and understand what it means to live under grace and to walk in grace. Pray for a revelation of Yeshua, the Capstone, the true Cornerstone, who came to extend grace to all who would receive this gift by His shed Blood on Calvary.

"For though we live in the world,
We do not wage war as the world does.
The weapons we fight with
Are not the weapons of the world.

> *On the contrary, they have divine power*
> ***To demolish strongholds."***
> *(II Corinthians 10:3-5)*

Crisis points in history are *gateways* for the enemy to invade, take advantage of a perceived need, advance his influence and establish *strongholds*. The Babylonian Exile (586 B.C.) and the Bar Kokhba Revolt (132-135 A.D.) were times of major crisis for the children of Israel. The mystical movement called *Chasidism* emerged out of the despair and chaos of the Middle Ages. As we investigate the rise and development of Chasidism, our purpose is to identify strongholds that need to be confronted through prayer so that the captives can be set free.

Strongholds are ways of thinking that become entrenched due to generations of demonic intrusion into the culture and religious system of a people.

Chasidism rose to prominence in the midst of tremendous tension between the sophisticated, learned *urban Jews* and the less educated and cultured *rural Jew*. Rabbi Israel ben-Eliezer (1700-1760), the founder of Chasidism, appeared on the scene in the mid-1700's when Eastern European Jewry was in a *desperate* state. Poverty, persecution, and pogroms had reduced the average Jew to peasants in constant fear for their lives. Sadly, the Church, who should have been reaching out with the love and compassion of God, turned a deaf ear to the continual outbursts of anti-Semitism and often approved of them. Jewish faith was growing weary.

At this opportune moment, Rabbi Israel, an unlearned man, given to visions and revelations, to meditation in the countryside, and having an intense fascination with Kabbalah (to be discussed later), *revealed himself* on his 36th birthday as a healer and leader. He later became known as the *Ba'al Shem Tov* ('Master of the Good Name'), a title bestowed upon him because of his alleged healing powers and miracles he performed by "invoking the name of God." The *revelations* of the Ba'al Shem Tov and the spread of Chasidim filled a perceived need in European Jewry and served as an *awakening* from an era Jewish writers describe as "spiritual unconsciousness." The attraction of

Chasidism at such a dark time was that it attempted to create a Judaism that was slightly more *personal,* more *attainable* for the average Jew who wasn't a scholar, and emphasized *joy* in prayer.

> *"... for Satan himself*
> *masquerades as an angel of light."*
> *(II Corinthians 11:14)*

The birth of Chasidism can best be appreciated in an *experience* the Ba'al Shem Tov shared in a letter to his brother-in-law, who was living in Israel at the time. This letter was first printed in 1781 and appears in many sources of Chasidic thought. In the letter, Rabbi Israel describes an *ascent of soul* that he achieved into the *upper worlds,* using *holy names,* where he purportedly receive knowledge that laid the foundation of Chasidism. The Ba'al was supposedly *guided* through this experience by a teacher and master and entered the *Chamber of the Messiah,* where the Messiah was *studying Torah* with the Sages of the Mishnah and other righteous ones. Rabbi Israel (the Ba'al) claims that he asked the Messiah when He would come and was told that He would not come until his teachings (referring to Rabbi Israel's teachings) would be *revealed* in the world, although he was forbidden by the Messiah to reveal the secrets of these teachings during his lifetime. Rabbi Israel also mentions encountering three *segulot* (described, in Chasidism, as beings possessing mystical powers).

Now that your head is spinning, let's focus in on a few points. Although Chasidism has grown and matured as any spiritual movement will, we are taking the time to analyze this experience because Chasidic theology builds upon and flows from this deceptive encounter. The Ba'al Shem Tov claimed that he was accompanied by a "teacher and master" on his dangerous ascent.

The practice of "guidance" by the soul of a prophet or saintly person from former times is common in kabbalistic thought.

This reliance on *spirit guides* can be traced at least as far back as R. Yitzchak Luria (1534-1572), perhaps the most famous kabbalist of Safed, also known as the *Arizal ("blessed memory").* Who was the mysterious escort that assisted the Ba'al Shem Tov to the upper worlds? Chasidic tradition says this master was the *Prophet Achiya HaShiloni*, whose soul was first revealed to him on his twenty-sixth birthday. Maimonides (a famous Jewish commentator) contended that Achiya Ha Shiloni received the Oral Tradition from Moses, was subsequently a member of the Rabbinical Court of King David and was also the master of Elijah the Prophet (talk about a guy who gets around!).

> *"Behold, I will send you*
> *The prophet Elijah*
> *Before that great and dreadful*
> *Day of the Lord comes."*
> *(Malachi 4:5)*

Another teaching of Kabbalah is that an especially *worthy person* (also known as a *Tzaddik, or righteous one)* may receive a revelation of Elijah the Prophet as a means of divine inspiration. The Chasidim are most zealous for the coming of Messiah. Is it any wonder that the spirits visiting "worthy ones" pose as the prophet whom Micah said would come before the Messiah?

Cry out to God to reveal to the Chasidim, however disturbing it may be, that the Ba'al Shem Tov was visited by a demonic spirit posing as the "soul" of Achiya HaShiloni. In the Name of Yeshua, bind the spirit of Achiya HaShiloni and every familiar spirit that would masquerade as the spirit of Elijah (or any prophet or sage) from visiting, communicating with, imparting knowledge or revelation, or working miracles among the Chasidim. In love for God's people, and even as a warning, pray that the Lord would allow these spirits to reveal themselves as the hateful, grotesque creatures they really are. Pray that the Holy Spirit would unmask these evil spirits so that the Ultra-Orthodox will know they are not hearing from the heavenly realm, but rather from the very depths of hell.

> *"For unto us a child is born,*
> *To us a son is given,*
> *And the government will be on his shoulders.*
> *And he will be called*
> *Wonderful Counselor,* **Mighty God,**

Everlasting Father,
Prince of Peace."
(Isaiah 9:6)

Interestingly, Rabbi Israel's *ascent* takes him to a chamber where he meets a Messiah who needs to *learn Torah* with the sages and the righteous ones. (For those unfamiliar with the term "Torah," it encompasses the **Written Law,** which are the five books of Moses, and the **Oral Law,** which includes the Mishnah, the Talmud, Midrash, and Halachah, all of which are commentaries based on the Written Law or expositions of Jewish Law based on the interpretations of the rabbis), as well as all the prophetic writings of the Old Testament. Torah also embraces the teachings of the Zohar, a major literature of Kabbalah.

Satan's greatest desire since his rebellion against God in heaven has always been to exalt himself and be worshipped. His attack on the authority and divinity of God, with the goal of deceiving mankind into believing that he could be "like God," is as old as the garden. The Word of God says that the Messiah of Israel will be called *Mighty God* and *Everlasting Father*, but here we see the old serpent revealing a messiah who *needs to learn Torah* with the rest of the sages.

"Therefore the Lord himself
Will give you a sign:
*The **virgin** will be with child*
And will give birth to a son,
*And will call him **Immanuel**."*
(Isaiah 7:14)

What is Satan's strategy here? After all, if the Messiah is merely human and needs to learn Torah along with Moses and the sages, *then the messiah could potentially be anybody.* Biblical prophecies, which speak of a miraculous birth and a child who would be called *God With Us,* no longer serve as guideposts to who Messiah might be. Rather, they have been usurped by *observations* of the rabbis as to who might *qualify* to be messiah based on their living the lifestyle of a Torah-observant Jew and having received special revelations. This helps us understand how the Habad Hasidim (popularly known as

Lubavitchers) could be misled into thinking that Rabbi Menachem Schneerson (1902-1994) was the Messiah. Although Rabbi Schneerson never visited Israel once in his life, let alone being born in Bethlehem (Micah 5:2), he is still considered by many in the Lubavitcher movement to be the anointed one that will return and redeem Israel!

Pray that the Spirit of Revelation and Truth will expose this deception and remove the veil from the eyes of the Chasidim to see that Yeshua, the Holy One of Israel, is Messiah and also "God with us," whose goings forth are from the days of eternity. Yeshua does not need to learn Torah because HE IS THE TORAH, the Living Torah, the Word made flesh, the Alpha and the Omega, the One "in whom are hidden all the treasures of wisdom and knowledge." (Colossians 2:3) In the Name of Jesus, bind every lying and deceptive spirit attached to this false revelation of Messiah that diminishes His glory and deity. Yeshua fulfilled 100 primary Old Testament prophecies in His first advent 2,000 years ago. Pray that the Chasidim will return to BIBLICAL PROPHECY as the only source of truth revealing who Messiah is. Pray they will repent of accepting mystical experiences as truth over and above the Word of God. Pray they would be freed from distorted interpretations of Messianic prophecies in the Jewish commentaries and would search the Scriptures for themselves to see the fulfillment of these prophecies in Yeshua.

"Therefore God exalted Him
To the highest place
And gave Him the name that is
Above every name,
That at the Name of Jesus
Every knee should bow,
In heaven and on earth and under the earth,
And every tongue confess
That Yeshua the Messiah is Lord,
To the glory of God the Father."
(Philippians 2:9-11)

I praise the Lord for this declaration of Scripture that there is no name higher than the Name of Yeshua, and the assurance that one day, at the Name of Jesus, every knee shall bow *in heaven, on earth* and *under the earth.* Referring to his experience in the upper worlds, Rabbi Israel shared that he achieved his ascent of soul using *holy names.*

What exactly are these *names* that Rabbi Israel used to bring about an ascent of soul? Oral tradition says that two of the Holy Names are **_yichuda ila'ah_** *(the upper unity, in which all of creation is nullified in the all-encompassing Being of God)* and **_yichuda tata'ah_** *(the lower unity, in which Godliness permeates all of creation, including spatial and temporal dimensions).* In everyday street language, this boils down to the pantheistic jingle "God is everything and everything is God." The third holy name is **_Ein Sof_** (which means "Infinite").

Satan *masquerades* as an angel of light (II Corinthians 11:14). He is a created being and, therefore, cannot create anything original. He merely *imitates everything godly,* but it is important to appreciate that he can only imitate something *real.* Satan cannot counterfeit a $3 bill because there is no such thing. It is simply fascinating to watch him imitate and pervert every major truth. In these end times, it is the heart of God to rescue His people from the grasp of the enemy and bring them into His marvelous light.

Although the word "trinity" never appears in the Bible, the Scriptures reveal that the Godhead is expressed in *three persons* or personalities. These persons have **names** - God the Father (Yahveh), God the Son (Yeshua), and God the Holy Spirit (Ruach Ha Kodesh). It should come as no surprise that the Father of Lies would attempt to pervert the triune Godhead, attribute descriptive names for God *to himself* and then bequeath them to someone as "passwords" into the so-called *upper worlds.* After all, the desire of Lucifer is to *ascend* above the tops of the clouds and make himself like the Most High (Isaiah 14:14).

> *"Hear O Israel, the Lord our God is one."*
> *(Deuteronomy 6:4)*

The Shema, perhaps the most famous Jewish prayer, is recited twice daily by Orthodox Jews all over the world. The Hebrew word for "one" in Deuteronomy 6:4 is "echad" which is plural and signifies a *compound unity*. In the same way that water is one substance yet can manifest as a liquid, a solid (ice), or a gas (vapor or steam), there are three personalities in the Godhead, each expressing itself in a different form, yet all one.

Rabbi Israel mentions *three segulot*, which Chasidism describes as *beings* possessing mystical power or means of transmitting mystical power. It is clear in Scripture that there are only *two sources of power* in the universe: power from God, through the *Holy Spirit*, the Spirit of Messiah Jesus (II Corinthians 3:17-18) freely available to those who are *in relationship with Yeshua,* or power from the *"unholy" spirits* of hell. We can easily recognize these *beings* that the Ba'al Shem Tov encountered as demonic spirits. It is an interesting observation that the founder of Chasidism also has *three names*, Israel ben-Eliezer, the Ba'al Shem Tov, and "the Besht," using the acronyms of his bestowed name, which he was affectionately called by his disciples.

Pray that this doctrine of demons concerning the holy names of God and the three segulot, this clever imitation of the triune nature of God, will be exposed, uprooted and replaced with the TRUTH of the compound unity of the God of Israel who is Father, Son, and Holy Spirit. Pray for a revelation of the life-giving truth that a Holy Name has been given to all mankind, Jew and Gentile alike, a Name that grants us a new and living way into the very Holy of Holies. Declare to every principality and power, in heaven, in earth and under the earth that Jesus is the NAME ABOVE ALL NAMES. There is only one Name we have been given, the Name of Yeshua (Jesus). There is salvation in no other Name, healing in no other Name, deliverance in no other Name. Pray that these blessed truths would be revealed to the Ultra-Orthodox. Let us cry out to the Lord for a great spiritual awakening among the Ultra-Orthodox in these last days that will bring them back to the God of Israel and His Word and deliver them from mystical experiences.

The Ba'al Shem Tov did not put his teachings in writings, but passed the mantle of leadership to his senior disciple Dov Baer (known as the *Maggid of Mezhirech)* before his death. The Hebrew word *maggid* means "preacher," but is also the word for "angel." Most of what is known about the Besht was passed down primarily through the Maggid, who died in 1772, through legends, stories, and books of praises, which were first published in 1814. Although the Maggid of Mezhirech was a Talmud scholar and practiced an ascetic lifestyle, concepts clashing with the teachings of the Ba'al, a debilitating illness led him to seek healing from the Besht, after which he became one of his chief disciples. He then attracted many learned scholars of his day to Chasidism.

In the Ba'al's teachings handed down by the Maggid, he stressed *love of one's fellow Jew* (even one who has strayed and needs to be brought back to faith), *spreading the wellspring of knowledge* concealed in the hidden wisdom of Torah, and *preparing the world and oneself for the coming of Messiah.* The Maggid himself stressed humility as a major virtue, a teaching we could heartily embrace, but he also taught there *was no such thing as absolute evil, only degrees of good.* The Maggid taught that sin contained repentance even as the olive contains oil.

The traditional rabbis fiercely opposed Chasidism, particularly because of the movement's ecstatic mode of worship, the change in prayer ritual and Torah study, and perhaps mostly because youth were abandoning the yeshivas and flocking to Mezhirech to study Chasidism.

Jacob Joseph of Polonnoye succeeded the Maggid and published the first Chasidic book, *Toledot Ya'akov Yosef* ("The History of Jacob Joseph") in 1780. This controversial work expressed the basic views of Chasidism, and also rendered sharp criticism of the great disparity between the Jewish leadership and the common people, an unfortunate reality that fueled the Chasidic movement. The book aroused the anger of the Mitnagdim in Brody and copies of it were burned.

*"The knowledge of the **secrets**
of the kingdom of heaven
has been given to you, but not to them.*

Whoever has will be given more,
and he will have an abundance.
Whoever does not have,
even what he has will be taken from him."
(Matthew 13:11-12)

Everyone loves a secret and God has *secrets* He longs to share. But Scripture tells us that He only shares them with sons and daughters *in His Kingdom* who enter the Kingdom through *the one and only Gate, Yeshua* (John 10:7-9). It is dangerous to seek heavenly secrets outside the Kingdom and even Rabbi Israel sensed that before his mystical journey. If Jesus is the Gate, then any source of secrets *outside of Him* is not a heavenly source.

During the Ba'al Shem Tov's mystical experience, he encountered a *soul* that he believed to be the Messiah. This Messiah told him that he would not come until Rabbi Israel's teachings would be revealed in the world. Oral tradition says that the Ba'al Shem Tov was forbidden to reveal the *secrets* he learned during his lifetime. Thus, he transmitted them to his disciples *after his death.*

We may safely say that once the door has been opened for demonic activity, however unwittingly, that activity is sure to continue in the next generation. How did the Ba'al Shem Tov's teachings reach the Chasidim after his death and the death of the Maggid, his successor? Chabad tradition relates that a certain Rabbi Shneur Zalman was *visited,* while in prison, *by the Ba'al Shem Tov* and the *Maggid of Mezritch.* In a nutshell, these two familiar spirits visited Rabbi Zalman and *gave him permission to reveal the esoteric secrets of Kabbalah — that is, the transmission of mystical experience and power* communicated to the Besht, which were not permitted to be revealed in his lifetime.

<u>According to Chasidic tradition, the purpose for revealing these "secrets" was to prepare the Jewish people for the advent of the Messiah.</u>

As mentioned earlier, the Ba'al Shem Tov appeared on the scene when Jewry in Eastern Europe was in a desperate state. Religious, social, and economic discrimination against the Jewish people had turned into outright persecution. Chasidism filled a spiritual vacuum and the Ba'al and his colleagues traveled throughout the villages uplifting and revitalizing the people. Chasidism teaches that, in former generations, the secret teachings of Kabbalah were concealed even from learned Torah scholars, but that in these *latter generations* it is permitted and is also a *mitzvah* (good deed) to reveal this wisdom. The Lubavitcher Rebbe Menachem Schneerson (1902-1994) taught that, in the messianic era, the study of the *esoteric aspects of the Torah* (meaning, the knowledge of God) will be the **primary focus** of Torah study.

If the secrets of Kabbalah are the primary focus of Torah study and these secrets are supposedly preparing the hearts of the Chasidim for the coming of Messiah, and those secrets are being revealed by demonic spirits, then, in truth, the "messiah" they are being prepared for is the Anti-Christ.

Pray for a revelation that the secrets of God are shared only with those who are His own (Matthew 13:11) in the Messiah, those who come to Him as little children (Matthew 11:25-26). We need to pray that the eyes of their hearts will be enlightened to understand that the SOURCE of Kabbalah is demonic and that it can never lead them to the true Messiah, only to a counterfeit, as it already has in the case of Rabbi Schneerson. Pray that all hope will be lost in the return of Rabbi Schneerson, that the Lubavitcher Chasidim will turn to Yeshua and not to any other false messiah. Pray that they will know the hope to which the God of Abraham, Isaac and Jacob has called them, the only Messianic hope there is - Yeshua. Pray that the veil will be lifted from their minds to realize what Kabbalah really is and renounce its theology which has superceded study of the Bible, the Word of God.

> *"...My people are destroyed*
> *From lack of knowledge..."*
> *(Hosea 4:6a)*

As we pray for the Ultra-Orthodox, it is important to realize that every Chasid is not necessarily studying the foundational teachings of

Chasidism, or Kabbalah, any more than the average Catholic studies the early writings of the church fathers. At this point in history, we are practicing a religion. If you were to ask a rabbi if the foundation of Chasidism is based on an occultic experience of the Ba'al Shem Tov, he would deny it as vehemently as a priest would deny that Mary worship is a basic component of Catholicism. Unfortunately, the Word of God says that ignorance of the *spirit behind the religion you are practicing* does not protect you from its influence on your life.

Pray that the Lord would open the spiritual eyes of the Chasidim (just as He opened the eyes of Elisha to see the angelic armies of God) and cause them to SEE and BECOME AWARE of the presence of evil spirits (segulot) in the mystical religion they are practicing, that they would become skeptical, curious, dissatisfied, hungry for the truth and would search the Hebrew Scriptures diligently for themselves.

> *"And do not be conformed to this world,*
> *But **be transformed***
> *By the renewing of your mind,*
> *That you may prove*
> *What the will of God is,*
> *That which is good and acceptable and perfect."*
> *(Romans 12:2)*

The Lord drew my heart to pray for the Chasidim because the longings of the Chasidic soul are, in some ways, similar to the believer's hunger for holiness and intimacy with God. We are *so close* and yet *so far*. The Chasidim are also extremely zealous for the coming of Messiah.

__The three major pillars of traditional Chasidic theology are Devekut, Ecstatic Prayer, and the Tzaddik, concepts rooted in Kabbalistic literature. However, the utmost goal of Chasidism is to transform the nature of a person's emotional attributes, such as fear, or any limiting characteristic. Tikkun, or self-rectification, is the pursuit of Chasidic thought.__

Chasidism teaches that the *soul is supreme* and we can trace the source of this teaching to Rabbi Israel achieving an *ascent of soul* into the *upper worlds.* This is an indication the rabbi believed his soul was ascending to a heavenly place, a world or place where the knowledge of God is. Chasidism contends that each person actually has *three souls* (godly, intellectual, and natural) in descending order of quality. The natural soul is referred to as the "animal" soul which cannot be improved, but needs to be transformed completely. Since the ability to transform the animal soul is not immediately attainable, the *natural inclinations toward evil* must simply be broken by forcing oneself not to say or do what the animal force wishes. This is about as close to the concept of *original sin* as you will find in Chasidism or any other branch of Judaism. It is said that true Divine service comes through *tikkun*, which means mending or rectifying, and begins in the intellectual soul. It is taught that both the godly and the intellectual soul have emotional attributes, but the desire of the intellectual soul is toward *self-fulfillment* and *self-expression*, which is beneath it, whereas the desire of the godly soul is drawn towards that which is above it, or *self-transcendence*. As we can see, whichever soul is dominant, *self* is still very much in the forefront.

> *"May your whole **spirit, soul and body***
> *Be kept blameless*
> *At the coming of our Lord Jesus the Messiah."*
> *(I Thessalonians 5:23b)*

In Luke Chapter 6, Jesus said that if the foundation of your faith is faulty, then everything else you build on it will be unstable and vulnerable to sudden collapse. As Yeshua Himself (the Creator) is the very foundation of our faith, a building block upon that truth is that man (the created being) is made up of a spirit, a soul, and a body. This could be loosely compared to the godly, intellectual, and natural soul. However, right here, at the very foundation, we discover a root error in Chasidic theology that cries out for intercession- *the exaltation of the soul life, or the ability of the intellectual soul to attain self-rectification.*

Kabbalah speaks of a soul and a body. It teaches that inner peace and harmony can only be achieved through the supremacy of the soul over the body. In his classic work, the *Tanya,* Rabbi Schneur Zalman explains that the entire Torah aims to establish the supremacy of the soul over the body; spirit over matter; quality over quantity; and thereby manifest Godliness in the world. Instead of our physical desires and needs being the driving force in our lives, the soul should be the driving force and the body its vehicle.

"But I say, walk by the Spirit,
And you will not carry out
The desire of the flesh."
(Galatians 5:16)

These are complex issues indeed and it may appear to be splitting hairs, but it is a crucial distinction to recognize that when we are born-again and enter new life in Messiah, it is our *spirit* that is birthed and reborn. Our soul (housing our mind, emotions, and will) must be cleansed and restored. The soul is the place where sin, wounds of the past, and bondage resides and needs healing and deliverance. The New Covenant teaches that our soul and body need to come under submission to our spirit. It is heading in the right direction for our body to submit to our soul, but they both must submit to our human spirit, which must then be submitted to the Holy Spirit. We are admonished that if we *"walk in the Spirit"* we will not gratify the desires of the flesh. Walking in our soul is a *tormenting* and *defeating* walk because the soul is incapable of overcoming the works of the flesh. The heart of God is looking with compassion on the Chasidim and longs to free them from the torment of fighting the losing battle to transform their nature.

__Only God, through the power of the Holy Spirit and the Blood of Messiah, can transform our nature and conform us to the image of Messiah.__

Pray that every deception convincing the Chasidim that "tikkun" is possible in their own strength will be exposed by the light of God's Word. Pray that God will reveal to them the true condition of their soul. Jeremiah 17:9 says that the heart (or the soul) is deceitful above all things and __beyond cure__. Pray that the Lord will reveal to them His desire is to give them a new heart. Pray the Lord will open their eyes to this basic truth that will set them free and be the beginning of healing and deliverance.

Deception at the beginning easily leads to further deception along the way. Chasidic theology also embraces the notion that *inanimate objects have a soul,* which is nothing more than age-old pantheism and New Age Hinduism. While we might agree that animals have a soul, to say that a brick or a chair has a soul is floating in mystical unreality. The belief that everything has a soul elevates the significance of the soul to divine quality. This belief is confirmed in Chasidic writings, which state this *spark of Godliness* is the true essence and reality of *all things,* and this spark is released and revealed when *physical matter* is used for a sublime purpose or deed in accordance with the Will of the Creator — as, for example, in *the performance of a commandment (mitzvah).*

Pray the Lord will open the understanding of the Chasidim to see through the deception that everything has a soul, and that the soul is somehow sacred and should reign supreme. Pray also that the stronghold of relating to God through WORKS rather than faith in the FINISHED WORK of Messiah will be completely shattered. When Yeshua said, "Take my yoke upon you. My yoke is easy and my burden is light (Matthew 11:28-30)," He was referring to His yoke of grace. Daily, the Ultra-Orthodox put on the yoke of Torah (including 613 commandments). As a prophetic act and declaration to every principality in the spirit realm, lift off the yoke of Torah (a burden which neither they nor their fathers could bear) and place upon them the yoke of Messiah, the yoke of grace.

Devekut (meaning "adhesion" or "cleaving" to God) was a foundational teaching of the Ba'al Shem Tov, declaring that "faith is the adhesion of the soul to God," and he demanded that devekut be present in all daily acts.

Cleaving to God, in Chasidic thought, applies to every aspect of life. At first glance, this sounds wonderfully biblical (Deuteronomy 10:20, 11:22-23, Joshua 23:8), and we might even describe *devekut* as an attempt to *know God.* But we will soon see that Chasidic cleaving is altogether different from the spirit of these Bible verses. The Ba'al Shem Tov emphasized the element of *joy in worship* as paramount and opposed any form of asceticism and fasting. *Physical pleasure,* he maintained, could give rise to spiritual pleasure (or *devekut*) if the person performing it intends to worship God and the act is performed in a state of *devekut.* Jacob Joseph (one of the Ba'al successors) taught that the ultimate purpose of man is to *cleave* to Him, and this union is only possible through joy. Fasting and any form of self-affliction bring sorrow, he said, and *sorrow is the root of all evil.* The underlying purpose of *devekut* is *union with the Divine*, to make contact with the supernatural world.

Chasidism teaches that, through prayer, man can attain devekut and make contact with the divine worlds. The way to devekut in prayer (as also in the study of Torah) is through concentration on the mystical meaning of the Hebrew letters.

In the attempt to avoid the danger of melancholy, the Chasidic gospel stressed *joy*, *optimism*, and *self-worth* through religious experience. Rabbi Nahman of Bratslav contended that depression was a major reason for man's drifting away from God, leading to sin. He stressed that, even over his sins, a man should not grieve much, recognizing that the *evil inclination* leads him to think he has committed a serious sin when the intention of his action was only to bring him into a state of melancholy, creating a hindrance to serving and worshipping God. Other rabbis taught that repentance comes essentially out of joy and delight. These teachings fly in the face of passages such as Joel 2:12-27, Job 42:1-17, and Isaiah 32:9-20, just to cite a few examples, which describe a deep, heart-rending repentance preceding tremendous blessing and restoration.

Pray that God would reveal to the Chasidim that in the presence of Jehovah there is FULLNESS OF JOY and the ultimate purpose of worship is to usher us into His Presence so that we may adore Him and be changed from glory to glory by His marvelous light, not to achieve oneness with divinity. Pray that the God of Israel would restore the gift and power of genuine, deep repentance to the Ultra-Orthodox and that out of the ashes of repentance would come a hundredfold blessing and the joy of the Lord as their strength.

"We are destroying speculations
And every lofty thing
Raised up against the knowledge of God,

*And we are **taking every thought captive***
To the obedience of Messiah."
(II Corinthians 10:5)

The Bible says that "lofty things" and "speculations" will rise up and attempt to hinder our efforts to know God. The Ba'al Shem Tov discovered this truth of *distraction in prayer*. He taught that prayer that leads to the attainment of *devekut* can be disturbed by *alien* thoughts which try to hinder a person's spiritual efforts. Scripture teaches that victory over these thoughts can only be realized by *taking them captive to the obedience of Messiah*, which means that you need to *know the Messiah*. A person attempting to fight the battle of the mind in their own strength ends up frustrated and exhausted. Nevertheless, the Ba'al Shem Tov's particular *recipe* for dealing with these distracting thoughts caused many to join his group and accept his authority.

The Besht taught that alien thoughts were derived from a *heavenly* source as the result of cosmic forces related to the doctrine of *fallen holy sparks*. We may safely say there is no thought whatsoever which hinders prayer or the knowledge of God that comes from heaven. Nevertheless, Kabbalist Isaac Luria taught that holy sparks of *divine light* are hidden in irrelevant, or sinful, thoughts that aspire to rise up and be redeemed. The holy spark conveys the undesirable thought to the human heart and the person who chooses to suppress the sinful thought helps the spark return to its divine source, thereby uplifting the *element of divinity latent in man's soul*. The transformation of this spark from a *latent* to an *active* condition is understood as *true union with God*, the state marking the climax of *devekut*. Thus, Chasidic prayer becomes a ladder by means of which a man may ascend to union with the Divine.

Since Chasidism presumes that everything that exists partakes of the divine essence, there is no room for melancholy or despair in the life of a Chasid, but rather he should feel joy and a burning enthusiasm for life, expressed in ecstatic prayer and group singing and dancing.

Some Chasidic sages maintain that the whole universe is a manifestation, or garment, of God, and the separate existence of living things was an illusion. Through piety and fervent prayer any Chasid, however, lowly, could attain a state of exultation in which he could experience personal communion with God. The pathway to this communion was the attempt to eliminate his own ego.

> *"For there is one God*
> *And **one mediator** between God and men,*
> *The man **Messiah Yeshua**,*
> *Who gave himself as a ransom*
> *For all men..."*
> *(I Timothy 2:5-6)*

The question of whether every Chasid is *capable of devekut* brings us to the issue of the *Tzaddik.* Jacob Joseph set forth the controversial doctrine of the tzaddik *(a righteous or holy one)* in his book *Toledot Ya'akov Yosef.* Most Chasidim, it is believed, will never achieve devekut on their own, much as they may strive, and they need the tzaddik to carry their prayers up to heaven. *Their faith is in the tzaddik and the hope that he truly is a righteous one.* The tzaddik was regarded as having a mystical relationship with God granting him powers to bring his disciples closer to their Creator. The tzaddik was reverenced by his disciples and had absolute authority over them, even in their personal and business affairs.

The role of the tzaddik is to teach the people to worship God by means of devekut and to bring sinners to repentance. The intermediary role of the tzaddik is key to the pervasive control they have over their disciples. The life of the Chasid is intimately connected to the tzaddik just as the life of a believer is intimately connected to Jesus.

According to Jewish tradition, the true meaning of the Scriptures were *kept hidden* from the masses and only revealed to those who were *spiritually ready* to receive it through Kabbalah. This was one of the ways the rabbis, or the tzaddiks, maintained power over their followers.

R. Shimon bar Yochai, author of the Zohar, alleges that he was granted permission to reveal the secrets of Torah only to his disciples, known as *chevraya kadisha ("the holy fellowship")*. As the tzaddikim grew in power, it became customary in Chasidic sects to imitate their characteristics, even their mannerisms. The Ba'al Shem Tov smoked a pipe and so it became a ritual of early Chasidic rabbis to smoke pipes. The mediating role of the tzaddik, the frustrating inability of individual Chasids to achieve devekut, and the tremendous faith that must be placed in the tzaddik that he is truly carrying your prayers to heaven, helps explain why there is such a heaviness in Chasidic neighborhoods where "joy in prayer" is a major component of their theology.

Pray that the Holy Spirit will reveal the truth that Yeshua alone is the mediator between God and man. He has made the way, through His Blood, to intimate communication with God. Heaven wants a personal relationship with the Chasidim. Pray that the tzaddikim, who serve as mediators, would be given a strong revelation of the deception in which they have been partaking and a profound revelation of their own sin in allowing themselves to be exalted to the position of gods in the lives of their disciples. Pray that they would repent, humble themselves before God and release their flock to seek and find a personal relationship with the God of Israel through Yeshua the Messiah.

"In that day, a fountain will be opened
For the house of David and for
The inhabitants of Jerusalem,
For **sin** and for **impurity.**
And it will come about in that day,"
Declares the Lord of hosts,
"That I will cut off the **names**
Of the idols from the Land,
And they will no longer be remembered;
And I will also remove the
Prophets and the **unclean spirit**
from the Land."
(Zechariah 13:1-2)

This Scripture reveals that there are *idols, impurity,* and an *unclean spirit* in Jerusalem. Praise God for His precious promise that, in the last days, just before the return of Jesus, a *fountain* will be opened for cleansing of sin and impurity and that He will remove the unclean spirit from the Land!

Prayerwalkers frequently experience the idolatry and unclean spirits in Mea Shearim which can be traced to the doctrine of the tzaddik and holy sparks.

The *tzaddik,* or the founding sage of any particular Chasidic group, because of his exalted status of holiness, essentially becomes an idol for his sect. He becomes the *channel* through which *the* spiritual outpouring from heaven is transmitted to his followers. The challenge the tzaddik faces is that he must simultaneously *sustain devekut* while *maintaining contact with the world* around him. He is the center of the community and influences it, but is also influenced by it. The sinful thoughts of his contemporaries affect him, reducing his holy stature, while, at the same time, his sinful thoughts may encourage others to sin.

It is taught that, for the sake of remaining unified with his disciples, and so that he may be able to lift them up, the tzaddik must occasionally descend from his high spiritual level and sin, thus identifying with his followers.

The deceptive *channeling* role of the tzaddik is further complicated by the doctrine of *holy sparks* (the notion of divine light hidden in sinful thoughts which man must redeem). If sin can somehow be *sanctified,* then the tzaddik is actually performing a mitzvah by sinning if it will redeem his followers.

Whatever his good intentions, if the tzaddik (who is the supreme symbol of righteousness) is engaging in unclean activities because his disciples are engaging in them and they need his sin to somehow redeem them, then the stronghold of impurity becomes that much stronger every time someone sins.

When it comes to the issue of *holy sparks*, there is no gentle way to say this doctrine is pure nonsense. Sinning will never *purify* or *redeem* anyone of their sinful, alien thoughts, whoever is doing the sinning. The notion that the tzaddik *must occasionally sin* in order to lower himself to the level of his disciples and pull them up from depravity sheds light on why there is such a massive gathering of *unclean spirits* hovering over Ultra-Orthodox neighborhoods.

Yeshua was sent to earth as a *spotless lamb* and never compromised His walk of holiness to "identify" with His followers by sinning. He who *had no sin* was *made sin for us* that we would no longer be slaves of sin. Jesus came to set the captives free so they might have new life in the Spirit. Because of this holy sacrifice, our prayers ascend to heaven through Yeshua, our High Priest, Intercessor, and Redeemer, not through any special *"holy person."*

Pray that God would graciously reveal to the Chasidim the truth that Yeshua has made a new and living way for their sin to be removed and for their prayers to reach heaven. Pray that God, according to His promises, would remove the idols and the unclean spirits from Jerusalem and that a spirit of purity and repentance would be released. Pray that Yeshua, the only pure and true Tzaddik, will be revealed, and that they will adore Him and cleave only to Him.

The Mitnagdim

The chief opponent of Chasidism was Rabbi Elijah ben-Solomon Zalman, also known as the *Vilna Gaon* (1720-1797), whose movement thrived in Lithuania. He was the Talmudic genius of his age and all the traditional Jewish scholarship rallied behind him. His anti-Chasidic groups became known as the *Mitnagdim* ('Opponents').

__The Ba'al Shem Tov and the Vilna Gaon were contemporaries in a bleak season of Jewish history and their movements developed alongside one another although they were fierce opponents.__

From the second half of the 18th century, the personality and activities of the Vilna Gaon, who attracted many disciples, had a lasting impact on Lithuanian Jewry. His movement developed into the most stimulating religious and spiritual center in Vilna and had a profound influence on Judaism in the sphere of both *Halakha* (Jewish Law) and *Kabbalah* (Jewish Mysticism). In 1772, the Vilna Gaon excommunicated the Chasidic congregation formed in Vilna. By the end of the 18th century, Vilna became the center of religious Jewish study. Bitter opposition continued against the Chasidim throughout the lifetime of the Gaon.

The term *"gaon"* originated in the Jewish academies of Sura and Pumbedita in Babylonia. The geonim were recognized as the highest authority of instruction from the end of the sixth century to the middle of the eleventh century. Eventually, *Gaon* became a title of honor for the head of a Talmudic Yeshiva, a great rabbi, or genius who had a profound knowledge of Torah. *Rebbe* or *Rav* was the title of honor for the spiritual leader, or tzaddik, of a Chasidic group.

__One of the main issues of division was the traditional lifestyle of the many Chasidic groups dominated by the special role of the tzaddik,__ *the spiritual leader of the group. The Mitnagdim also opposed the Chasidism in the areas of prayer and repentance.*

The Mitnagdim accused the Chasidim of rejecting the *values* and *traditions* of Talmudic study, adopting superstitious practices, and building a personality cult around their *tzadikkim* that nearly amounted to idolatry. The Mitnagdim generally reject tales of rebbes having supernatural healing powers, regard direct mystical communication with God as presumptuous, and consider elevating *prayer* over *study*, and *emotion* over *intellect* as neglecting true Torah study.

The Mitnagdim consider themselves the genuine Torah scholars, while the Chasidim are frowned upon as perhaps too ignorant to study Torah, instead placing all their faith in a charismatic leader they blindly follow.

The Ba'al Shem Tov contended that the prayers and devotions of the *amei ha'aretz* (unlearned folk) should be valued as highly as the *Talmidei Chachamim* (learned elite), even though the common folks did not know the meaning of the words they prayed. The scholars maintained that all tragedies of society can be traced to encouraging the ignorant masses, resulting only in arrogance and a lowering of the dignity of the learned class.

The Ba'al Shem Tov also believed that even a Talmud scholar and a saintly *tzaddik* (righteous one) needed to do *teshuvah* ("repent"). Repentance (in Chasidism) redeems the *holy sparks,* raises humanity to a higher spiritual level, and prepares the world for Messiah. The Mitnagdim argued that this view diminished the honor of the Torah and Torah scholars, and that repentance was only required for those who had "sinned."

Nevertheless, Chasidism survived and, although a legal reconciliation of the two groups later occurred, the hearts of the two groups have remained divided. In a humorous sort of way, these groups could be loosely compared to the two camps in the modern-day Church: the *Evangelicals* and the *Pentecostals*. Although it is a simplistic comparison, it may help us to relate to these camps.

_**What binds the Chasidim and the Mitnagdim together in a
community sense is their Ultra-Orthodox lifestyle and passion for
Torah as they each pursue it. Reduced to its simplest terms, the
raging conflict is between Poland and Lithuania, between the Gaon
and the Tzaddik.**_

Both groups are prominent in Mea Shearim and, from outward
appearances, they appear very similar, since they all wear black, unless
you know what you are looking for, especially in hats. The high,
narrow fur hat (called a _spodik_), or a flat, low hat with a wide brim
(called a _felush_), or a _shtreimel_ (really a large skullcap surrounded by
thick animal fur of fox or mink), would identify a person as Chasidic
(even the sect they belong to), whereas the Mitnagdim tend to simply
wear large, stylish black hats and black suits, although there are groups
that wear large furry black hats. This is only one of many ways of
distinguishing one another. In general, the Chasidim wear longer
sidecurls (payot), while the Mitnagdim tend to have short curls or
simply longer sideburns.

_**For purposes of prayer, it is essential to appreciate the reality that,
while these groups have their differences, both the Chasidim and
the Mitnagdim embrace Kabbalah, and the consciousness of the
serious nature of sin and value of deep repentance as described in
the Scriptures has been greatly diminished.**_

_**Pray for an outpouring of the love of God and a spirit of true
repentance upon the Chasidim and the Mitnagdim. Pray also for a
breaking of the spirit of intellectualism and superiority among the
Mitnagdim. Pray for deliverance from mysticism for both groups
and a return to the Word of God as the highest source of truth.**_

News reports speculated that the attack on the apartment of the Swiss
ladies in 1998 was likely perpetrated by a group of the Mitnagdim
called the _**Neturai Karta**_ (which means "Watchmen on the Walls" in
Aramaic). They are an extremely zealous fringe group of the Ultra-
Ultra Orthodox and one of the oldest groups living in Jerusalem for
over 200 years. From the age of three, the boys study Torah full-time
all their lives. They do not study any other subject. They study and
speak in Yiddish, as they believe Hebrew to be a sacred language.

They have a strict dress code: the men wear big furry black hats, black coats, and long side curls. The women shave their heads and wear scarves, long-sleeved dresses with black stockings. There are hundreds of Neturai Karta living in and around Mea Shearim.

Pray that the Lord will turn the zeal of the Neturai Karta toward the gospel as He did with Saul of Tarsus, who persecuted believers every bit as much as these "watchmen" before He met Yeshua on the Damascus Road. Pray that even one of them will receive a powerful revelation of the Messiah and be turned completely around. Pray that they will fulfill the call to be intercessors on the walls of Jerusalem and witnesses for Messiah.

Kabbalah

"The fear of the Lord
Is the beginning of wisdom...."
(Psalm 111:10a)

Man's desire for _hidden wisdom_ is as old as the Garden. Adam and Eve enjoyed a pristine environment, had dominion over all the earth, and experienced unbroken fellowship with their Creator. In these pure surroundings, intimacy in marriage and intimacy with God was healthy and unhindered. This thrilling fulfillment in relationships and harmony with nature was also known as _Paradise._ But the moment Adam and Eve tasted of the _Tree of the Knowledge of Good and Evil,_ intimacy with God was severed and _self-centered knowledge_ came alive. Man became aware of himself and afraid of God. He would be banished from His Presence and begin seeking the wisdom of men and even the revelation of evil spirits.

All history from this moment forward is the unfolding of the magnificent purpose of our Heavenly Father to restore the fellowship and intimacy of the Garden, re-possess all that was relinquished to Satan through sin, and rescue mankind from humanism, idolatry, and the occult. In Rabbinic Judaism, the _occult_ manifests in the form of Kabbalah.

Kabbalah is an occult theosophy that developed among the Jewish people in Babylonia, and later Italy and Spain, between the 6th and 13th centuries A.D., that explores hidden wisdom in the Scriptures concerning the attributes of God, the Messiah, Creation, and the inherent powers of certain combinations of Hebrew letters and numbers, a system known as Gematria.

> "There shall not be found among you
> *Anyone who makes his son or his daughter*
> *Pass through the fire,*
> *One who uses divination,*
> *One who practices witchcraft,*
> *Or one who interprets omens, or a sorcerer,*
> *Or one who casts a spell,*
> *Or a medium, or a spiritist,*
> *Or one who calls up the dead."*
> *(Deuteronomy 18:10-11)*

The children of Israel are starved for supernatural encounters and spiritual experiences. *"Reincarnation, Dybbuks, Past Lives, Messiah & Millennium"* was the title of a lecture series, including a Kabbalah Tour, advertised in a popular kosher restaurant in Jerusalem, inviting "all thinking adults of all religions" to this 4-day seminar. Other posted activities included *Ascent of Soul* (a mystical weekend in Safed), *Torah Dance,* and *Higher Dreaming.*

Pray that the God of Abraham, Isaac, and Jacob would satisfy the hunger of His precious chosen people for supernatural experiences with a revelation and visitation of Yeshua, the only One who can fulfill the deepest longings of our soul. Pray their eyes would be opened to the verses in Deuteronomy that strictly forbid witchcraft, sorcery, and consulting the dead (even dead sages). Pray the Ultra-Orthodox will come to recognize the dangerous occultic nature of Kabbalah.

The simple definition of the Hebrew word Kabbalah is "tradition," and is understood to mean the mystical trend the rabbis say has existed in the Jewish faith since antiquity. Kabbalah means "to receive" and refers to heavenly revelations passed on to succeeding generations through oral tradition.

Sadly, I am discovering that the subject of Kabbalah is a *sensitive* one, even in sectors of the Messianic Body. I have received discreet and concerned responses to prayer letters by Jewish believers confessing that their spiritual leader has a flair for Kabbalah, even teaches them a bit, leaving them feeling uncomfortable, and in a quandary what to do. I have also heard the remark that Kabbalah is impossible to fully comprehend and appreciate unless it is studied with a rabbi.

I want to make it very clear to all readers at the very start of this chapter *that I have not and have no desire to study Kabbalah.* What I have studied are the *components of the system* and the *fruit of its beliefs.* One need not experiment with cocaine to discover the effects of the drug. Once the *chemical makeup* is unmasked, we may safely conclude that this white powder is a narcotic and, if used often, will become addicting. We do not need to ingest the drug to arrive at this truth, nor do we need to wander the twilight labyrinth of Kabbalah on a personal search for enlightenment. Rather, we can take the essence of Kabbalah, place it under the microscope of God's Word and ask the Holy Spirit for discernment. Once the ingredients are examined, it becomes clear that Kabbalah is a branch of the occult, that if you open yourself up to it, you will be taken captive by the enemy, and likely need deliverance to get out of it.

__Kabbalah became popular after the 12th century when Talmudic legalism, ritualism, and intellectualism reached its peak. Kabbalah opened an approach to religion that seemed more pleasurable, more immediate, and less restricting.__

The Dark Ages gave rise to *mystical movements*, both within Christianity and Judaism. The link between the rise of Kabbalah and the birth of the Chasidic movement in the 17th century is a strong one. Persecution, poverty, the loss of momentum in traditional Judaism, a messianic fervor that lingered beyond the failure of Shabbetai Zevi's claims to be the Messiah (to be discussed later), and a sense of alienation, rising from the growing division between the *learned class* and the *common people*, gave the enemy a brilliant opportunity to enchant the Jewish people into Kabbalah. While the framework of Judaism had been firmly established, Kabbalah gave a secker hungry for the mystical tremendous freedom to wander, even into dimensions of experience forbidden by Scripture itself.

__The purpose of Kabbalah, in Jewish thought, was to broaden the dimensions of Torah so that the laws of the descendants of Abraham,__

Isaac, and Jacob would be extended to the inner secret law of the universe. Thus, we are seeing Kabbalah becoming popular far beyond the borders of Judaism.

For the kabbalists, Judaism in all its aspects was a system of *mystical symbols* reflecting the mystery of God and the universe, and their purpose was to *discover and invent keys* to the understanding of the symbols. Thus, the kabbalists became the *gatekeepers of secrets*, the guardians of hidden wisdom, not to mention the *supernatural powers* surrounding their contact with the spirit realm. This gave the kabbalists tremendous influence over their disciples and Judaism worldwide.

*"**Beware** that no one takes you captive*
through philosophy and empty deception,
according to the tradition of men,
according to the elementary principles of the world,
rather than according to Messiah.
*For **in Him** all the fullness*
Of Deity dwells in bodily form."
(Colossians 2:8-9)

It became widely accepted that Kabbalah was the *esoteric* (secret, mysterious) part of the Oral Law given to Moses at Sinai. Later, the Kabbalah (which embraces aspects of *Gnosticism)* became a Jewish mystical system of theology. Hence, mysticism was *sanctified* in Judaism simply by attributing it to Jewish history and proclaiming it to be "Jewish," even to the point of attributing its origin to Moses. Although Kabbalah has permeated every sector of contemporary Judaism, it is most closely associated with the Ultra-Orthodox due to its rise in popularity after the birth of Chasidism.

When approaching the subject of Kabbalah, we want to ask: "What spirit is behind it? What is the source of this hidden wisdom? Do these revelations agree with God's Word?"

We will find that the concepts of Kabbalah vastly conflict with the revelation of Scripture and one place where they clash head-on is in the teaching of *reincarnation*. In a summer weekly radio sermon in the Year 2000, Rabbi Ovadia Yosef, spiritual leader of the Ultra-

Orthodox Shas Party in Israel, sparked controversy by suggesting that the six million Jews who died in the Holocaust were *reincarnations of sinners.* While referring to the Nazis as "evil," Rabbi Yosef went on to say that Holocaust victims were, "souls of sinners, people who transgressed and did all sorts of things that should not be done. They had been reincarnated in order to atone." While disturbing, this remark is perfectly consistent with kabbalistic theology. Chief Rabbi Yisrael Meir, himself a Holocaust survivor, concurred that Judaism has a concept of reincarnation and of the *righteous dying to atone for sins in a previous life,* but he did not believe this accounted for the Holocaust and had no reasonable explanation for it.

A few basic definitions will serve to shed light on the *occultic nature* of Kabbalah.

Occultism is a belief in the power of various practices, based on hidden knowledge about the universe and its mysterious forces, such as astrology (prediction of events by the stars), alchemy (medieval chemistry, or potions), divination (fortune-telling), and magic (art of using supernatural powers).

Theosophy is a religious philosophy usually translated as "divine wisdom" and emphasizes mystical experience, esoteric doctrine, occult phenomena, and enjoys an affinity with Asian thought. It's defining feature is the belief that a deeper *spiritual reality* exists and that man may establish direct contact with that reality through intuition, meditation, revelation, or other states transcending man's normal consciousness.

Mysticism is the quest for hidden truth or wisdom, the goal of which is *union with the divine or sacred* (the transcendent realm). At its core, mysticism contends that man is more than one-dimensional and, therefore, may *progress* to his spiritual goal of communion ("one with God") through various stages, usually designated as purgation, purification, illumination, and unification. Mysticism shares a common world with magic, metaphysics (transcendent levels of reality), and science, also embracing disciplines of prayer (even ecstatic and erotic forms), worship, contemplation, fasting, breath control, autosuggestion and rituals.

The process of self-realization in mysticism, or the ascent of man to union with the divine, corresponds to the Chasidic precept of cleaving.

By nature, mysticism is knowledge that cannot be communicated directly but may be expressed only through symbol and metaphor. The Jewish kabbalists stressed this mysterious aspect by imposing all kinds of limitations on the sharing of their teachings, either with regard to the age of the initiates, the ethical requirements, or number of students permitted to study. Tradition teaches that the sages used to transmit statements to their students and other sages privately, in a whisper, through Kabbalah. I was told by an Ultra-Orthodox yeshiva student that only married men over the age of thirty are permitted to study Kabbalah directly, and only with a rabbi and by invitation.

Gnosticism is a theological and theosophical belief system in which matter is viewed as evil and the spirit as good, and salvation to be gained by esoteric (secret) knowledge, or gnosis. Gnosis was the divine nature and it's *emanations*, and is traditionally associated with powers and magic.

The fundamental presupposition of Kabbalah is that the world is an emanation of the spiritual essence of God.

The definition of *emanate* is to "issue forth from a source," much as fragrance emanates from a flower. We might agree insofar as the heavens *declare* the glory of God and the skies *proclaim* the work of His hands (Psalm 19:1). But this is where the analogy ends. The Bible does not speak of creation emanating from God. He is *separate* from His creation, which is declaring His invisible attributes and eternal power by the things that have been made (Romans 1:19-20).

Kabbalistic theology describes God as the *Ein Sof* (Endless One) who is infinite and transcendent and, therefore, can have no direct contact with finite beings. Here we find a contradiction with Scripture. Enoch *walked* with God (Genesis 5:24), God *spoke* to Abram (Genesis 12: 1-3), He *appeared* to Isaac (Genesis 26:23-24), He *spoke to Jacob in a dream* (Genesis 28:10-17) and *wrestled* with him in the form of a man (Genesis 32:24-30), He *showed His glory* to Moses (Exodus

33:18-23) and *spoke* with him face to face (Numbers 12:6-8). The Bible abounds with the theme of a *personal* God who desires a *personal relationship* with man and *can be known.*

The Zohar (Book of Splendor), is the central literature of Kabbalah and was written largely by R. Shimon bar Yochai (mid-second century A.D.), who was known as the master of the inner dimensions of Torah.

The Zohar became the basis for all later Kabbalistic writings. After the Spanish Inquisition in 1492, leading Kabbalists settled in the Galilee city of Safed. R. Yitzchak Luria (also known as Ha'ari) became the key figure and his teachings, transmitted by his disciples, gave Kabbalah a widespread impact on the Jewish world. Luria's teachings were studied by the Ba'al Shem Tov and, along with the revelations he received in his own personal *ascent of soul*, were absorbed into the beliefs of Chasidism.

As the centuries progressed, it was no longer necessary to study Kabbalah directly or individually because it was kneaded into the dough of Judaism and taught as basic components of Torah.

Safed gave the world many influential kabbalists. While Mea Shearim is the stronghold of religious and rabbinic spirits, Safed is the stronghold of Kabbalah and is regularly visited by Ultra-Orthodox Jews from all over Israel and all over the world because of the many *"tombs of the righteous"* which are there. A window into the mystical mind of the Ultra-Orthodox, and its startling implications, is shared in a fascinating legend. In 1570, it is said that Rabbi Haim Vital was walking from Safed to a cave where the Babylonian sages were buried. As he stopped along the way to prepare the prayers he intended to pray at the gravesites, he suddenly began shaking and words like "Torah" and "wisdom" came from his lips. When he returned to Safed, Rabbi Ytizchak Luria (Ha'ari) greeted him with great honor. When asked why he was being treated with such respect, the Ha'ari said he was not addressing Rabbi Vital himself, but the *spirit* of Righteous One Benaiah ben Yehoyada, who had just entered his (Rabbi Vital's) soul. After this, Rabbi Vital became one of the Ha'ari's chief disciples.

Pray for the mercy and compassion of God upon the Ultra-Orthodox. Pray for deep revelation and profound discernment against permitting any "spirit" other than the Holy Spirit of the Living God to "enter their soul." Pray their eyes will be opened to the demonic spirits behind this belief system and that they will close the door of their hearts to any supposed spirit of a past sage. Pray that their hunger for spiritual fulfillment, wisdom, and revelation will be found only in a living relationship with Yeshua the Messiah.

"Trust in Him at all times,
O people;
Pour out your hearts to him,
For God is our refuge."
(Psalm 62:8)

Pilgrimages to Safed are commonplace, especially during certain holidays, such as Lag B'Omer. The 4th century sages instructed religious Jews to visit the graves of "righteous ones" when faced with a national calamity, particularly a drought or a plague. It didn't really matter who the grave belonged to because any grave would cause the "worshipper" to contemplate death and repentance. These tombs are sprinkled all over Safed and it is immensely popular to pray at these gravesites because it may be easier (it is said) to pour out our fears, despair, hopes and gratitude next to a tombstone than to pray more abstractly to God.

How the enemy loves to reduce personal intimacy with God to the *abstract* and lead the lost into the deception of dead tradition and religion, even idolatry! God longs to hear our heartfelt prayers. His lovingkindness endures forever to those who put their trust in Him.

Pray for an outpouring of the love of God upon the Ultra-Orthodox that touches their heart and convinces them of God's great personal concern for them. In the Name of Jesus, bind every spirit of idolatry that exalts any sage to a level of holiness where his graveside would be worthy as a place of prayer. Pray that the Chasidim will discover Psalm 62 inviting them to pour out their hearts to the God of Israel, who is their refuge in times of trouble. In the Name of Yeshua, bind every lying spirit that would suggest that God is abstract and cannot be touched by human sorrows - in other words, the sages are really there for us, but God may not be. Pray that the lovingkindness of the Lord will lead them to repentance.

Kabbalah is divided into theoretical and practical branches. The theoretical is concerned with philosophies about God and His attributes. The practical brings this speculation into the realm of everyday life through prayers, ascetic practices, and drawing upon numerology, talismans, amulets and incantations of divine names and words.

The claim of some writings is that Jewish mysticism *separates* the speculative and the practical, encouraging and focusing on the philosophical aspect. However, it is clear that in kabbalistic circles down to the present day, both elements are preserved in their secret doctrine, acquired by means of revelation or initiation rites.

The Ba'al Shem Tov claimed to achieve his ascent of soul by using *divine names*. This experience led to "revelations" that became foundational to Chasidism. The user-friendly appeal and acceptance of practical Kabbalah was later evidenced by the invasion of *superstitions* and *magic charms* into Judaism. A vast array of *amulets* is displayed in the Israel Museum in Jerusalem that have been embraced in Judaism through the centuries down to the present day. All over Israel, the *hamsa* (hand with an eye in the center) is prominently displayed in business, buses, and taxis, and worn as an amulet to ward off the "evil eye."

Astrology also crept into Judaism through Kabbalah. You will find several reconstructed synagogues at the Israel Museum with the Zodiac clearly represented on the walls or ceilings.

In Kabbalistic Astrology, the stars are seen as the messengers or transmitters of God's will.

Since humans, it is said, suffer from spiritual short-sightedness, God created the heavenly bodies and stars as a spiritual computer screen that reflects our true nature back to us. In *Sefer Yetzirah* (Book of Creation), the sign of Taurus is connected to the energy of the Hebrew letter Vav, "a nail." The earthly energy of Taurus serves to nail and yoke things together, uniting separated entities into one.

"The night is nearly over;
The day is almost here.
So let us put aside the deeds of darkness
And put on the armor of light."
(Romans 13:12)

As we pray for the Ultra-Orthodox, we have taken the time to zero in on Kabbalah because it has served as an *entryway for false doctrine and familiar spirits* to tamper with the people of God. We want our prayers to be informed, but we also need to be convinced that Kabbalah is a *doctrine of demons* if we are to pray from the heart with fervency. If we were to permit ourselves to entertain certain patterns of New Age thought, which have crept into the Body of Messiah, we could easily find ourselves in the mire of confusion. After all, haven't we, as believers, had personal encounters with God that some would define as "mystical?" What about "words of knowledge" and "discerning of spirits?" Wouldn't these be considered "occultic" by those who didn't know the difference? Didn't Jesus say that the "mysteries" of the Kingdom of God are "hidden" from the wise and only revealed to little children? Didn't Jesus Himself appear to His disciples and give them final instructions after His death? The enemy has been sowing in this mine field of deception since the Garden and loves to entangle God's people in a knot with so many loose ends we simply want to throw our hands up and quit. But let's not. Let's try to sort through this mixed bag and get to the truth so the truth can set us free.

We want to start by clarifying that Jesus did not appear to His disciples after His DEATH. He appeared to His disciples after His RESURRECTION, which is quite different. Only Jesus can appear to people because only Jesus is in a resurrected body. He is the firstfruit of those who are asleep (I Corinthians 15:20). On the Mount of Transfiguration, Moses and Elijah spoke only with Jesus, not with the disciples (Matthew 17:1-3).

It is critical to observe in the Mount of Transfiguration passage that Jesus *led the disciples up on a high mountain.* They did not *seek* this experience, not did they *conjure up* Moses and Elijah. We may also ask the questions, "Why Moses and Elijah? Why not David and Daniel? Great king. Great prophet." It was of the utmost importance that *Moses* and *Elijah* commune with Jesus in this *vision* so that the disciples of Yeshua would be given the revelation that *Jesus is **greater** than both Moses and Elijah,* along with the effect of evoking the question of when Elijah would come (v.10).

The key to discerning the nature of Kabbalah is the *combination of belief systems* woven into the overall tapestry: mysticism, theosophy, gnosticism, astrology, reincarnation. Theosophy believes in a spiritual *reality* that can be *contacted* through various mystical pathways. *This is quite different from believing in God, with whom we may have a personal relationship <u>only by means of Yeshua, His Son, and no other way</u>.* Furthermore, as believers, we experience a personal *relationship* with God, but we are not God. Messiah is *in us* and we are *in Him*, however, we are separate entities. I am not Jesus and He is not me. As believers, we are being transformed into *His likeness*, we are becoming more *like* Yeshua, but we are not becoming Yeshua. We will rule and reign with Him in eternity, but He alone is *Lord, King,* and *Creator.*

<u>The Shema declares that there is only one God, but it does not declare that all is God. The Bible clearly teaches the concept of absolute evil as distinct from the pure holiness of God.</u>

The revelations of Kabbalah are essentially *pantheistic,* teaching that all reality *springs* directly from God's own *essence,* which would include evil. The God of the Bible, on the other hand, has always existed separately from creation, and created everything out of *nothing, not out of Himself.* We are created in His image and likeness, but we are not divine in the same sense that He is divine. We *partake* of the divine nature, but we are not divine in and of ourselves, nor can we attain to divinity, however many levels we may progress spiritually. Man was created to have dominion over the earth and the animals. All creation *praises* the Lord, all creation *declares the glory and existence of God,* but all creation is not the image and likeness of God, or even the essence of God.

> *"...Attaining to all riches*
> *Of the full assurance of understanding,*
> *To the knowledge of the **mystery of God,***
> *Both of the Father and of Messiah,*
> ***In whom are hidden all the treasures***
> ***Of knowledge and wisdom."***
> *(Colossians 2:2b-3)*

To be sure, there are *mysteries of God*, there is *hidden wisdom*. But Scripture says that all the hidden treasures of wisdom and knowledge are *in Messiah*. Satan is a *created being* and everything he does is an imitation or a counterfeit of something *real* that was created by God. Hidden wisdom cannot be revealed apart from a revelation of Messiah (I Corinthians 2:6-16). The hidden mysteries of Scripture speak of His Kingdom and the blessings prepared for those who love God. The *spirit of the world* begets worldly, even demonic, wisdom that *glorifies men* and leads them away from Messiah. But the *Spirit from God* reveals heavenly mysteries that *glorify God* and lead men to Yeshua. When we have the Spirit of God, we have the Spirit of Messiah (II Corinthians 3:17) and can understand the mysteries of God as the Spirit reveals them to us because we have the *mind of Messiah*.

There are real mysteries, real hidden wisdom, real intimacy and real spiritual encounters with God. The key distinction is that all the mysteries and hidden wisdom of God are designed to bring us to the knowledge of Messiah, they exalt Yeshua, not man, and they conform with the written, revealed Word of God. They are not extra-biblical.

Kabbalah is extra-biblical revelation, sanctioning approaches to spiritual experiences and power forbidden by Scripture, and teaching doctrines that blatantly conflict with it. The Word of God must be the *final word* on truth or we can be easily swept into the force field of deception, even in the pursuit of God.

> *"Behold, I have given you authority*
> *To tread upon serpents and scorpions,*
> *And over **all the power of the enemy,***
> *And nothing shall injure you."*
> *(Luke 10:19)*

A fascinating event in the late 1990's caused quite a stir of controversy in the Chasidic community, not to mention creating some confusion among the believers. A kabbalist rabbi in Jerusalem supposedly cast a *dybbuk* (the Yiddish word for demon) out of a widow who claimed to be possessed by the spirit of her late husband. We are told that his spirit was "floating around between heaven and hell unable to find a resting place" and that he was tormenting his wife and wanting to draw her into the spirit world where he is. This "exorcism" was broadcast live on Chasidic radio and a tape recording of the "voice of her husband" speaking through her was also played. The trouble was, every time the demon would start to leave, it would grab the throat of the woman and start choking her in an attempt to kill her (not an unusual occurrence when a spirit of witchcraft is involved), at which point the rabbi would back off and the demon would calm down. Finally, the rabbi commanded the demon to exit the widow through her little toe, causing her to let out a horrible shriek. Afterwards, she testified that she experienced relief from the spirit.

This incident sent shock waves throughout the Chasidic world because it proves there are evil spirits that must be contended with. That's the good news. The bad news is that it is compounding deception in the Chasidic world and also creating confusion among believers in the form of, "Isn't it wonderful how God answered the prayers of the rabbi? See, God answers everyone's prayers." To be sure, God loves this rabbi and I also love him with the love of God. The fact remains that this rabbi is neither a believer in Yeshua, nor was he using Yeshua's name to address the spirit. Jesus said, "ALL AUTHORITY IN HEAVEN AND ON EARTH HAS BEEN GIVEN TO ME." (Matthew 28:18) He also said, "In My Name you will cast out demons." (Mark 16:17) If these words of Jesus are true, then evil spirits do not have to obey any other name or authority.

Therefore, the question must be asked: Was this a genuine deliverance? Can an unbeliever cast out demons? What about the sons of Sceva? They were trying to cast out demons using the name of Jesus "whom Paul preaches" even though they didn't have a relationship with Jesus themselves (Acts 19:13-16). The demons knew Jesus and they knew Paul, but they didn't *know* these other men (meaning, they didn't recognize them as followers of Yeshua) and so they beat them and left them naked and humiliated.

This incident also sheds a new light on the passage where Jesus is being accused of casting out demons by the power of Satan (Matthew 12:22-28). He throws the accusation right back at the Pharisees, asking, "And *by whom* do your people cast them out?" Jesus quickly points out that a house divided against itself will not stand, yet apparently, *it is possible* to cast out demons by the power of Satan, not only because *he can counterfeit everything spiritually real*, including deliverance, but especially knowing that the house will be vacant and swept clean, they can soon return with all their friends, leaving the person in a worse state (Matthew 12:43-45). It would be even more desirous for demons to fake a deliverance if it will reinforce the lie that a person doesn't need Yeshua to exercise authority over evil spirits.

In the Old Testament, there are no accounts of anyone casting out demons. The best one could hope for was *relief*. When Saul was tormented by a spirit,, he called for David to play the harp and the spirit left him. (I Samuel 16:22-23) However, it always came back and no one can deny the state of Saul was eventually worse at the end than at the beginning. It would be interesting to monitor the progress of this widow. Today, she may be riding high on the waves of talk shows and unexpected celebrity, but I am not personally convinced she has seen the last of this spirit posing as her husband or even other spirits. When Yeshua came, the demons left, never to return because he whom the Son sets free is free INDEED!

Pray for the salvation of this widow and for lasting freedom from all demonic oppression through Messiah Yeshua. Pray for the salvation of the rabbi and a genuine gift of discerning spirits. Bind deception and confusion. Pray that the Body of Messiah will not allow emotionalism, or other sentimentalities, to cloud, dilute or compromise the truth of the Word. There is no question that God loves the widow and the rabbi and desires the widow to be free. That is one aspect of the truth. Another aspect of the truth is that ALL OF US are lost until we are found and salvation is found in no other name than the Name of Jesus and deliverance, in the Name of Jesus, is only one of the many blessings of salvation.

We can praise the Lord that, through this incident, the Chasidic community is being roused from a deep sleep to the reality of *evil spirits*. Although Chasidism was founded on revelations imparted by the "souls" of past sages in various visitations, these spirits were considered to be anything but evil and it is considered the utmost blessing if you should be worthy to receive wisdom and guidance from any of these "righteous ones" from the past.

The fact that this spirit claimed to be hovering between heaven and hell is actually a cause for rejoicing because this demon unwittingly confirmed that there is such a place as hell.

The truth of eternal punishment, even though it is clearly mentioned in the Tenach, has been resisted by Jewish thought and labeled as a "Christian" scare tactic for ages, simply to protect people from turning to Messiah. Now, this spirit is talking about hell, and who, *in their thinking,* can refuse to believe a spirit? We who know the Lord are expressly warned *not to believe every spirit*, but to test the spirits to see if they are of God. (I John 4:1-3). However, in this case, we can pray that the tiny slice of truth this spirit spoke will be used by God to open their eyes to the realization that heaven and hell are both very real places, bring them to repentance and into the fullness of blessing that God has for them.

Pray that the Lord will give the Body of Messiah wisdom so they will know how to minister the truth to the Jewish people regarding Kabbalah. There is much spiritual confusion in Jerusalem and perhaps around the world. For example, in witnessing to and praying for a secular Israeli woman, I was sharing that God answers prayer, which is simply conversing with the Father in Yeshua's Name, and He will answer her prayers in Yeshua's Name just the same as mine. I have no "special powers." When I pray, it is not "my Kabbalah" as opposed to "someone else's Kabbalah." Please pray that the Lord will give her understanding.

Kabbalah is also used to *impart blessings* for good luck. In the Jewish Quarter, particularly at the Western Wall, Orthodox women abound with *tzedaka* (charity) boxes and handfuls of *scarlet threads*. What is the significance of these scarlet threads? Tradition says that, in Temple times, on the Yom Kippur (Day of Atonement), there were two large strips of cloth hanging in front of the Temple. One was white and the other was red. The color red is a symbol of God's judgment. When the High Priest went in to offer the blood of the sacrifice, if the High Priest was clean and the repentance of Israel was acceptable, then God would grant forgiveness and the red cloth would turn white. If forgiveness was declined, then the white cloth would turn red and that's how the people would determine God's decision for that year.

Today, long scarlet threads are taken to Rachel's tomb in Bethlehem or the tomb of Shimon Ben Yochai in Meiron. The thread is wrapped around the tomb seven times and seven "blessings" recited over them. Then the threads are cut into smaller strips to be distributed for "good luck" or protection from the "evil eye." *The hope is that, like the red cloth over the Temple, the scarlet thread will turn white (in the spirit realm) and the wearer will enjoy good fortune.* Why Rachel's tomb? Rachel died in childbirth, thus, it is believed, she "suffered for us."

At the heart of this tradition is the inference that someone wiser, more holy, or someone who has suffered, can approach God on your behalf, appease His wrath, and rescind punishment.

> *"Now there have been many*
> *Of those priests,*
> *Since death prevented them*
> *From continuing in office;*
> *But because Jesus **LIVES FOREVER**,*
> *He has a **permanent priesthood**.*
> *Therefore, He is able to save **completely***
> *Those who come to God **through Him**,*
> *Because He always lives to intercede for them."*
> *(Hebrews 7:23-25)*

There's a gold mine in these few verses and I encourage you to keep them close by whenever you pray for the Ultra-Orthodox. Yeshua is *alive!* He ever lives to stand before the Father as our Advocate, Mediator, and Intercessor. His Blood redeems us and turns the wrath of God from us completely.

Pray that these precious truths will be graciously revealed to the Ultra-Orthodox. Pray for the mercy of God to lift the veil so they may know there is protection from evil forces, provided exclusively by the Blood of Yeshua. We have AUTHORITY over the enemy because of the Blood of Messiah. We do not need to depend on "luck." We have been given POWER in the Holy Spirit. Pray that every lie of the enemy, deceiving the Ultra-Orthodox into believing that anyone (man or woman, dead or alive) other than Jesus can stand before the God of Israel as a mediator on their behalf, will be exposed and renounced.

> *"Bless those who persecute you;*
> *Bless and curse not...*
> *Do not be overcome by evil,*
> *But overcome evil with good."*
> *(Romans 12:14, 21)*

Kabbalah is also used to *speak curses.* In 1995, an Ultra-Orthodox group cursed Prime Minister Yitzak Rabin thirty days before he was assassinated. In 2000, Rabbi Ovadia Yosef (Shas Spiritual Leader) came under sharp criticism for cursing Education Minister Yossi Sarid, primarily for opposing exorbitant government funding of Shas religious schools. Sarid eventually resigned from the Knesset. It is not unusual during prayerwalks to experience small children cursing us simply because we are strangers and they are taught to fear and curse anyone who is not from their community.

Pray that the Lord will deliver the Ultra-Orthodox (and all Judaism) from the system of kabbalistic blessing and cursing and bring them into the Light of Messiah.

> *"For those who guide this people*
> *Are leading them astray;*
> *And those who are guided by them*
> *Are brought to confusion."*
> *(Isaiah 9:16)*

Confusion is the fitting word for this complex, mystical maze of philosophies.

In the final analysis, the questions must be asked, "What is your highest and final standard of truth? Is it the Scriptures, OR the Talmud, the Zohar, and the words of the rabbis? What is your source of power? Is it the Holy Spirit OR the spirit behind Kabbalah? Any honest inquirer will quickly realize you cannot have both. You must choose which of the above sources will be your final authority.

Father, we thank You that you are not the author of confusion. We thank You that the Ultra-Orthodox are hungry for communion with You. You are greater and mightier than any false system of revelation and you knew the devices the enemy would use against your people even before the foundation of the earth. Father, we pray in the Name of Yeshua, that you would unveil the deception of Kabbalah to your Jewish people, particularly the Ultra-Orthodox, that you would unmask the evil spirits behind it, that you would expose every inconsistency of this occultic system with Scripture. We pray for your mercy, grace, and compassion upon every person who has become ensnared and taken captive by the enemy through Kabbalah and we pray, in the Name of Jesus, that you would lead them to freedom. We pray for the convicting work of the Holy Spirit and your lovingkindness to lead to repentance for exalting esoteric teachings above your Word, for entertaining false doctrines, for accepting reincarnation, astrology, using amulets, and seeking spiritual experiences beyond the boundaries of Your revealed Word. We pray for the full restoration of the Word of God to the position of highest, ultimate authority, the final word of truth in their lives. In the Name of Jesus, we bind confusion away from the Ultra-Orthodox and loosen a sound mind upon every genuine seeker to read and understand the intent of Scripture as inspired by the Holy Spirit. We pray for the full restoration of an intimate, personal relationship and fellowship with You through Yeshua, the Messiah, the Holy One of Israel. We pray that every high thing the enemy has planted to lead the Ultra-Orthodox astray will be torn down and that the Kingdom of God will be planted in their midst.

Tzimtzum

"I testify to everyone who hears the words
Of the prophecy of this book:
*If anyone **adds to them,***
God shall add to him the plagues
Which are written in this book;
*And if anyone **takes away** from the*
Words of the book of this prophecy,
God shall take away his part from
The tree of life and from the holy city,
Which are written in this book."
(Revelation 22:18-19)

The Book of Revelation *warns* that no words should be added or taken away from the prophecy given to John the Apostle on the island of Patmos. This may well be said of any portions of Scripture. This is crucial in avoiding deception. Jesus said in Luke 6:46-40 that the *foundation* we build on determines the stability of the structure. Our faith must be built on the **ROCK** of Yeshua and the **SOIL** of the Word.

Removing words (such as Isaiah Chapter 53, which is never read in the yearly Torah portions in the synagogues) hinders the truth and adding words (such as quotations from the Zohar) distorts or perverts truth.

When the devil seeks to deceive, he is very *particular* about which passages of Scripture he wants to distort. He does not arbitrarily snatch a verse from here and there, but zeros in on verses that shed light on the *identity* and *nature* of Messiah.

"Holy, Holy, Holy is the Lord of hosts,
The whole earth is full of His glory."
(Isaiah 6:3b)

Amen and Amen! Isaiah chapter 6:1-7 presents perhaps the most awesome, powerful images of *Messiah as Lord and King.* Isaiah says that he *"saw the Lord sitting on a throne"* (v.1) and later that *"my eyes have seen the King, the Lord of hosts."* (v.5). If we can envision this in our minds, what Isaiah is actually seeing in this glorious heavenly vision is Yeshua, exalted and seated at the right hand of the Father. He is *seated* because the work of redemption on Calvary has been *finished.* After Jesus fulfilled the will of the Father, became the sacrificial Lamb for Israel and for all mankind, and ascended into heaven, He *sat down* at the right hand of majesty. When Jesus stands up from the Throne of glory at the end of the age, it will not be as the *Lamb,* but as the *King,* the *Lion of Judah.* Isaiah is beholding the *Risen Saviour* and it drives him to immediate despair of his own sinful condition. Even the great prophet Isaiah is overcome by the revelation that he needs his sin, his unclean lips, purged right then and there or he will not survive this encounter with Glory.

Is it possible to combine Scripture with extra-biblical sources and arrive at an interpretation that remains true to the spirit and intent of Scripture? Let's consider one example of the disastrous effects of *mixing.*

Kabbalistic theology combines Isaiah 6:3 with a passage from the Zohar.

"The whole earth is full of His glory,"
(Isaiah 6:3b)
and
"there is no place that is empty of Him."
(Tikkunei Zohar 57)

The first quotation (Isaiah 6:3b) is Hallelujah true! The glory of God fills the earth, but not in the sense that Kabbalah interprets it. As we zero in on the word *"full,"* the mystery unfolds. If God's glory or essence *fills the earth* in the sense that a car *fills a parking space,* then this poses a problem for God when it comes to creation. He must first *create the space* to put things like trees and oceans and elephants before He can create the objects themselves. We will leave this thought simmer on the stove and move along.

The second quotation (Tikkeunei Zohar 57) is *not* true. God is everywhere in the sense that His eyes roam to and fro in the earth searching for those whose hearts seek after Him. He is watching over all things at all times. However, His *glory, His manifest Presence,* is not everywhere. Psalm 5:4 (only one of many examples) is clear that God does not dwell, inhabit, or abide, in places were there is *SIN.* His *glory* does not dwell in houses of prostitution, abortion clinics, Buddhist temples, or gambling casinos.

If you *mix* these two statements together, out comes *Tzimtzum.* The *foundational error* of misinterpreting the Isaiah verse and adding the Zohar quote led famous kabbalist R. Isaac Luria of Safed to develop the doctrine of *tzimtzum* in his description of *creation.*

Kabbalistic theology asserts that God *withdrew* or *contracted within Himself* in order to create a "parking space" for His creation. He limited Himself, or shrunk, so that the *worlds* (plural) could be created. Then, within this *divine vacuum* now available for creation, God (the Ein Sof or "Infinite") *radiated* a thread of His Light, which turned into 10 Vessels (or *worlds*, Upper and Lower worlds). These Vessels became known as Siferot, or Angels. At first, these Sefirot (in reality, demonic angelic beings) were empty, just as the body of Adam was initially empty of the life of God, but then the Ein Sof *poured some His own essence* into the 10 Vessels, thus giving them life.

This *encounter* or *collision* between the Light of the Ein Sof and the *limited nature* of the Sefirot resulted in a *cosmic catastrophe,* known as the "*Breaking of the Vessels,*" which were unable to contain the Infinite fullness. The *overflow of sparks (or "holy sparks")* resulting from this collision fell into a variety of *shells (called "kelipot").* This incident could be likened to pouring water into a glass until it overflows. These *shells* are symbolic of the non-divine, the *potential for evil,* which must be redeemed **by man** through *service to God, performing mitzvoth, study of torah, and kabbalistic meditations.*

When all the "sparks" have been redeemed from their servitude to the *base nature* (or evil inclination), they will have been *elevated to their source,* the Messiah will come, and the world will be redeemed.

The gnosticism in Kabbalah manifests in its interpretation of the interrelationship between the Ten Sefirot (or "divine emanations") of God.

The Sefirot inhabited four realms (or levels), in descending order: *Atziluth* (the heavenlies), *Briah* (the world of creation), *Yetzirah* (the world of formation), and *Assiah* (the world of material action). Each *emanation* (listed as Crown, Wisdom, Intelligence, Greatness, Strength, Beauty, Firmness, Splendor, Foundation, and Sovereignty) would be further removed from the Ein Sof, and thus *further away from God's perfection and transcendence* (His beyond-ness).

Taking on a personal form, the Sefirot, as angels, served as intermediaries between God and man, providing a wide open door for demonic activity.

By simply taking the beauty of "The whole earth is full of His glory" and *mixing it* with a few words of error, we were easily transported to this mind-boggling fantasyland! Even a casual glance at the disintegrating moral condition of the world today reveals we are farther away than ever from "redeeming the sparks" if it depends on the goodness of man.

If you found this exhausting reading, I can assure you it was challenging writing! This material is *heavy*, to say the least, and there is a demonic presence surrounding kabbalistic literature so that even reading it can be oppressive. While doing the research, I was diligent to pray protection over myself, read only small portions at a time to get what I needed for purposes of prayer and saturate myself in the Word afterwards to recover.

What does the Word of God say?

First, Genesis chapter 1 reveals that God created the heavens and the earth, but does not say He created *worlds*. It also says that God *spoke* and created all things. Verse 2 says the *Spirit of God* was hovering over the waters, revealing that God is a *Spirit* that does not take up space as we know it.

Second, Scripture often interprets Scripture and Psalm 19 presents a magnificent rendering of "The whole earth is filled with His glory." There is no place on this earth you can go where the glory of God is not *manifest in the things He created.* The stars, the mountains, the flowers, the redwoods, the wildlife, the waterfalls, all rise to give praise to the existence and majesty of the Almighty. Wherever you are on this planet, it is impossible to escape the voice of God speaking to all humanity through His spectacular creation.

Third, the Bible presents a vastly different picture of the *origin of evil*, not the *potential* for evil. Scripture does not speak of a cosmic collision creating "holy sparks," but describes a *rebellion* and *disobedience*, first in heaven and then in the Garden. Evil was already in existence in the form of pride *before* God created the world and evil is never *holy or divine in any sense.* God cast Lucifer (Satan) out of heaven, meaning out of His presence, just as He cast Adam and Eve out of the Garden, after iniquity was found in him. Satan is now known as the "prince of the power of the air." Tzimtzum would have us believe the *vacuum* created by the Ein Sof to make room for the worlds was *divine*, thus ascribing an inherent divinity to everything subsequently created within the divine vacuum.

Fourth, we are redeemed from sin, from *evil,* that is, from the sin nature we inherited from Adam at birth, by the *Blood of the Lamb*. We are redeemed by a **REDEEMER** whom God promised to send by the word of His prophets, not through man's performance of anything. Redemption comes through repentance and receiving the gift of forgiveness and eternal life from Messiah Yeshua.

Fifth, in Scripture, angels are *worshipping spirits* before God's throne (Isaiah 6:1-3, Revelation 5:11-14), *prophetic messengers* sent at *God's* command in response to prayer *to God* (Daniel 9:20-27) or to deliver a prophetic utterance (Luke 1:8-17, 26-34), or *ministering spirits* at *God's directive* (I Kings 19:4-8, Matthew 4:11, Acts 5:17-20). Angels may serve *as God's invisible army* (II Kings 6:15-17, II Chronicles 32:20-21), but they are never intermediaries and the Bible never encourages us to seek contact with or revelation from the angels.

Pray for FREEDOM from all doctrines of demons (such as holy sparks) and an IMPARTATION of discernment to separate truth from error. Pray that the Lord will deliver the Ultra-Orthodox from MIXING the Word of God with any other source, however sacred it may be to Judaism, however many centuries it has been considered precious, however it may depart from unquestioned traditions. Pray that the Lord will untangle the web of deception that surrounds the BASIC APPROACH to Scripture. Nothing is too difficult for Thee! Pray that the Lord will grant revelation knowledge that every angel is not necessarily a "good angel." Pray that the Light of Messiah Yeshua will penetrate the darkness of Kabbalah and draw the Ultra-Orthodox into a personal, intimate relationship with the God of Israel.

> *"Then the glory of the Lord*
> ***Departed** from the threshold*
> *Of the temple and stood*
> *Over the cherubim."*
> *(Ezekiel 10:18)*

Pray for a revelation that, while the glory of God is everywhere present in His glorious creation, the MANIFEST PRESENCE of God does not abide in all places. We can know this for sure because the glory departed from the Temple and even from the Old City of Jerusalem (Ezekiel 11:23) and always departs in the presence of sin, evil, and idolatry. His glory returns whenever there is a returning to God in repentance with all our heart, soul, and mind and approach to Him through the provision of the new and living way of His Son and Mediator, Messiah Jesus.

> *"But even though we, or an angel*
> *From heaven, should preach to you*
> *A gospel contrary to that which*
> *We have preached to you, let him be accursed."*
> *(Galatians 1:8)*

These strong words of the Apostle Paul were meant to pierce our souls like shock waves, to serve as a wake up call. There is *another gospel*. There are *angels preaching* that which is contrary to the truth of Scripture. Drawing together everything we have learned, we could say that the false gospel of Kabbalah, as expressed in Chasidism, presents a *Tzaddik* as a substitute mediator, a *trinity* of holy names that were used by the Ba'al Shem Tov to ascend into the upper worlds, counterfeit manifestations of the Holy Spirit in the form of *spirit guides* and a *soulish joy* expressed in ecstatic prayer that can easily appear to be the joy of the Lord.

Pray for a profound revelation of this false gospel to the Ultra-Orthodox. Pray they would recognize the deception, the demonic source of these doctrines, repent of opening their hearts to it, and turn to the gospel of salvation in Messiah Yeshua.

> *"For a child will be born to us,*
> *A son will be given to us;*
> *And the government will rest on His shoulders;*
> *And His name will be called*
> *Wonderful Counselor, Mighty God,*
> *Eternal Father, Prince of Peace."*
> *(Isaiah 9:6)*

Pray for a revelation of the blessed truth that there was ONE TIME when God voluntarily LIMITED HIMSELF, but not by contracting. There was one time when, in miraculous fulfillment of prophecy, God chose to humble Himself by taking on the form of man, even of a baby. There was ONE TIME when God took up space in the sense that, if the Messiah was sitting on a chair, you could not sit on the same chair He was sitting on. Yet, at the same time, He CREATED everything composing that chair (the wood, the nails, the elements, every last molecule). If Yeshua would cease to exist for even a moment, that chair would instantly disintegrate because ALL THINGS were created by Him and THROUGH HIM all things consist, literally hold together (Colossians 1:16-17).

> *"For He delivered us from*
> *The domain of darkness,*

And transferred us to the kingdom
Of His beloved Son,
In whom we have redemption,
The forgiveness of sins.
*And He is the **image***
Of the invisible God,
The first-born of all creation."
(Colossians 1:13-14)

*Pray that the Ultra-Orthodox would be **TRANSFERRED** from the Kingdom of Darkness to the Kingdom of Light through the Blood of Messiah Yeshua. Pray they will come to acknowledge that the Son of Man and Son of God came as the **REDEEMER** and to **REVEAL THE FATHER** (John 14:8-10), to be the very image and expression of the invisible God, so that Israel (and subsequently all mankind) could draw near and enter the very Holy of Holies by His Blood. He Himself **MADE THE WAY** and **IS THE WAY** to the Father (John 14:6) so that man need not (nor cannot) ascend through a complex maze of sefirot redeeming sparks all along the way to reach the Divine Majesty and thereby secure his own redemption.*

The Rabbinic Spirit

"...And they (the chief priests, scribes, and elders)
Spoke to Him (Jesus) saying,
*'Tell us, by what **authority***
Are you doing these things,
Or who is the one
Who gave you this authority?"
(Luke 20:2)

We cannot hope to comprehend the *rabbinic spirit*, and how it gained entry into the fabric of Jewish culture, without first understanding the *roots of Rabbinic Judaism* and what authority God established in the Scriptures.

The rabbinic spirit has to do with the question of authority. The rabbis and religious leaders asked Jesus who gave Him the authority to do what He was doing. It is only fair that we ask from where the rabbis get their authority. Is it from God or from man?

"God, who at various times
And in various ways
Spoke in time past to the fathers
By the prophets,
Has in these last days
Spoken to us by His Son,
Whom He appointed heir of all things,
Through whom also He made the worlds."
(Hebrews 1:1-2)

God *spoke* to the patriarchs or *appeared in a vision* to various Biblical characters in the Tenach (Old Testament), particularly in the first five Books of Moses through to Judges, constantly revealing Himself, initiating relationships, and intervening in the lives of men and women. Throughout Israel's history, God spoke to His people through His *appointed servants,* the *prophets,* until Messiah. Today He speaks through His Son, *Yeshua.*

Kings, priests, and prophets were the established offices of God in the Bible.

While the patriarchs were the founding fathers of the faith and an honored class in themselves, the kings governed the nation and led the army in battle, the priests ministered before the Lord, and presented offerings for the nation, and the prophets spoke the Word of the Lord to the kings and priests. There is no mention of rabbis anywhere in the Tenach. So where did the rabbis come from? How did they come to possess the awesome, unquestionable authority they have today?

To solve this mystery, we will be taking a look at four *"Crisis Points"* in the history of Israel going all the way back to Moses. Admittedly, the whole of Jewish history reads like a series of one crisis after another, however, these four specific points will highlight *precedents* that were set and developments that took place which ultimately secured the tent pegs of rabbinic authority:

1) *The Golden Calf* (Wandering in the Wilderness Experience)
2) *The Exile to Babylon* (Seeds of Oral Tradition & Rise of Babylonian Sages)
3) *The Bar Kokhba Revolt* (Rise of Rabbinic Judaism/Rabbi Akiba)
4) *The Dark Ages* (Birth of Mystical Movements and Chasidism)

The gospel of Matthew tells us that there were fourteen generations between Abraham and David, fourteen generations between David and the exile to Babylon, and fourteen generations between the exile and Jesus the Messiah.

These generations can be seen as eras of the growing distance between God and His people before Yeshua arrived on the scene.

Each *era* symbolizes a gradual moving away from the abiding Presence, the Shekinah Glory of God presiding over the nation, the personal involvement of God in the daily affairs of the people, ultimately resulting in an inaccessible, ineffable, impersonal *theory* of God accompanied by a intellectual forest of commentary which would prevent the Jewish people from approaching the Living God who created them for personal, covenant relationship. The three eras are:

Abraham-David	Era of Covenant Relationship
David-Babylon	Era of Persistent Idolatry & Resulting Exile
Babylon-Messiah	Era of the Rise of Oral Tradition & Rabbinic Authority

In the first era, the patriarchs were walking with God in ***personal relationship***. Subsequently, the nation of Israel was repeatedly lured from intimacy into idolatry, but whenever the people cried out in their distress, God raised up *judges* to rescue them. During the reign of King David, the people followed the Lord with all their heart because David followed the Lord with all his heart. After the nation was split into Israel and Judah, and Solomon's heart was seduced away from the Lord by his many wives, Judah moved further and further away from personal relationship, first into the idolatry of the nations, and eventually into their own traditions. Yeshua strongly challenged this unfaithfulness in His teachings throughout His earthly ministry.

Inevitably, the love relationship the Father desired to flourish between Himself and His people Israel had been replaced with legalistic religion. The rabbis were assuming power and the people did not know God anymore.

> *"Come, **make us gods***
> *Who will go before us.*
> *As for this fellow Moses*
> *Who brought us up from Egypt,*
> *We don't know what has happened to him."*
> *(Exodus 32:1)*

As we consider the *crisis of the Golden Calf*, we may need to be reminded that when we look at Israel, we are actually looking into a *mirror*. If we are honest, we must confess that we see our own sins in the failures of the people of God and we also see the mercy and faithfulness of God. Israel broke covenant with God before the law was even presented, yet God invited Moses to journey up the mountain to receive a *new covenant*.

"Come, make us gods" is the source of all religious folly. There is a crisis, we are at a standstill in our journey toward the Promised Land, we have been waiting for what seems like forever for an answer from God and the heavens appear as brass. He's keeping us waiting and, in the meantime, things are getting out of control. This is a matter of *survival.* If we don't *do something*, the people will begin to scatter. Saul, Israel's first king, caved in under this very pressure (I Samuel 13:11-12). Samuel was late in coming, the Philistines were closing in, the army was scattering, and Saul felt *compelled* to sacrifice before Samuel arrived. It resulted in his downfall and the destruction of his entire family.

Wilderness experiences can easily lead to embracing or creating human solutions or systems of worship that replace or re-define God so that we can continue on with our journey.

When we are in the midst of a crisis, our vision of reality becomes distorted. The Israelites thought that *Moses* had brought them up out of Egypt (Exodus 32:1). In their view, "this fellow" had led them into the wilderness and now he's disappeared into the mountains and if he doesn't come back, what will become of us? Here we are, stranded in the middle of nowhere, without a clue where we are supposed to be going and there's no word of direction. Ever been there? So, what do we do? We begin to *make us gods* to rescue us from our predicament - plans and solutions of our own making.

Whenever we "make gods" to rescue us, we separate ourselves from God, disconnect from His heavenly source of provision, and compromise our faith. In other words, we break covenant with Him.

We will see how the urgent need to keep the nation of Israel together during crises experiences at the tragic expense of preserving *relationship* with the God of Israel, has determined the behavior of God's chosen people even up to the present day. But the precedent was set in the wilderness with the golden calf.

Pray that God will reveal the sin of breaking covenant with Him, of manufacturing our own gods in order to preserve our identity, our nation, our family, our career, or our ministry. I invite you to repent with me for any times in our walk with God where we have "broken covenant" with Him by resorting to our own methods of deliverance in a crisis and failing to depend completely upon Him. Let us repent for the sin of constructing religious substitutes for waiting on God until He comes back down the mountain.

Pray that God will create an insatiable hunger in the hearts of the Ultra-Orthodox for a personal relationship with Him, as the patriarchs had, a hunger that won't take no for an answer, a hunger that desires beyond the outward covenant of circumcision, and ignites a passion in the heart to hear the voice of God and have the assurance of redemption that Yeshua promises to all those who put their faith in Him.

> *"By the rivers of Babylon*
> *We sat and wept*
> *When we remembered Zion."*
> *(Psalm 137:1)*

<u>The Babylonian Exile was a monumental crisis and tragedy in the history of God's chosen people because, for the first time, they were separated from the Promised Land and from the Temple, which was the center of spiritual and ritual life.</u>

If Satan cannot prevent us from entering the Kingdom of God, then his next strategy is to *defile* and/or *derail* the purposes of God for our lives by somehow drawing us into his domain. If he can lure us or *take us captive* into **HIS** camp, then we will never be able to drive him out of **OUR** camp. Tragically, the idols of the nations prevailed over Israel and captured their hearts so that Israel was never able to turn the hearts of the nations to the God of Israel. If we are not diligent to guard our hearts, this can easily happen to us.

*"When the Lord brought back
the captives to Zion,
we were like men who dreamed.
Our mouths were filled with laughter,
Our tongues with songs of joy."
(Psalm 126:1-2a)*

The books of Ezra and Nehemiah record the lists of exiles that returned from Babylon. In this first exile from the Land, the captives that returned had only been separated from Jerusalem for *seventy years* and were then given permission to rebuild the walls of the city. Can you imagine the utter exhilaration it must have been to re-capture the Old City of Jerusalem and the Western Wall in 1967 after *2,000 ye*ars of diaspora? There are no words in any language to describe this miracle and the faithfulness of God to His people. Sadly, of the scores that went to Babylon in 586 B.C., only a handful returned. The first wave of aliyah (priests and heads of families) totaled 42,360 (Ezra 2:64-66, Nehemiah 7:66-68) and the second group who returned with Ezra numbered far less (Ezra 8:1-20, Nehemiah 12:1-26).

In preparing to write this prayer guide, the Lord led me on a fascinating study from the call of Abram in Genesis 12 through the fall of Jerusalem and subsequent exile to Babylon in II Kings 25. The birth of the nation of Israel unfolds like the miracle of a rose and the Scripture records all the events and circumstances that caused this precious flower to be divided, uprooted, and eventually carried off into captivity. After Solomon's death, but previous to the Babylonian exile, the Bible refers to the people of God collectively as *Israel* or *Judah*, depending on what kingdom they were born into. Israel went into captivity to Assyria and Judah went to Babylon.

It is the history of Judah that most profoundly influenced the course of the history of God's chosen people.

In the Land, there was an *ordained system, a way of approaching God through the Temple sacrifices.* Suddenly, in Babylon, the people of Judah did not have a system of approaching God, and the vacuum created by captivity inspired the need to develop a *new man-made system.* The Babylonian Exile highlights a spiritual principle, namely that, whenever the enemy can cause us to be driven out of God's protected boundaries, he will have a distinct advantage over us, unless or until we repent.

__Safe and secure within the boundaries of our personal Promised Land, we are under God's canopy of protection, but beyond these borders, we are in enemy territory and much more vulnerable to his deception.__

Certainly, the teaching of the ways of God by word of mouth to the next generation had already begun before the exile. However, it was not the *Hebrews* who ultimately transmitted the Bible to succeeding generations or other peoples, but their descendants, the *Jews*. The *patriarchs* had long since passed into eternity and the *prophets* were taken captive to Babylon and neither would have a say as to *how* their encounters with God would be communicated to future generations.

Interestingly, we do not find a reference to "Jews" in the Bible until after the Babylonian exile. The *kingdom of Judah* went into exile and *Jews* came back. What happened? During the traumatic years of exile, early seeds of the "*Oral Tradition*", the rise of the sages, and a religion called "Judaism" began to take shape.

__The Bible itself does not speak of any form of "Judaism," rather only a personal and covenant relationship with God.__

However, Jewish history describes *three progressive stages* as follows:

Biblical Judaism	(20th-4th century B.C.) (Age of Patriarchs, Kings, Priests, & Prophets)
Hellenistic Judaism	(4th century B.C. – 2nd century A.D.)
Rabbinic Judaism	(2nd century A.D. – Present)

The kingdoms of both Israel and Judah were destroyed, but only Judah succeeded in re-establishing themselves in the Land, because of Judaism. Israel never restored their kingdom.

__The Jews are the last remnants of the Hebrews and Israelites, and they are the ones who developed and promoted Judaism in the 2,500__ *years from the Babylonian exile to the present day. The oral tradition developed into Judaism, later maturing into Rabbinic Judaism.*

One might ask: "What's the problem here? So Judaism developed. What's the big deal?" The big deal has to do primarily with Israel's *origin, relationship, calling,* and *inheritance* and the ultimate *fruit* of the development of Rabbinic Judaism.

God birthed the people and nation of Israel for His purposes and His glory. The sages birthed the oral tradition, for their purposes, namely keeping the people together, and their glory, for which they receive praise even to this day.

What God was looking for and calling for through any number of prophets during the season preceding the exile and even after it, was *repentance*, not *glue*. He had birthed the nation, delivered it out of Egypt, protected it in the wilderness, and brought it into the Land of Canaan. He was more than able to keep the people together in exile if they would return to Him with all their heart, forsake their own ways, and learn His ways. *Reform* triumphed over *repentance*, which is a pattern of history, not only of the Jews, but also of all mankind. Rather than humble ourselves, we *re-define our faith and culture*, and bypass the highest calling of God on our life.

God's purpose for creating Israel was to bring them, as a special people, into a personal covenant relationship with Him, reveal to them His plan of salvation (atonement), initially through the blood of the Passover lamb, and then commission His people to be witnesses who would share this personal relationship and plan of salvation through Yeshua, the Lamb of God, with the entire world.

The calling upon the children of Israel to be a witness to the nations (Isaiah 43:10) was circumvented by the ultimate creation of Rabbinic Judaism, the seeds of which were planted in Babylon. Rabbinic Judaism, as a *self-preserving religious system,* would ultimately serve to turn the focus of the Jewish people *inward* (on their Jewish identity) so that they could not minister *outward* to the nations. Tragically, this may even occur in sectors of the modern Messianic Body when *Jewish identity* is exalted above *pure devotion to Yeshua Himself* and the Great Commission to *make disciples* of all nations (Matthew 28:19-20).

If Rabbinic Judaism is, indeed, a man-made religion, then the roots of our faith are Hebraic, not Jewish, an extremely critical distinction, because whichever roots you embrace will be what you manifest spiritually.

> *"And if the first piece of dough*
> *Be holy, the lump is also;*
> *And if the root by holy,*
> *The branches are too."*
> *(Romans 11:16)*

A *holy* and *healthy* root produces holy, healthy branches. Yeshua is the pure *Root* (Romans 15:12, Revelation 22:16) and *Branch* (Isaiah 11:1/Jeremiah 23:5-6) of our faith. But Yeshua is also a physical descendant of the Hebrews through the line of David. Our *Hebraic roots* lead to the *patriarchs (Abraham, Isaac, Jacob, David)* and the *source of truth* for the patriarchs is the *pure Word of God*. Abraham was declared righteous *by faith* before the law was given (Romans 4:1-3) and it is of the utmost significance we realize the root that is *holy* is Yeshua Himself (who existed before the foundation of the world) and the *faith* of Abram, the patriarch, which was credited to him as righteousness because of the relationship Abram had with God. Isaiah 41:8 calls Abraham a *friend of God*. Romans 11:28-29 expresses that the gifts and callings of God are irrevocable and that even the present unbelieving Jewish nation is beloved for the sake of the *fathers* with whom He made a covenant (Genesis 17:4-8, Genesis 26:3-5, Genesis 28:12-14). Those of us who are grafted-in to the olive tree are enriched as we embrace the Hebraic roots of our faith.

Jewish roots, on the other hand, lead to the *rabbis* and the *source of truth* for the rabbis is far beyond Scripture (the Talmud, the Kabbalah, and so on). The basis of righteousness is *good works, not faith*. Relationship with God is expressed more through a life of Torah study than a walk of faith. To the degree that we embrace *relationship* or *religion*, we reap *intimacy* with God or *legalism*, and we *release* or *hinder* the flow of God's *anointing* and *purposes* for our lives.

Identity is a deep and binding issue for many and often prevents us from coming into the *fullness* of God's blessings. We are raised in a certain environment and atmosphere, absorbing customs and traditions that we assume are healthy and holy. The ultimate question every believer in Yeshua must answer is, *"What is most important in our hearts?"* Are we more concerned about an identity rooted in the expectations of ourselves, the expectations of others, the pleasure we may enjoy in that particular identity, the influence of the world, our cultural history, the influence or pressure from family or friends, the customs and traditions of our particular race, *OR* cultivating a personal, intimate relationship with our Heavenly Father, being conformed to the image of His Son Jesus, walking in the freedom and power of the Holy Spirit, and fulfilling the destiny upon our lives so as to bring glory to Him?

__Our identity in Messiah Jesus is the only identity that will ultimately bring us peace, joy, and fulfillment, and glorify our Father in heaven.__

Pray that the God of Israel would impart a fresh revelation of the Hebraic roots to the Ultra-Orthodox, even to Messianic believers (and to the Church), and re-direct their focus towards the God of Abraham, Isaac, and Jacob, the Word of God itself, and Yeshua, the promised Messiah. Pray that He will reveal to them their high calling and destiny to bring Jesus, not Judaism, to the nations. Pray for FREEDOM from every false identity defined by man and an EMBRACING of their true identity as a Covenant people of God, an identity that can only be fulfilled and enjoyed in Messiah Yeshua Himself.

Along with the political and military systems that must be rendered powerless in these last days, so the *religious system* will also be brought to bankruptcy before the return of Yeshua. Rabbinic Judaism will most certainly assert itself for one last battle, as well as the political and military arm of flesh, in the attempt to save the nation. But God will not share His glory with any human system. He will rescue Israel from destruction with His own hand as He has always done. Judaism will not hold the Jewish people together in this final hour when God is shaking everything that can be shaken, but God Himself will hold the nation together, as He did in the wilderness. There is today a spiritual Jacob that is being transformed into Israel.

Pray for the total collapse of every system of "power and might." As God wrestles with His people to subdue their strength and change them as He did the patriarch Jacob, pray they will yield to Him, resist anger, cynicism, and dependence on worldliness or humanism, and cry out to Yeshua, who is their only salvation. We may want to take a moment to repent for any times in our own lives (even as we stand in the gap for Israel) where we have created life-rafts to help God keep us or something in our lives afloat, where we have mixed together a glue of seeming godliness that results in thwarting His purposes for us and hindering our relationship with Him.

Pray the Lord will do a deep work in the hearts of His people (even believers) to come completely out of the bondage of Egypt and into the Kingdom of Light. Pray He will grant discernment to be able to separate the truth of Scriptures from rabbinic conjecture.

What is the Oral Tradition? Although there is nothing at all in Scripture to justify this assertion, nevertheless, it is said that the Oral Tradition (or Oral Law) is the authoritative interpretation of the Written Law (or Torah) which was regarded as given to Moses on Sinai, and therefore equal with the Written Law.

> *"This people honors Me with their lips,*
> *But their heart is far away from Me.*
> *But in vain do they worship Me,*
> *Teaching as doctrines the precepts of men."*
> *(Matthew 15:9)*

Jesus spoke these piercing words to the Pharisees and scribes who challenged Him for refusing to *obey the traditions* of the elders. Yeshua came to die for our sins, give us eternal life, and also to give us a *new heart*, a heart after God. This is the essence of all the prayers we pray for the Ultra-Orthodox.

The view that the Oral Law was given to Moses on Mt. Sinai was a fundamental principle of the rabbis. There is a strong *bond*, we are told, between the Written Law and the Oral Law, and neither can exist without the other—both from the dogmatic point of view and from that of historical reality. The rabbis say that the Oral Law depends on the Written Law, but, at the same time, the Written Law cannot exist without the Oral Law.

> *"All authority has been given to Me*
> *In heaven and on earth."*
> *(Matthew 28:18)*

This brings us to the question, "What is a *rabbi* and where did they get the authority to make such an outrageous and binding statement?" The word "rabbi" does not appear anywhere in the Tenach, thus there is no divine position of authority granted to them by God. The earliest pairs of ancient teachers, called *zugoth*, appear approximately 250 years after the last period recorded in the Hebrew Scriptures. They were followed by the *sages*, a term designating the spiritual/religious leaders who molded every aspect of Jewish life and flourished from the Second Temple period until the destruction of the Temple in 70 A.D. The sages included the scribes, Pharisees, members of the Sanhedrin, and heads of academies (teachers of the law), and served as jurist, judge, and prophet.

Jesus the Messiah strategically stepped onto the stage of history when there was a power struggle raging between the schools of Hillel and Shammai and the era of the sage was transitioning to the Tannaim.

The word "tanna" means *to hand down orally*. The Tannaim were sages who shaped Jewish thought from the period of Hillel to the completion of the Mishnah by Judah Ha-Nasi (*"Patriarch"*) in the first and second centuries (20-200 A.D.). His death closed the period of the Tannaim. Rabbi Akiba was the dominant Jewish sage among the *tannaim*. Other key figures were Rabbi Yochanan ben-Zakkai and Rabbi Meir. From Moses through the Tannaim (sages) until after the Bar Kokhba Revolt, the inspiration for all Jewish learning and authority *originated in Israel*. It was Judah Ha-Nasi's intention that it remain so, thus he prohibited any ordination of spiritual leaders outside of Jerusalem, so the *chain of tradition* would remain linked to the Holy land.

The Babylonian scholars who were active in the period from the completion of the Mishnah (200 A.D.) until the completion of the Babylonian Talmud in the 5th century were called *Amoraim* (meaning "spokesmen" or "interpreters"). The *link* that connected the chain of teachers in Babylonia with the Tannaim was *Abba Arika*, or *Rav*, a student of Judah the Prince. Naturally, the first and foremost *Amora* of Babylonia was *Rav* and his traditions were preserved and then transmitted to *European scholars*. Thus, modern-day Ashkenazi rabbis may also consider themselves *links* in the Chain of Tradition. Pumbedita and Sura eventually became the centers of Jewish study in Babylonia. The discussions and debates of the *amoraim* in these two satellite cities constitute the bulk of both the Jerusalem and the Babylonian Talmud, although the Babylonian Talmud eventually gained dominance.

The Talmud is a massive compilation of sixty-three books divided between the Mishnah and the Gemara. The Mishnah is a collection of interpretations and commentaries on the Biblical laws (Five Books of Moses), also known as the "Oral Law," which the rabbis say is "one" with Scripture. The Gemara is a vast collection of commentaries on the Mishnah. Together, the Mishnah and Gemara form the Talmud.

The title *Rabbi* derived from the noun *rav*, which in biblical Hebrew means "great," but the literal meaning is "my master." During the generation after Hillel, the term was used as a title for sages. Yeshua addressed the use of this title in Matthew 23:7, likely referring to its recent introduction and prophetically anticipating the power it would later command. The talmudic rabbi was an interpreter and expounder of the Bible and Oral Law, and usually had an occupation from which he derived his livelihood. In the Middle Ages, however, the title took on the form of teacher, preacher, spiritual head of the Jewish community or congregation, as we are familiar with today.

God's ways are so much higher than our ways and far beyond our understanding. While Rabbinic Judaism is clearly a man-made religious system that created and awarded rabbis indisputable authority, yet, it also served a divine purpose for a *season* of Jewish history. Although the nation of Israel was destroyed in 70 A.D. and the people scattered across the globe, the Jewish people survived, not only because of the promise and faithfulness of God to preserve them, but also because the *"Jewish Idea,"* or Judaism, was exalted above that of the Jewish Land, Jewish national life, even the Hebrew Scriptures.

__God permitted the system of Judaism to yoke the nation together in the Diaspora. Nevertheless, just as He promised to gather His people from the farthest corners of the earth and free them from their wanderings, He will also free them from the yoke of Rabbinic Judaism in these last days, return them to their original Hebraic roots, from whom the Messiah springs forth (Isaiah 11:1-2), and give them "a new heart," a heart to follow Him.__

"Truly, I say to you,
Whatever you bind on earth
Shall be bound in heaven;
And whatever you loose on earth
Shall be loosed in heaven."
(Matthew 18:18)

The rabbis say the Written Law and the Oral Law cannot be separated. In other words, they are __bound together.__ *The Word of God says that He has given believers authority to bind and loose, in Yeshua's Name. Let us agree in prayer to LOOSE (to sever) the bonds of the Written Law and Oral Law, to separate them in the spirit realm, to break the unholy and unauthorized connection between the two established by the rabbis, and BIND (tie, attach) to the hearts and minds of the Jewish people only the Written Word of God. Pray that the deception and lie that the Oral Law was given to Moses on Mount Sinai and is equal to or even above the Scriptures will be exposed and rejected by the Ultra-Orthodox.*

Pray that every unholy, unhealthy soul tie will be broken between rabbis (and their yeshiva students) and the Talmud, the Zohar, and Kabbalah. Pray also that soul ties between the tzaddikim and their disciples would be severed. Pray that the Holy Spirit will reveal the divine inspiration of Holy Scripture ALONE and create a hunger to return to the pure Word of God in the yeshivas.

"For false messiahs
And false prophets will appear
And perform great signs and miracles
To deceive even the elect—
If that were possible."
(Matthew 24:24)

If the exile to Babylon was a crisis, the *Bar Kokhba Revolt* was a catastrophe of unparalleled proportions. Solomon's Temple was destroyed in 586 B.C. Many Judeans went into exile, but the remnant that returned rebuilt the Temple. Even after the *Great Revolt* (66-70 A.D.), led by the Zealots in an attempt to break free from Roman dominance, and the destruction of the Second Temple in 70 A.D, Jews were allowed to inhabit the Land.

After the failure of the Bar Kokhba Revolt (132-135 A.D.), Jews were strictly forbidden to live in Judea or come anywhere near Jerusalem, the Romans changed the name of Israel to Palestine, and a final split occurred between the followers of Jesus and the followers of the rabbis, which also laid the foundation for the church to ultimately disconnect from their Hebraic roots.

The long-term consequences of this tragedy are staggering. More Jewish lives would be lost in this uprising than all previous battles, and for nearly 2,000 years afterwards the Jewish people would be scattered to the nations and relentlessly persecuted, as the framework for indisputable rabbinic authority would be nailed down.

The sages had been gaining prominence over the priests since the exile to Babylon. During the reign of Herod, the status of the priests was reduced, which served to further elevate the sages, now known as *Pharisees*. The Pharisees and the Sadducean priesthood struggled for dominance, the Pharisees ultimately winning. The Pharisaic scholars in the schools of Hillel and Shammai wrestled for authority, the school of Hillel emerging victorious. By the time the title of Pharisee was changed to "Rabbi," the priests were entirely eliminated as a significant influence. The destruction of the Second Temple served to heighten the rationale for rabbis and rabbinic institutions of learning. *Yavneh* became the center of rabbinic authority when the Sanhedrin was *transferred* from Jerusalem to this coastal city in 70 A.D.

> *"And the axe is already laid*
> *At the root of the trees;*
> *Every tree therefore*
> *That does not bear good fruit*
> *Is cut down and*
> *Thrown into the fire."*
> *(Matthew 3:10)*

The ultimate purposes of God reach their fulfillment in the *fullness of time* (Ephesians 1:9-10). He is seeking those who will worship Him *in Spirit and in truth*. Jesus came to earth at just the perfect moment. Strategic transfers of power were in progress, perhaps at their peak, when Yeshua appeared on the scene. An overview of the cataclysmic transfers and consolidations of authority over the course of Jewish history were from *Priests to Sages, Sages to Pharisees, Sadducees to Pharisees, School of Shammai to School of Hillel, Pharisees to Rabbis, then a consolidation of all Rabbinic Groups into one Sect.* Ultimately, there would be the consolidation of all Rabbinic views into the Talmud, confining the views of the victorious sect within certain boundaries.

As the foundation of the Oral Law was being birthed, as the power struggle was being played out in the rivalry between the Pharisees and the Sadducees, Jesus announced that "the Kingdom of God is at hand." (Matthew 4:17)

Talk about upsetting apple carts and stealing the thunder! When the Bible speaks of the Pharisees coming to "question" Jesus or "test" Him, it is important to understand who these men were. They weren't just local rabbis from down the street. They were the foundation-layers of what would later become Rabbinic Judaism. Yeshua was neither a disciple of Hillel or Shammai, was gathering disciples of His own, performing awesome miracles all over the country which none of the followers of the sages could keep up with, and all Israel was flocking to Him.

John the Baptist, whose call for repentance prepared the way for Messiah, said that the axe was already being laid at the *root*. The true disciples were being separated from the hypocrites. So it is in this day as the Lord prepares His spotless Bride. As the time approaches for the return of Jesus, and the restoration of all things, He is moving upon His army of intercessors to dig down deep to the very *root of demonic strongholds*.

We can be sure the God of Israel is restoring all things and laying the axe at the root of rabbinic authority because of what happened in Yavneh. In May 1999, a group of American Messianic Jews, Gentile Christians, Israeli Messianic Jews and Messianic pastors traveled to the city of Yavneh to repent, uproot what had been planted in history and plant, in the spirit, the seeds of healing and restoration. Yavneh was the city of the great scholars and rabbis, known as *tannaim*, between 70 A.D. and 132 A.D.

After the fall of the Second Temple, the Sanhedrin (the Jewish governing body consisting of seventy elders who ruled on certain theological, ethical, civil and political matters) relocated to the biblical harbor city of Yavneh, initially under Rabbi Yochanan Ben Zakkai. Some historic decisions were made at Yavneh which have affected the Jewish people up to this day. Among them were the arranging of the definitive canon of the Bible, the formulation of the 18 blessings of the Amidah (silent reading prayers) and the several "blessings" against Christians and *other heretics*.

We want to take a closer look at this last decision. Up until the Bar Kokhba Revolt, Christianity was considered a Jewish movement, a branch or sect of Judaism, just as Chasidism is a sect within Judaism. After the failure of the revolt and the loss of the Temple, the Sanhedrin ruled at Yavneh that Jews who believed in Jesus were no longer to be considered Jewish. It was a final severing of ties with the Jewish followers of Yeshua and a punishment for those Jewish believers who were partners in the revolt up until Simon Bar Kokhba (the leader of the revolt) was proclaimed by one of the sages to be the Messiah, but withdrew from participating because of this proclamation. Up until this point, a person could believe in Jesus and still be Jewish. All that changed in Yavneh. This *redefinition of who is Jewish* also seemed to make things a lot easier for the Church and, based on the decision of the Sanhedrin, the Church Fathers also taught that once a person "converts" to Christianity they are no longer Jewish and must disconnect from their Hebraic roots.

Blessings <u>against</u> people are commonly known as *curses*. At Yavneh, these curses were formed not only against Christians, but other heretics as well, namely, Jewish believers. This recent gathering of Christians and Messianic Jews at Yavneh was for the purpose of standing together as a Body to repent for the sins of the Sanhedrin and of the Church, break the curses that were spoken over both groups, renounce the lie that both groups perpetuated down through history, take back what the enemy has stolen, proclaim the truth of the Word in the place where the lie was generated and sing praises to God for the victory.

Praise God for the strategic spiritual warfare He is inspiring in Israel in our day. God is digging down and pulling up the roots that are hindering revival. Pray that the victory experienced in the spirit at Yavneh will be manifested in the natural and that the power of the decision at Yavneh will be BROKEN over the Jewish people. This lie has been a major stumbling block for centuries. The Lord is taking the obstacles out of the way of His people and preparing a highway for His coming!

Perhaps as significant as the curse against heretics, Yavneh also served as the battleground for the spiritual war that ultimately exalted *Rabbi Akiba ben Joseph* (40-135 A.D.) above every other rabbinic voice.

<u>**The greatest tragedy of the Bar Kokhba Revolt is that, in the midst of it, Rabbi Akiba, who would become the father of Rabbinic Judaism, declared Simeon ben Kosiba to be the Messiah.**</u>

The details of how ben Kosiba's name became Kokhba give us an insight to the precedent that was set by Rabbi Akiba to *adjust the facts* to suit his purposes. Rabbi Akiba changed a letter in *Kosiba* so it became *Kokhba* and then substituted *bar* (Aramaic for "son) for the Hebrew version *(ben)*. The result was "Bar Kokhba" which means "*son of the star*." The manipulations of Kosiba's name were intended to give him messianic legitimacy based on Numbers 24:17. It was only after the Bar Kokhba died in Bethar, exhausted in battle, that his followers realized he wasn't the Messiah.

__Perhaps more than any other, Rabbi Akiba's influence over the centuries shaped the religion practiced by Orthodox Jews today. R. Shimon bar Yochai (author of the Zohar) was a favored student of Rabbi Akiba.__

Rabbi Akiba methodically challenged and defeated all the traditional rabbis of his day, and achieved an indisputable position based on his promotion of the concept that the *decision of the majority is binding.* This view finds its source in a twisted interpretation of Scripture. Exodus 23:2 says "You shall not follow a multitude in doing evil." The rabbis interpreted this to mean that, while we should *not* follow a multitude for evil, the implication is that we *may* follow a multitude for good. Consequently, this gives the majority the power to define what is *good.*

The Bar Kokhba Revolt presented the perfect moment to capture the crown of authority. The belief that Messiah was born on the day the Second Temple was destroyed fueled longings for a Messianic deliverer, who was seen as a political savior and this set the stage for someone to seize the day and proclaim a Messiah.

__Rabbi Akiba's declaration at this strategic moment enforced the authority of the rabbis and also forced the followers of Yeshua to withdraw from the revolt, causing them to be declared traitors, and effectively cutting them out of the Jewish loop.__

Repentance precedes revival and revelation. John the Baptist emerged from the wilderness, preaching, "Repent, for the kingdom of God is at hand," and the multitudes came, confessing their sins, and were immersed (baptized) preparing the way for Messiah. Shortly thereafter, Yeshua was revealed as the "Lamb of God." Repentance begins in the house of God. How we interpret Scripture is an indicator of our maturity and the depth of our relationship with the Living God. It can have a powerful effect, even a "binding" effect, on those we influence.

I entreat each one of us to humbly and honestly come before God and repent of any times we have forced or concocted an interpretation of God's Word to advance our own interests. Repent for any damaging effects our conclusions may have had on others. As the One New Man, let us repent on behalf of the rabbis, going all the way back to Rabbi Akiba (even the sages who influenced him), for distorting God's Word for the purpose of securing power over their disciples and even over the Scriptures themselves, and also repent for faulty interpretations of the Church (such as replacement theology) which have caused it to disconnect from its Hebraic roots.

In Jesus' Name, cancel every effect of these soulish decisions that have "bound" the Jewish people to the decisions of the "majority" and loosen freedom to pursue the pure and undefiled truth of God found in Scripture, even if it means standing alone. Pray that the manipulation of Torah to further the power of the rabbis would be exposed. Pray that the rabbinic SYSTEM of interpretation would be challenged in the yeshivas by those who are hungry for an honest, personal relationship with God.

> *"How can you say, 'We are wise,*
> *For we have the law of the Lord,'*
> *When actually the lying pen*
> *Of the scribes*
> *Has handled it falsely?"*
> *(Jeremiah 8:8)*

According to Jewish tradition, Rabbi Akiba, along with contemporaries of his day, and later Judah Ha-Nasi, *systematized* (or codified) the Mishnah, the Midrash, and the Halakah, *fixed the canon* of the Old Testament books, *authorized a new translation* to replace the Septuagint (the Greek version of the Old Testament) and also *authorized a new paraphrased version* of the Scriptures.

We'll need to unpack this box to fully appreciate the impact these actions would have on future generations. Let's begin with a few definitions. The *Mishnah, Midrash,* and *Halakah* are all *commentary,* not Scripture. The Mishnah is the systematized core of the *Oral Law* (based on the Five Books of Moses) and is one of the two basic parts of the *Talmud*, the ultimate statement of rabbinic authority. The *Midrash* is a vast collection of over one hundred books containing complex, esoteric interpretations of the Tenach, which attempt to bring out the "spirit" of a verse. *Halakah* is codified Jewish Law, based on the decisions of the sages.

__Systematizing or codifying means to arrange it into a framework so that everything following it also needs to be confined within that framework.__

The system *laid the foundation* for Rabbinic Judaism, even in the compiling of Scripture. Although there were others whose influence played a major part, Rabbi Akiba apparently made the final determination which books would be included and excluded in the Tenach. As believers, we are extremely grateful and indebted to the early Jewish scribes for faithfully recording and guarding the Hebrew Scriptures which comprise the Bible we read today. There is no doubt that the hand of God was guiding the decision of the final canon. However, Rabbi Akiba stepped beyond the sacred boundaries of selecting books and also authorized a *new translation* of these books. The *Greek Septuagint* had been accepted for centuries in the Diaspora, since Greek was the common language of the people, and the Greek version of Tenach was especially vital for those Jews living outside of Israel, although Greek and Aramaic were both used in the Land.

__Why would Rabbi Akiba need a new translation of the Bible? Simply because the followers of Yeshua often quoted the prophecies in the Septuagint to prove that Jesus is the Messiah. These truths clashed with the rabbinic authority structure Akiba was in the process of creating.__

The new paraphrased version was specifically intended to *disarm the believers* and provide the Greek-speaking Jews with a *rabbinical Bible*. Thereafter, in whatever language you were reading the Tenach, you were reading Rabbi Akiba's translation. His system served as a lens through which Judaism would thereafter be viewed and sealed the authority for rabbis to *revise* the Scriptures if they couldn't get them to fit in to their teachings.

"But each one should be careful
How he builds.
For no one can lay any foundation
Other than the one already laid,
Which is Messiah Yeshua."
(I Corinthians 3:10b-11)

When the Apostle Paul wrote these words, he was not merely addressing divisions within the Body of Messiah. Saul of Tarsus was previously a "zealous Pharisee" (Philippians 3:4-6) and well aware of the rise of rabbinic authority in Judaism. Even as these power struggles were in motion, Jesus taught about laying a foundation upon the rock and not upon sand. These Scriptures speak spiritually to *another foundation*, a *sandy foundation* that was being laid at precisely the same time as the Rock, the Chief Cornerstone, was being set into place.

The faulty foundation of the Oral Law (exalting the words of men over the Word of God) could also be described as a FENCE around the Torah. A fence has a dual purpose: it protects property (indicating ownership) and restricts access. This is precisely what the rabbinic system did with the Scriptures.

The Talmud speaks of *erecting a safeguard* around the Torah (Aboth 1:1), which is nowhere commanded by God, so that it would not be willfully trespassed or damaged. In reality, the fence restricted the Jewish people from getting to the heart of the Scriptures, but it didn't restrict the rabbis, who apparently crashed the fence whenever it was deemed *reasonable or necessary.* This truth is borne out when speaking to Israelis, many of whom have no idea that what *Judaism* teaches and *what the Bible says* are very often two entirely different things.

In the Name of Yeshua, we tear down the fence in the spirit realm that restricts God's people from His Word and from discovering the Living Torah. We proclaim that access to the Scriptures is now unlimited! We invite God's people to CHARGE towards the Word. (The image the Lord gave me is similar to the Berlin Wall coming down. People were tearing it down brick by brick with their bare hands, pulling away the barbed wire, and leaping over the wall to freedom.) Let us declare FREEDOM to the captives, liberty to approach the Scriptures and be led by the Spirit to interpret it after the heart of God.

> *"For there is one God*
> *And **one mediator** between God and men,*
> *the man **Messiah Yeshua**,*
> *Who gave himself as a ransom*
> *For all men..."*
> *(I Timothy 2:5-6)*

The question may be asked, "How does the rabbinic spirit affect the everyday life of the Ultra-Orthodox?" Primarily, in exerting excessive *control* over the minds and lives of their followers. Hospitals in Israel are experiencing increasing conflicts with Ultra-Orthodox patients who are relying more on the advice of the rebbe than the diagnosis of the medical doctor, often to the detriment of their health.

While waiting for an intercessor to arrive for a prayerwalk one day, I struck up a lively conversation with a young yeshiva student at the bagel shop on Mea Shearim Street. At one point, he remarked, "You really understand a lot of things. What rabbi do you study with?" I honestly replied that I didn't study with a rabbi. He was shocked and blurted out, "It's impossible to study Torah without a rabbi!" I innocently asked, "Why?" but by this time he was offended. "It just is!" He quickly ended the conversation and left.

This incident gives us a glimpse into how much control the rabbis have on the minds of their followers. The truth is, this young yeshiva student did not know *why* he couldn't study Torah without a rabbi and I was perhaps the first person in his life who questioned it. This also helps us understand the complications a person will encounter who is attempting to escape from Chasidim. The Ultra-Orthodox who go to their rabbis for medical advice also seek their counsel on buying a car or who to marry, which shows that the fingers of the rabbi are on virtually every aspect of their lives. To be sure, there is a place in God's order for godly counsel, but these controlling relationships far exceed the boundaries of that biblical order. The *mind control spirit* (which is usually associated with drugs, alcohol, and transcendental meditation) also includes *passive submission*, which can give a person a sense of security by relieving them of the responsibility of making difficult moral and ethical decisions by transferring all the responsibility onto the authority figure.

In the Name of Yeshua, bind the spirit of mind control from operating in the lives of the Ultra-Orthodox and pray that the rabbis will be freed from the control the kingdom of darkness has over their own minds and the minds of their followers through them. Pray the Ultra-Orthodox will desire to break away from this unhealthy system of bondage and desire to pursue the truth prayerfully through honest personal study of the Scriptures. Pray for a revelation of Yeshua among the rabbis, that they would be blessed with the "mind of Messiah" and the heart of a shepherd after the Lord's own heart. Pray that they would repent, humble themselves before God and release their flock to seek and find a personal relationship with the God of Israel.

The *Dark Ages* gave rise to *mystical movements* both in Judaism and Christianity. We have already addressed *Chasidism,* the major mystical movement in Judaism. We will now focus on an extra-biblical Jewish holiday called *Lag B'Omer,* an annual festival that sheds light on the mystical influence of the rabbinic spirit.

Lag B'Omer (which means "counting the omer") is celebrated with bonfires ablaze in every Ultra-Orthodox neighborhood. It is not a biblical holiday, but occurs between Passover and Pentecost (Shavuot).

In Deuteronomy 16:9-11, God commanded Israel to count seven weeks from the time they put the sickle to the standing grain until the Feast of Weeks. This *forty-nine day period* begins with the second day of Passover, when the *omer* (a sheaf of new barley) was traditionally brought to the Temple in Jerusalem as an offering, and ends on Shavuot, the feast of the wheat harvest. These days of counting have also become *days of mourning* in remembrance of the many persecutions, martyrdom and suffering of the Jewish people throughout history. *Yom Ha Shoah* (Holocaust Remembrance Day) in Israel is observed during this season, along with a day of remembrance for all the fallen soldiers since 1948. Celebrating during these days is forbidden and no weddings are scheduled, *except on the festival of Lag B'Omer,* which falls on the 33rd day, and has become a day of rejoicing.

Why is Lag B'Omer a day of rejoicing? Shortly after the destruction of the Second Temple, during the first 33 days of counting the 49 days towards Shavuot, there was a *horrible plague which killed 24,000 of Rabbi Akiba ben Joseph's disciples.* I was told this happened because these men were unkind and unwilling to share. We have already established that Rabbi Akiba is the father of Rabbinic Judaism and was also a very instrumental voice in persuading the Jewish people to ultimately reject Yeshua as Messiah.

> *"Truly I say to you,*
> *All these things*
> *Shall come upon* **this generation.** *"*
> *(Matthew 23:36)*

The death of 24,000 disciples in 33 days sounds like an awfully harsh punishment for mere selfishness. The more likely explanation is that the words Yeshua spoke *to the generation who knew Him and/or were in powerful positions of leadership to influence the people against Him at that time or shortly thereafter* were being fulfilled.

The first reason for rejoicing on Lag B'Omer is that after 33 days, the deaths from the plague stopped. The second reason for rejoicing is that the famous kabbalist Shimon Bar Yochai (author of the Zohar) died on this 33rd day.

Normally, when someone dies, rejoicing is hardly the proper emotion. However, the Ultra-Orthodox say that Rabbi Shimon Bar Yochai was a very great and holy sage and that when a sage dies, it is cause for rejoicing because *"his soul goes to higher levels after death."* One person explained to me that, in the upper worlds, the next world (or heaven), Rabbi Yochai is *"an advocate"* for the Jewish people.

We have already established that Rabbi Shimon Bar Yochai lived in the second century and was a major student of Rabbi Akiba. He is also the author of the *Zohar (Book of Splendor),* the mystical foundation stone for all later mystical movements in Judaism, including Chasidism. The precepts of Kabbalah are most fully articulated in the Zohar.

Why all the bonfires? When Rabbi Yochai died, a *"supernatural fire"* suddenly appeared over his grave site. This "miracle" caused people to believe that he was surely a holy sage because (they explained) *fire is a symbol of the Torah and the fire of the Torah is the Jewish people.* Hence, the death of Shimon Bar Yochai is celebrated annually with bonfires. On the eve of Lag B'Omer, hundreds of thousands of Ultra-Orthodox Jews travel to a city called *Meron,* near Safed in Northern Israel, to gather and pray around the tomb of Rabbi Yochai.

Oh Lord, send YOUR FIRE, the true fire of Pentecost, to the Ultra-Orthodox! Send the fire of the Holy Spirit! Cry out to God that their thirst for the FIRE OF TORAH will be quenched in Yeshua, the Living Torah. Pray that the veil of Rabbinic Judaism, which has blinded the eyes of the Jewish people, kept them in bondage to mysticism and the false holiness of the "sages," keeps them distanced from their Heavenly God who loves them and hinders them from discovering the precious Messianic promises in the Scriptures, will be torn away and every deception will be exposed. The Bible says we have an Advocate with the Father (I John 2:1) who ever lives to intercede for us (Hebrews 7:25) and His name is Yeshua! Pray that they will be delivered from idolatry and the LIE that any person, other than Yeshua, can "intercede" for them in heaven.

> *"Therefore, as a tongue of fire*
> *Consumes stubble,*
> *And dry grass collapses into the flame,*
> ***So their root will become like rot***
> *And their blossom blow away as dust;*
> *For they have rejected the*
> *Law of the Lord of hosts,*
> *And despised the word of*
> *The Holy One of Israel."*
> *(Isaiah 5:24)*

These are harsh words that should break our hearts and move our spirits to compassion when we consider their fullest implication. As intercessors, we are sometimes called to be *gardeners*. We have seen how the root of the rabbinic system is rotten, yet, we serve a God who is *a REDEEMER*. In these last days, it is God's heart to *restore the vineyard,* to re-plant what has been ruined and rotted by past sin or the deception of the enemy. This is where the privilege of prayer and spiritual warfare finds its highest fulfillment. It is the will of God to *replant the root, re-build the foundation, tear down the fence* that barricades His people from the promises and provisions of Messiah, and *build up a highway to Zion.*

We have taken the time to research the roots of Rabbinic Judaism because the rabbinic spirit, which hovers like a spiritual chuppa (canopy) over Mea Shearim and every Orthodox community, is not simply an obscure nameless, faceless spirit. The sages who laid this foundation have names and their spirits to this day exert tremendous influence over the community.

Certainly Rabbi Yokhanan Ben Zakkai had a major influence, founding the strategic academy at Yavneh. But Rabbi Akiba eventually surpassed him. Those readers who saw the awe-inspiring *Transformations* documentary may recall that in Almolonga (Guatemala) there was a patron saint who had become an object of idol worship. Although this saint came to exist in the form of a mannequin and his face was only a wooden mask, *his spirit ruled over the people* because of their devotion, and revival did not come until the ancestral spirit ties were broken with him.

As the army of the Lord, it is our privilege to partner with Him as an expression of our love for the descendants of Abraham, Isaac, and Jacob. We pray with understanding for those who do not how to pray for themselves. The enemy has done great damage, but his time is short, and there is a Redeemer, Hallelujah! Let us speak prophetically to Jerusalem (and all Israel) and proclaim that Yeshua is the pure and true Root of their faith and ours (Revelation 22:16). Yeshua is the Lamb that was slain before the foundation of the world, the Offspring of David, the bright Morning Star, and the Branch that will reign in righteousness forever. Let us declare that Jesus is the Solid Rock of Israel, the Firm Foundation, Chief Cornerstone, the Author and Finisher of our faith.

> "But yet a tenth will be in it,
> And will return and be for consuming,
> As a terebinth tree or as an oak,
> Whose stump remains when it is cut down.
> So the holy seed shall be its stump."
> (Isaiah 6:13)

Rabbinic Judaism is an *oak* that grew in stature and might over centuries, yet the Scripture says it will be cut down and a *holy seed* will be its stump. This *stump* will produce a tree of life and a tree of righteousness.

Praise the Lord for this precious promise for the remnant. In the Name of Jesus, we call forth the holy seed and we come against every name that has been exalted to a position of undisputed authority, even to idolatry, in the history of Israel going all the way back to Egypt. In the Name of Yeshua, we break every soul tie and spirit tie with the founders and sages of Rabbinic Judaism and Chasidism, in particular Rabbi Yohanan ben-Zakkai, Rabbi Akiba ben Joseph, Rabbi Israel ben-Eliezer (the Ba'al Shem Tov), and Rabbi Shimon Bar Yochai. In the Name of Yeshua, we break the power of the rabbinic spirit over the lives of the Ultra-Orthodox. We place upon them the authority of Yeshua and the freedom and liberty of the Holy Spirit. We uproot the OAK of Rabbinic Judaism, the tree of false religion, that the enemy has planted and, in its place, we plant the OLIVE TREE of the patriarchs, the tree of relationship with the God of Israel, and the vineyard of new wine and new life in Messiah Yeshua.

The Religious Spirit

"What shall we say then?
That the Gentiles, who did not pursue
Righteousness, attained righteousness,
Even the righteousness which is by faith;
But Israel, pursuing a law of righteousness,
Did not arrive at that law.
Why? Because they did not pursue it by faith,
But as though it were by works.
They stumbled over the stumbling stone."
(Romans 9:30-32)

The religious spirit is the source of all spiritual pride and has to do with issues of self-righteousness, seeking to establish your own righteousness before God through works, inevitably leading to pretension and hypocrisy.

The characteristics of the religious spirit are highlighted throughout the teachings of Jesus as He encounters the Pharisees.

The religious spirit is *proud and separate* (Mark 2:16). Jesus came to save sinners and to heal the sick. But the Pharisees felt themselves too holy to associate with sinners. It is clear in the example of Yeshua that, while we are not to engage in the *activities* of sinners, we must be willing to place ourselves where they are to share the gospel. The religious spirit *lacks the compassion* to reach out to those that are not within their own devout circles.

The religious spirit is *legalistic and cannot comprehend the spirit behind God's laws, creating hardness of heart* even towards their own flock (Mark 2:23-28). In Mark 3:1-6, Jesus asked if it was *lawful* to do good, to save a life on the Sabbath. He then proceeded to heal a man with a withered hand, but the Pharisees went out and counseled with the Herodians how they might destroy Him. His mercy violated their man-made traditions.

The religious spirit *performs so as to be seen by men* (Matthew 6:1-6 / Mark 2:18). Yeshua stressed the beauty of practicing our acts of righteousness *in secret before God* so that our reward in heaven would be great. The religious spirit prays, gives, fasts, eats certain foods and avoids certain foods, studies, and so on, to be *recognized and approved by men.*

The religious spirit *cannot flow with God's Spirit* (Mark 2:21-22). Yeshua came to proclaim the Kingdom of God and transact a New Covenant. This new kingdom and new covenant required *new wineskins.* New wine bursts the old wineskins of religious tradition. Rabbinic tradition is set in its ways and cannot flow with the river of God. It is a *fixed system* and not flexible so as to receive fresh revelation from heaven that conflicts or jeopardizes it authority structure. Jesus had to break the mindset even of His disciples so they could even begin to comprehend the reason for His coming to earth at that particular time of their visitation (Matthew 16:21-23). Peter rebukes the Lord and tries to protect Him from going to the Cross because his traditional understanding of the Messiah is that he would be a King, a Deliverer, a Redeemer from the oppression of the Romans, not a Suffering Servant.

The religious spirit *cannot see the Kingdom of God.* Yeshua challenged Nicodemus to be *born again by water and the Spirit* in John 3:3-12. Nicodemus could not understand this because anyone under the influence of the religious spirit closes their eyes to anything that is not confined within the boundaries of its own system of interpretation. Stephen was stoned to death for charging the Pharisees with resisting the Holy Spirit (Acts 7:51-58) and sharing his open vision of the Son of Man standing at the right hand of God.

The religious spirit *resents grace* and relentlessly drives its victims to strive towards the unachievable goal of *perfection* (Luke 18:18-27). The story of the rich young ruler begins with the question, "Good Teacher, what shall I do to inherit eternal life?" Jesus first straightens him out by declaring there is no such thing as a *good person*. Only *God* is a good person, so if you're calling me *good*, you're calling me *God*. Although the young ruler excelled in keeping the Ten Commandments, Yeshua zeroed in on the *heart issue* where he was lacking. Legally speaking, he had *kept all the commandments*, but his *greed and possessiveness* prevented him for having a *pure heart* towards God. He could not give up his many properties, revealing his love for treasures on earth. This encounter with the rich young ruler illustrates why it is *impossible* to inherit eternal life through the law. Even if a person is successful in perfectly keeping the Ten Commandments, which we should all strive to keep, a secret, selfish sin or indulgence would be enough to deny us entry into eternal life without the Blood of Messiah. Even the disciples were questioning Him afterwards, "Who then can be saved?" This is why Yeshua said, "The things impossible with men are possible with God." Hallelujah!

> *"Come to Me, all who are*
> *Weary and heavy-laden,*
> *And I will give you rest.*
> *Take My yoke upon you,*
> *And learn from Me, for I am*
> *Gentle and humble in heart;*
> *And you shall find rest for your souls.*
> *For My yoke is easy,*
> *And My burden is light."*
> *(Matthew 11:28-30)*

There is a yoke of slavery that the *religious spirit* has placed upon the Ultra-Orthodox. The burden of this horrible oppressive spirit can be vividly observed and experienced on every prayerwalk. The heart of God yearns to free the Ultra-Orthodox from this yoke and bring them into the freedom and light of Messiah and His beautiful yoke of grace. Each day, in the morning prayers called *Shacharis*, the Ultra-Orthodox take upon themselves the *yoke of Torah*. As they put on a *tallis* (prayer shawl) and *tefillin* (frontlets or phylacteries worn of the forehead), they are *binding themselves to 613 commandments*. The promise of Yeshua is to give His people *rest for their souls*. The *yoke of Messiah* is easy and light, but the only way to access this yoke is to *come to Him*.

As we come to Yeshua through faith, He sets us free from the *Law of Sin and Death* so that we can enter in to the *Law of the Spirit of Life* in Messiah (Romans 8:2). The Bible says that the Law brings *wrath* (Romans 4:15-16) because we cannot live up to it, but faith brings *grace*. The Old Covenant is a *law of works* while the New Covenant is a *law of grace* (Romans 3:27-28) and it is impossible to be under both laws. The great apostle Paul described his own struggle trying to keep the law (Romans 7:14-25). He discovered that the law is *spiritual* and our inner man joyfully agrees with it, but our flesh, in its weakness, wages war against the spirit desiring to fulfill it. The purpose of giving of the law was to *reveal sin* and *serve as a schoolmaster*, so that we would recognize our spiritual depravity and hopelessness and be brought to Messiah and into the grace of God (Galatians 3:22-25).

Faith is in accordance with grace and the religious spirit ridicules grace because it wants to receive glory for its own righteousness.

This does not mean that faith and grace lead to lawlessness. The wonderful new life of the Spirit we are born into creates *peace with God* (Romans 5:1) and empowers us to *reign in life* through Messiah Jesus (Romans 5:17). As we serve the Lord in the *newness of the Spirit,* we *bear fruit* for His Kingdom (Romans 7:4-6). As the love of God grows in our hearts, the *fruit of the Spirit* is produced in us, *against which there is no law* (Galatians 5:22-25).

Love is the fulfillment of the law (Romans 13:8-10) because love does no wrong to his neighbor. The law of the Spirit is a higher and more perfect law and we cannot fulfill it without the power of the Holy Spirit.

The Bible says if we are *led by the Spirit* we are the *sons of God* (Romans 8:14). It is easy to put on a prayer shawl, keep feasts, and eat only certain foods. It is not so easy to love unlovable people, to forgive those who wound you, or to bless those that curse you and persecute you. Love is the highest expression of the heart of God in every circumstance and there is no law that love breaks in its kindness and mercy.

Pray for mercy to pour over the Ultra-Orthodox. Pray that they would be led by the Spirit and so become sons of God. Pray for a breaking of the yoke of the religious spirit and for freedom from self-righteousness and hypocrisy, the never ending, tormenting cycle of living a lie. Pray for the Holy Spirit to gently and lovingly convict their hearts of sin (even original sin and absolute evil, not simply an "evil inclination"), righteousness, and judgment, to convince them that they can never enter the Kingdom of God through good works, that a fountain of grace is open to them in the Messiah. Pray they will be granted a vision of Yeshua, who is the righteousness of God, the One through whom we stand justified and righteous before a Holy God. Pray for a revelation of the GIFT of salvation freely available by FAITH. This gift cost the Heavenly Father everything, even His only Son. Pray for an impartation of the spirit of humility and the power to receive this amazing gift of grace and not disregard it as a "cheap means" of redemption. Pray that they will run to Yeshua in holy desperation and find rest for their souls. Pray for an outpouring of new wine into new wineskins.

Organized religion is the great enemy of the gift of God's grace. How did religion usurp the intimate relationship God desired to enjoy with man?

To discover the *roots of religion*, which is always a *works-based system,* we must go to the Garden. Once sin entered our world, the very first thing that man *"knew"* was that he was naked. Adam and Eve's first *religious act* was to sew fig leaves and make loincloths to cover themselves and hide from the Presence of God. This laid the groundwork for the development of religion. All religious systems are the *fig leaves* of man's attempts to cover his sin, appear righteous before a holy God, and keep a safe distance from His Presence.

The gospel was first preached in the Garden. God Himself covered man's nakedness with garments of skin as a symbol of His unyielding love and a foreshadowing of His eternal plan of salvation.

God created *a people* through whom He would bring redemption to all mankind. The Lamb was the plan. Satan's strategy to lure Israel away from *relationship* with God into the fig leaves of *religion* and the unfaithfulness of *idolatry* prevented them from fulfilling the high calling upon them to be a light and a witness to the nations. In these last days, the God of Israel is calling His people *home*, not simply to a homeland in the Middle East, but to a *place of intimacy* and restoring them to the *calling* and *anointing* reserved especially for them.

God is Creator of everything that was and ever will be, but so much more. He is the relentless pursuer, the lover of our souls, the initiator, and supreme romantic behind the greatest love story ever told. He created man in His image and desires intimate fellowship with His creation. Adam and Eve had daily fellowship with God *until* they listened to the serpent. They were cast out of the Garden, but God had a plan to redeem *a people* back to Himself through the Seed of a woman so that the broken relationship could be restored.

> *"So it came about in the course of time*
> *That Cain brought an offering to the Lord*
> *Of the fruit of the ground.*
> *And Abel, on his part also brought*
> *Of the firstlings of his flock*
> *And of their fat portions.*
> *And the Lord had regard for Abel*
> *And his offering;*
> *But for Cain and for his offering*
> *He had no regard."*
> *(Genesis 4:3-5a)*

In the next generation, we see the *religious act of Cain* in bringing the fruit of his own *works* and not a *sacrifice* from the flock. Cain's disregard for the *designated approach to God* to obtain mercy and atonement for sin, planted the seed of *paganism*.

Paganism, which is the ancient term for man-made religion, or worship inspired by demons, always re-defines God, so that He is less fearful and more controllable, and de-emphasizes judgment for sin. Re-defining God begins with rejection of God for who He really is.

New Age re-defines God as a neutral or female deity. A female deity symbolizes gentleness and nurturing. The reasoning is that a male god is too harsh, especially for those who have experienced absent or abusive relationships with their earthly fathers. God's solution for broken relationships with earthly fathers is *healing* (through forgiveness, repentance, and restoration), not re-defining God. In the natural realm, every seed that is planted produces fruit after its own kind. Apple seeds produce apples, not coconuts or heads of lettuce. In the spirit realm, the principle is the same. Whoever or whatever re-defines God *gives birth*, so to speak, and whatever is created is of the *same essence,* so that we end up worshipping the creation, not the Creator.

Throughout the history of religion, whether in Judaism or the Church, just as Cain manifested jealousy and hatred towards his brother, a defining feature of the religious spirit is that it will always want to murder the worshipper of God in spirit and in truth. The religious spirit will always attempt to suffocate or exterminate the anointing that God bestows on those whose worship is pleasing in His sight.

From the Garden, the *seed of Satan* (the Serpent) has been warring against the *Seed of a woman* (the Lamb) who was slain before the foundation of the earth. During the days of Noah, Satan tried to *defile the blood line of humanity* by seducing the "daughters of men" to bear children by the "sons of God," demonic spirit beings also known as the Nephilim (Genesis 6:1-13). Noah found favor with God and his generations (his blood line) had not become corrupted. God wiped out every living creature, except for Noah's family, and selected wildlife, to protect the *seed of a woman* that would come through the line of *Shem*, one of Noah's sons. This remnant served as a *new beginning* in human history. However, the line of *Ham*, one of Noah's other sons, produced *Nimrod* (Genesis 10:6-12). The beginning of Nimrod's kingdom was *Babel* (or Babylon).

> *"And they said to one another,*
> *'Come, let us **make bricks** and*
> *Burn them thoroughly.'*
> *And they used brick for stone,*
> *And they used tar for mortar.*

And they said,
*'Come, let us **build** for ourselves*
*A **city** and a **tower***
Whose top will reach into heaven…"
(Genesis 11:3-4a)

The ambition of "brick-making" and "tower-building" is the root of religion, the attempt to reach heaven by human endeavor. Humanism is the ultimate manifestation of brick religion.

"…And let us make for ourselves a name,
Lest we be scattered abroad
Over the face of the whole earth."
(Genesis 11:4b)

The clash between the concepts of *blood sacrifice* and *bricks & mortar* is irreconcilable. One is pleasing and acceptable in the sight of God and the other loathsome. God requires a *blood sacrifice* that He Himself provides (a lamb in a flock and, ultimately, the Blood of the Lamb) and any glory for the mercy extended through the sacrifice belongs only to Him. Brick religion always makes a name for itself. *Man* gets the glory for having built something that reaches heaven, for attempting to provide an acceptable offering of his own making, and essentially *becomes God* for his achievements. There is also a *false unity* in organized religion. The people of Babel were afraid they would be scattered, so they built a tower. But God will ultimately scatter false unity based on humanism or idolatry (Genesis 11:5-9). It is the *love of the brethren,* a love that can only be experienced in *Messiah Jesus,* that God is seeking, not the *unity of mankind.*

"I have loved you with an everlasting love;…"
(Jeremiah 31:3a)

Relationship is rooted in love. Religion is rooted in laws. Relationship is God-initiated. Religion is man-initiated.

Absolutely everything God does with Israel is fueled by the passion of this one desire: *"You will live in the Land I gave your forefathers; you will be My people, and I will be your God." (Ezekiel 36:28).* God desires *relationship*. He *loves* His people and desires to give them *life*. God breathed the *breath of life* into man (Genesis 2:7), but His ultimate purpose is to bring man to the *river of life* (Revelation 22:17). In the absence of relationship, you end up with only rules and rules, by themselves, create hardness of heart. Heartless religion. That's why God promises to *"remove the heart of stone"* from Israel (Ezekiel 36:26-27).

Pray that the Lord will draw Israel back into the intimate, bridal relationship that is her destiny, that the remnant chosen by grace will truly become God's people, and fulfill their calling to be witnesses to the nations. Pray that the heart of stone will soon be replaced by a heart of flesh in fulfillment of His promise in Ezekiel 36.

Satan's attempt to defile the *bloodline* of humanity failed. His next strategy, namely to lure Israel (and all mankind) from relationship with God into fruitless religion, proved much more successful.

"The earth is the Lord's,
And all its fullness,,
The world and those who dwell therein."
(Psalm 24:1)

The earth is the Lord's, so how did the *religious spirit* establish itself on earth? How does Satan *gain legal access* anywhere that he gains it? If Satan is "the prince of the power of the air" (Ephesians 2:2) and "the ruler of this world" (John 14:30), what does this mean? The Hebrew word for "earth" in Psalm 24 is *erets* which means ground, land, or soil. Everything of this *physical earth*, its produce, and inhabitants, belong to God. The Greek word for "world" in John 14:30 is *cosmos*, referring to *structures*, human systems of government and religion. In other words, what many of us were taught never to discuss at the dinner table, namely religion and politics, this is the world that Satan is the ruler of, including social structures, cultural distinctions, and so forth. The seed of religion in Babel *opened the door (gave legal access)* to the religious spirit.

During the life of Jesus, and up to the first and second centuries in

Judea, you could discuss religion and politics because they were *one and the same.* There was no separation of Church and State, so to speak. God's system of government for Israel was a *theocracy,* meaning "God-governed." This is vastly different from the so-called theocracies we find today. God was not the *oppressor.* God *delivered* the Israelites from Pharaoh, who was oppressing them. God was not only their Deliverer, but also their Father and King. He governed the Israelites through Moses, then Joshua, and set up the office of judge after the death of Joshua, which continued until the nation requested an earthly king.

What happened to the precious intimate relationship with God and the high calling God so deeply desired for his people?

First, let us establish that God created *a people,* a *special nation,* so that he could reveal Himself *first to that nation,* and through the fulfillment of His promises to that people and nation, reveal Himself and redeem *all peoples and nations.* How did God *create* this special people and nation?

> *"Now the Lord said to Abram,*
> *'Go forth from your country,*
> *And from your relatives,*
> *And from your father's house,*
> *To the land which I will show you..'"*
> *(Genesis 12:1)*

When God called Abram to leave Ur of the Chaldees (one of the largest towns in Sumer and later in Babylonia), He was calling him *out of paganism,* and *into covenant relationship.* God promised that He would make Abram into "a great nation." Abram is described in Genesis simply as a *Hebrew* (Genesis 14:13). When Abram was ninety-nine years old, God appeared to him, changed his name to Abraham and his wife's name from Sarai to Sarah, and gave him perhaps the most comprehensive overview of the promises and purposes of God recorded in the Bible. Along with the *covenant of circumcision,* God promised that Abraham would be the *father of many nations,* that nations and kings would come from him, and that the *whole land of Canaan* would be given to his descendants as an everlasting possession. He also promised that Sarah would become a mother of nations and that, even though she was barren and in her old age, she would bear a son, through whom the Lord would *establish an everlasting covenant* and that this son would be the father of twelve rulers (Genesis 17).

The first time we see the word "*Israel*" in the Bible, someone else is getting their name changed. God wrestled with Jacob in the desert, subdued his natural strength, changed his name to Israel and the *twelve tribes (rulers)* were born to him (Exodus 35:23-26). The tribes of Israel who went into Egypt were called *Israelites* or *Hebrews* interchangeably (Exodus 1:1-7, 15-19, 3:10-11, 7:16). Progressively, the Israelites became known as *Israel*. When Moses confronted Pharaoh to let God's people go, and the ten plagues were released upon Egypt, something exciting begins to happen. All of a sudden, the petals of the flower open and we behold the birthing, if you will, of a nation. The first three plagues (blood, frogs, and gnats) appear to have affected the whole land of Egypt. But when we come to the plague of the flies, God *begins to make a distinction*, first between "my people and your people" (Exodus 8:22-23) and then, in the next plague, between the livestock of Israel (as a nation) and Egypt (as a nation) (Exodus 9:4)!

This is the first time we see the Israelites given the same nation status as Egypt, although they are also described as a community, as is in Exodus 12:6, when God gives the ordinances for the first Passover.

Hereafter, God's people will be referred to interchangeably as *Israelites* and *Israel* for a short time and, ultimately, only as *Israel*. Exodus 18:1 paints a lovely picture of the concept of Israel as a *people* and a *nation*. Israel was first a ***person*** (Abram) who left paganism in obedience to God's call and became a father of the faith, then a ***patriarch*** (Jacob - who was changed by an encounter with the Living God), then ***tribes*** (who went into Egypt), then a ***people*** (known as Hebrews or Israelites), and finally a ***nation*** (dwelling in a Land whose borders were specifically defined by God). The forming of the nation of Israel can also be seen as an image of the *many stages of deliverance* the Lord works in the life of a believer as we yield ourselves to Him.

What is essential for our purposes as we focus in on the religious spirit, is that Israel was never a *religion,* but a *people* and a *nation* birthed by God. *"Judaism"* is never mentioned. Relationship, covenants, and personal encounters with Yahweh were key in every stage of Israel's development. The hand of God, who revealed Himself and moved miraculously in the lives of individual Hebrews and the nation of Israel, accomplished everything. The *tribes* went into Egypt, but *Israel* came out. What a mighty God we serve!

For readers unfamiliar with Jewish history, a brief overview is presented below, which can also be described as the *Seven Ages:*

Patriarchal Age   (Abraham to the Conquest of Canaan)

First Commonwealth   (1200-586 B.C.) (Age of Judges, Kings, Prophets, Priests)

Second Commonwealth   (586 B.C.-70 A.D.) (Babylonian Exile, Return & Rebuilding of Temple, Persian/Greek/Hasmonean/ Roman Empires)

Jews of the East   (Rise & Decline of Jews in Babylonia & Palestine first 1,000 years A.D.) *Rise of Religious Systems* (Development of Rabbinic Judaism among the Jews, and Catholicism and Islam among the Gentiles)

Middle Ages in Europe   (Jewish Settlement in Europe & Participation in the Development of European Culture/Crusades)

Ghetto Age   (1492-1880) Jews of Eastern Europe (Inquisition/Renaissance/Highest Cultural Activity in Jewish Life)

Modern Age   (1880-Present) Zionism

Three major man-made religious systems developed during the first thousand years after the death and resurrection of Messiah Jesus (Judaism, Catholicism, Islam). In using the word "man-made," I mean to say that these systems each developed ultimate authority figures other than God Himself.

The *Pope* became the infallible authority of Catholicism (the only expression of Christianity until the Reformation), the *Grand Mufti* for Islam, and the *Rabbis* for Judaism. The Hebrew Scriptures record the return of exiles from Babylon to rebuild the Temple in Ezra and Nehemiah, just as God had promised Jeremiah. However, only a remnant returned. Scores remained in Babylon and it is the history of those who did not return to Jerusalem that most affected the future course of Jewish history. Although it took hundreds of years for the tree to take root and spread its branches, the seeds for a *religious system called Judaism* and the *institution of rabbis as authority figures* were planted during the crisis of exile in Babylon.

> *"And a certain ruler questioned Him,*
> *Saying, 'Good Teacher, what shall I do*
> *To inherit eternal life?'"*
> *(John 18:18)*

Chasidic theology teaches that God can be comprehended better by *action* (performance of good deeds) than by *meditation*. This intellectual approach to God by *doing* is why the ruler asked Jesus, "What must we *do* to do the works God requires?" (John 6:28) Jesus shocked them by *not* giving them anything to do, but rather something to *believe and receive.* Walking with God is more about *being* than *doing* and this turned many away from Jesus.

Pray for a revelation of the precious truth that ONLY GOD can bring us safely into eternal life through the BLOOD OF MESSIAH and no other way. He has made the impossible possible and lifted the heavy yoke. Pray for understanding that the "works of God" are simple – to believe in the Messiah as Redeemer and Lord. Pray for the exposing and renouncing of the religious spirit among the Ultra-Orthodox and a complete deliverance from legalism and spiritual pride. Pray that as they come to faith in Messiah, a fresh anointing to pray, worship, and move in the gifts of the Spirit will be released.

> *"For if you believed Moses,*
> *You would believe Me;*
> *For he wrote of Me.*
> *But if you do not believe his writings,*
> *How will you believe My words?"*
> *(John 5:46-47)*

Moses was sent to deliver Israel out of Egypt. Moses wrote of a prophet that would be raised up from among their brethren and the words of God would be in His mouth. Anyone refusing to listen to this Prophet/Teacher would be accountable to the Almighty (Deuteronomy 18:15-19). The priests and Levites from Jerusalem asked John the Baptist if he was this prophet. He denied it, called for repentance to prepare the way for His coming, and pointed to the Lamb. Throughout His ministry, the multitudes recognized Jesus first as the Prophet and only later as Messiah.

All over Israel, particularly during the season just preceding Yom Kipper, on-going seminars called *Aracheim* ("Values of Life") are presented for the purpose of drawing Jewish people (especially young men) back to God. These seminars are also called *tshuva* (which means "repentance"). At first glance, this sounds great. Of course, these seminars are designed to draw them into Torah Judaism, Moses, and the Ultra-Orthodox lifestyle.

Pray that everyone attending these seminars would indeed find the God of Israel and the Moses of the Bible, because Yeshua said, "If you believed Moses, you would believe me." We can boldly pray that they find Moses, because if they TRULY find Moses and believe His words, it will lead them to Yeshua. Pray for FREEDOM from the laws and traditions of men that only create burdens and busyness and hinder intimacy with God. Pray that the strongholds of the mind would be broken, the notion that simply because something has been done for centuries it is necessarily good or godly. Pray especially that the rabbis leading the Tshuva movement would be encountered on the Damascus Road, find the God of Abraham, Isaac & Jacob, AND Moses and that God would bless them and use them to pioneer Messianic repentance seminars leading to salvation!

False Messiahs

*"Who do **men** say that I, the Son of Man, am?'*
So they (His disciples) said,
'Some say John the Baptist, some Elijah,
And others Jeremiah or one of the prophets.'
He said to them,
*'But who do **you** say that I am?'"*
(Matthew 16:13-15)

Ultimately, every person must answer this piercing question. It is a question that cannot be answered by popular opinion or even through the diligent research or speculation of scholars. It is worth noting that every answer given by men was the *wrong answer*. Even Peter was not given personal credit for his correct response.

"Blessed are you, Simon Bar-Jonah,
For flesh and blood has not revealed this to you,
But My Father who is in heaven."
(Matthew 16:17)

Praying for a revelation of Yeshua as Messiah, Son of God, and God the Son, is one of the most powerful prayers we can pray for the Ultra-Orthodox. Flesh and blood cannot reveal Jesus, but only the Father in Heaven.

We should also pray for *visitations*. Yeshua appeared to Saul of Tarsus on the Damascus Road, revealing Himself as Lord (Acts 9:4-5). The Apostle Paul later said that he did not receive the gospel *from men*, but rather *by revelation* (Galatians 1:11-12).

There are conflicting views of Messiah, or the Messianic Age, within Judaism, ranging from belief that the Messiah will come *when we are worthy* for him to come, to the broader view that the *messianic potential* is within every soul and the *messianic age* is a state of utopian paradise achieved after centuries of *progressive improvement.* According to Jewish theology, goodness that is not associated with *human endeavor* is not good in the most precise sense of the word. And so the rabbis ask, "What good is there in a messianic belief system that speaks of instant, supernatural change?"

A popular belief among the Ultra-Orthodox is that when we *"deserve it"* Messiah will come. From the perspective of Chasidic thought and Kaballah, the messianic ideal is the opposite of *sudden transformation.* It is a *process* that has taken as many years as humans have inhabited the planet to effect radical changes in the world.

__Kabbalistic theology contends that humanity's collective efforts over the course of millennia have paved the way for a New Age. These changes occur through the observance of good deeds referred to as mitzvoth. These collective acts have the capacity to transform the world.__

Maimonides affirms a Talmudic teaching that a *solitary mitzvah* is endowed with the power to alter the balance of the entire universe. The masters of Kabbalah assert that evil, by its very nature, does not enjoy the same longevity as the *forces* of goodness. With the passage of time, the evil of yesterday has already been dissipated, whereas the *positive energies* endure forever. To look at the world today, it would appear that, however much progress human endeavor has been achieved in the fields of education, science, and technology, the forces of evil are rapidly advancing. Conversely, the New Covenant teaches that, in the last days, perilous times will come and that men will be more evil than ever before as the coming of Messiah approaches (II Timothy 3:1-5). As evil increases on the earth, the Scriptures teach that, because believers are *new creatures in Messiah*, they should not be overcome by evil, but overcome evil with good (Romans 12:21).

"Beware that no one misleads you.
For many will come in My name,
Saying, 'I am the Messiah,'
And will mislead many.'"
(Matthew 24:4-5)

False messiahs have appeared throughout the ages, however, three major contenders contributed in shaping the course of Rabbinic Judaism and movements within Ultra-Orthodoxy. We have already mentioned *Simeon Bar Kokhba* ("Son of Star") who Rabbi Akiba proclaimed as the Messiah and the major impact this had on the rise of rabbinic authority after the destruction of the Second Temple and dispersion of Israel to the nations, as well as severing the Messianic Jews from the Jewish community.

__Chasidim was birthed in the wake of a religious crisis resulting from the failure of the messianic movement surrounding Shabbetai Zevi (1626-1676), who caused the greatest upheaval in Jewish life than any other false messiah in the history of the Diaspora.__

In 1648, at the age of 22, Shabbetai Zevi, the son of a prosperous Jewish merchant of Smyrna (Turkey), publicly proclaimed himself to be the Messiah and announced the imminent redemption of Israel. He was not taken seriously at first and was eventually banned by the rabbis for his messianic claims and strange behavior during "ecstatic spells." Nevertheless, Zevi later settled in Jerusalem and in 1665, was proclaimed to be the true Messiah by Nathan of Gaza, a well-known mystic and faith healer, arousing intense messianic fervor in Turkey, Italy, and Poland. To prove his messianic authority, Shabbetai Zevi violated biblical and rabbinic decrees. In 1666, on the eve of Passover, Shabbetai Zevi sacrificed a lamb and roasted it with its fat, which is forbidden in Scripture (Leviticus 3:16-17 / I Samuel 2:12-17), and encouraged his followers to eat the meat with the fat, pronouncing a peculiar blessing over it: "He who permits the forbidden."

In Smyrna, Zevi pronounced the Ineffable Name (YHVH or Yahveh), decreed the elimination of the Tenth of Tevet (a rabbinic fast) and also promised to free women from the "curse of Eve." Many of Zevi's disciples sold their houses to raise the funds to journey to the Holy Land, while others were convinced they would simply be transported on clouds. Shabbetai Zevi also abolished the fasts of the 17th of Tammuz and the Ninth of Av (commemorating the destruction of both the First and Second Temples), and instituted new festivals. The 17th of Tammuz became the "day of the revival of Shabbetai Zevi's spirit" and the Ninth of Av celebrated his birthday.

The Turkish government soon became alarmed by the growing messianic passion and gave Shabbetai Zevi two choices: either be put to death or convert to Islam. Zevi chose to convert, profoundly shocking the Jewish world. Still, many of his followers held to their belief he was the Messiah.

Drawing upon Isaac Luria's kabbalistic doctrine of the "holy sparks, and the messianic overtones of his teachings, which fueled expectations of a coming redeemer, Nathan of Gaza argued that, in his apostasy, Shabbetai Zevi was actually fulfilling a mission to lift up the holy sparks which were scattered among the Gentiles and now concentrated in Islam. Only the Messiah, Nathan explained, could redeem these sparks and, thereby redeem these lost souls, and now Shabbetai was acting as a spy in the enemy camp.

Ten years after his conversion, Shabbetai Zevi died suddenly on the Day of Atonement (Yom Kippur) at age 50. Even so, Shabbateanism died a slow death. Many of Shabbetai's followers proclaimed 1706 as the year of his second advent and hundreds of Jews immigrated to Palestine in 1700 with Rabbi Judah Hasid (likely Shabbateans) to await the arrival of Messiah. While God may have positively used the Shabbatean movement to spark a wave of aliyah in the early 1700's, the overall effects on Judaism were profoundly negative. The Ba'al Shem Tov (founder of Chasidism) was born in 1700 in Okop, a small town in Podolia, Poland. *Podolia* and *Volhynia*, where Shabbateanism had its strongest impact, was precisely the place where Chasidim was birthed.

It was a sect of Chasidism that promoted the most contemporary false messiah. Rabbi Menachem Mendel Schneershohn (1902-1994) was the head of the family dynasty that ruled the Lubavicher-Habad Chasidim, the largest Chasidic group, headquartered in New York.

The term "Lubavich" derives from the Belorussian village of Lubavich which became the center of Habad under the direction of Shneur Zalman's son, Dov Baer (1773-1827). Dov Baer (also known as the

Maggid of Mezhirech) was the senior disciple of the Ba'al Shem Tov, and under his leadership, Chasidism attracted many Torah scholars.

Rabbi Menachem Mendel Schneershohn was born in Niloaev, a Russian town, but settled in America in 1941 after completing his studies in mathematics and engineering at the Sorbonne in Paris. In 1950, he was called upon to assume leadership of the Lubavichers and, under his influence, the movement penetrated mainstream Judaism in many parts of the world. Although, generally speaking, Habad is a sophisticated branch of Chasidism that doesn't expect miracles from their ruling *tzaddik,* Rabbi Schneershohn is said to have healed a man of cancer by placing his hand on the mans' side and saying "Si'z gornisht" ("It's nothing."). The chairman of the village council of Kefar Habad also claimed that, during the High Holidays of 1973, when he left Brooklyn to return to Israel, Rebbe Schneershohn gave him a bottle of brandy to take to Zafriyyah, a village near Kefar Habad. Upon arriving in Israel, the chairman learned that one of the boys of Zafriyyah was lying unconscious in a hospital, seriously wounded in the Yom Kippur War. It turns out the soldier's watch stopped when he was hit by a missile, which was also the exact time the Rebbe handed the chairman the bottle of brandy. Upon hearing this, the doctors agreed to give the soldier a few drops from the bottle and the boy immediately opened his eyes, fully conscious.

Rabbi Schneershohn never proclaimed himself the Messiah, but he never denied it either. Although Rabbi Schneershohn died in 1994, never visited Israel once in his life, let alone being born in Bethlehem (Micah 5:2), he is still considered by many in the Lubavicher movement to be the Messiah that will return and redeem Israel.

> *"Either make the tree good*
> *And its fruit good,*
> *Or else make the tree bad*
> *And its fruit bad;*
> *For a tree is known by its fruit."*
> *(Matthew 12:33)*

Yeshua said that a tree will be known by it fruit. Rabbi Schneershohn suggested that R. Shimon bar Yochai (author of the *Zohar)*, was a *reincarnation of Achiya HaShiloni,* the spirit guide that accompanied the Ba'al Shem Tov on his *ascent of soul into the upper worlds.* Rabbi Yochai said the Jewish people will be redeemed from the Diaspora "in a compassionate manner" through tasting the secret teaching of the *Zohar.* Even a casual glance at history clearly reveals the return of the Jewish people to the Land of Israel was a fight from start to finish. The Ba'al Shem Tov believed that one of his missions was to prepare the world for Messiah, and Rabbi Schneershohn suggested this was his connection to the *Achiya HaShiloni* and the reason this "soul" visited him.

We may ask what the fruit of this visitation and the birth of Chasidism has been? Who have the Chasidim embraced as Messiah? Can we safely say that the teachings of Chasidism are preparing the world (or themselves) for the *coming of Yeshua*? Are they based even remotely on the *scriptural references* to Messiah?

Is the fruit of Chasidism a deeper knowledge of the God of Israel, His Word, or His Messiah?

Kabbalistic theology claims that the Achiya HaShiloni was the master and mentor of Elijah the prophet, thereby conjecturing that even the biblical prophets used spirit guides. How then will the Chasidim ever be able to recognize the true "Elijah" without a profound revelation of the extent to which Chasidism has strayed from the truth of the Tenach?

> *"But who can endure the day of His coming?*
> *And who can stand when He appears?*
> *For He is like a refiner's fire*
> *And like the fuller's soap.*
> *And He will sit as a smelter*
> *And purifier of silver,*
> *And He will purify the sons of Levi*
> *And refine them like gold and silver,*
> *So that they may present to the Lord*
> *Offerings in righteousness."*
> *(Malachi 3:2-3)*

The Bible says that when the Messiah comes to redeem Israel, He will come as a refiner's fire and sit as a purifier of silver. The prophet asks the question: "Who can *endure* the day of His coming?"

Simply stated, only the *priests*, the *Levities*, and the *remnant* that have consecrated their lives to the smelter will not be consumed by the holy appearing of Yeshua. A silversmith must diligently watch the furnace constantly, for if the time for refining is exceeded even in the slightest degree, the silver will be injured. When the silversmith can finally see his own image in the silver, then the refining process is finished. The faithfulness and compassion of God will permit His priestly kingdom to enter the furnace, but only to bring forth gold, only until His image is seen in the remnant of Israel. The coming of the Lord will be first for *purification of the remnant*, then for *restoration of Israel*.

In the Name of Yeshua, call forth the priests, the Levites, and the remnant (which will ultimately be the One New Man) from Israel and from the nations. Pray that the spiritual Zadokites (Ezekiel 40:45-46), who are called to minister first unto the Lord at the Golden Altar of Incense, will be raised up as intercessors for the remnant of Israel and for the nations in preparation for his glorious coming.

Pray for an utter disillusionment with false messiahs and a return to the prophetic Scriptures as the only source of revelation concerning the identity and dual purposes for the Messiah (Suffering Servant/Redeemer King).

Pray for a breaking of the generational practice of relying on spirit guides, particularly the familiar spirit of Achiya HaShiloni, and the perverting of the purposes and promises of God through false impersonations and visitations to past sages and rabbinic leaders. Pray that this stronghold, particularly as it relates to the identity of Messiah, will be completely defeated and that the Word of God will be restored as the only guidepost to every issue of life.

The Tabernacle

"You search the Scriptures,
Because you think that in them
You have eternal life;
And it is these that bear witness of Me..."
(John 5:39)

While traditional rabbinic theology and Kabbalah present a false, unbiblical, image of Messiah, prophecies of the true coming Messiah abound in the Tenach (Old Testament).

Some of the most powerful imagery illustrating the person and purposes of Messiah are seen in the construction of the Tabernacle, even in the dimension, colors, and positioning of the furniture. Every detail foreshadows some aspect of the life of Messiah and describes how we are ushered into the presence of God.

The pattern of the tabernacle was designed according to *specific instructions* given to Moses and he was warned not to alter the pattern in the slightest detail. (Exodus 25:9). Why would God be so concerned about a structure in the desert conforming so meticulously to a certain pattern unless there were deeper revelations behind it? We learn in the Book of Hebrews that the pattern God gave on Mount Sinai was a *shadow of what is in heaven!* God brought Israel out of Egypt first and foremost so they could be free to *worship Him* and their first assignment was to build the Tabernacle. God desires to *dwell* among His people and the tabernacle (also called the *tent of meeting*), was the place where God would put His presence in the camp. The tabernacle itself was a symbol of *Heaven*, and was divided between the *Outer Court,* the *Holy Place*, and the *Most Holy Place.*

Each furniture piece reveals an aspect of Messiah and represents seven stages of worship (or development) in the believer's life as we move closer to the Most Holy Place and the face of God. Three pieces are in the Outer Court, two in the Holy Place, and two in the Holy of Holies.

"For if the blood of goats and bulls
and the ashes of a heifer
sprinkling those who have been defiled,
sanctify for the cleansing of the flesh,
how much more will the Blood of Messiah,
who through the eternal Spirit
*offered Himself **without blemish** to God,*
cleanse your conscience from dead works
to serve the living God?"
(Hebrews 9:13-14)

The *Brazen Altar* was made of acacia wood overlaid with bronze. It was the first article of furniture a worshipper encountered in the Outer Court.

The Brazen Altar is the meeting place between God and man and foreshadows the Cross. It represents substitutionary atonement, the death of the innocent in place of the guilty.

The Sinai Covenant principle of atonement is *life for life.* The clear image here is *life poured out.* It costs something to remove sin and there is no other provision made for man. I cannot bring my life to the altar because my life has been condemned by sin. I can only bring an *innocent life.* Isaiah 53 cannot be referring to Israel as a nation because *no one* except Messiah is innocent of sin and *all* require atonement. Faith in the Blood of the Lamb is the only remission for sin, not works, charity, study, suffering, self-inflicted punishment, or any amount of religious activity or tradition. This faith is based purely upon the *fact of the Cross,* not our feelings.

"Through Jesus then,
Let us continually offer up
A sacrifice of praise to God,

> *That is, the fruit of lips that*
> *Give thanks to His Name."*
> *(Hebrews 13:15)*

The rabbis say that Hosea 14:1-2 is the contemporary pathway of atonement and that on Yom Kippur the Jewish people can bring their *words of repentance* to remove sin. The trouble with this concession is that the fruit of our lips *is not a life that can be exchanged.* The perfect lamb was a shadow of the *Lamb of God* who takes away the sin of the world. When Jesus said, "I Am the Gate," He was alluding to the entryway of the Tabernacle, where the Brazen Altar was positioned.

Our iniquity is removed right at the doorway so that we may present our words as an expression of worship. We offer the fruit of our lips as thanksgiving for what has been give to us as a gift by the Brazen Altar.

> *"...Let us draw near to God*
> *With a sincere heart*
> *In full assurance of faith,*
> *Having our hearts sprinkled*
> *To cleanse us from a guilty conscience*
> *And having our bodies washed*
> *With pure water."*
> *(Hebrews 10:22)*

Moving a step closer to the magnificent presence of God, we find ourselves at the *Laver*, also made of bronze and in the Outer Court. While the Brazen Altar and the Laver both speak of judgment for sin and are concerned with cleansing, the Brazen Altar is for *everyone,* but the Laver is only for *priests.* The Brazen Altar gives us *access to God's righteousness*, but the Laver grants us *access to God's holiness* in our daily walk.

What's more, the cleansing agents are different. For the altar it is *fire*, but for the laver it is *water*. The fire that burned the sacrifice yielded the blood that washes away our *sins of the past,* whereas the water is a present, practical provision for *daily sin.* The ministry at the Brazen Altar is done *for* the priest, while cleansing at the Laver is done *by* the priest.

The Laver represents Messiah as the Word of God as He cleanses us from daily sin. The Laver is God's provision for refreshing and cleansing from the defilement that is a by-product of ministering to people.

This is why Jesus washed the feet of His disciples. They were *positionally* clean, but they needed to be *practically* cleansed from the daily dust of serving. The Laver was designed with mirrors on the inside in such a way that it reflected the face of the priest. As we gaze upon Yeshua, who is the Word of God, He reveals ourselves to us, changes us, and refreshes us.

The Laver is extremely essential in the daily walk of the priest. The gifts of the Spirit will only flow through *clean vessels.* We cannot bypass the Laver and charge into the Holy Place. Ministering to people is "outer court" ministry and is only the beginning of God's blessings. We can minister to *people,* but we cannot minister to *the Lord* without the work of the Laver in our lives. A danger in the life of the believer is that the Word of God itself and daily feeding upon it can easily become replaced by traditions and substitutes, such as commentaries or even good Christian books.

> *"I am the Light of the world.*
> *Whoever follows Me will never*
> *Walk in darkness,*
> *But will have the light of life."*
> *(John 8:12)*

Entering the Holy Place, we delight in the beauty of the *Golden Candlestick,* or *Menorah.* This stunning work of art, hammered into shape from a talent of pure gold, displays seven branches representing the *seven Spirits of God* (Isaiah 11:2/Revelation 1:4). It would have been much easier to simply melt the gold and pour it into an iron cast, but this is not the way into God's presence. *Religion* pours us into a mold, but God beats us into shape, forms us into His image, as we walk with Him in *relationship.*

The lamp crowning each branch of the Menorah was kindled by a *live coal* from the Brazen Altar. God Himself ignited the wood by a flame of fire from heaven and only *His fire* could be used to light the oil lamps of the Menorah, which were to be kept *burning continually*. All *natural light* is excluded and everything is done in the *light of Messiah*. No human flesh or wisdom can survive in this sacred place.

__The Menorah symbolizes Messiah who is pure gold. He was beaten and hammered, yet the radiant glory of God shines through Him. He is the perpetual Light, whose Word is the lamp unto our feet and is a perfect manifestation of God. He is the living Ner Tamid (Eternal Light) gracing every Jewish synagogue.__

Three sets of almonds decorated each branch of the Menorah, making a total of nine, creating a lovely image of the *fruit of the Spirit*. The almond tree is also known as the "awakening tree" because it is the first tree to come to life after winter. The three stages of growth are the *bud,* the *flower,* and the *fruit*. Aaron's rod budded, blossomed, and brought forth fruit. The almond branch of the Menorah symbolizes the Rod of Jesse referring to Messiah spoken of in Isaiah 11:1.

> *"Then Jesus declared,*
> *'I am the bread of life.*
> *He who comes to Me*
> *Will never go hungry,*
> *And he who believes in Me*
> *Will never be thirsty."*
> *(John 6:35)*

Moving deeper into the Holy Place, we see that the Menorah illuminates the *Golden Table* and the *Shewbread* resting upon it. Each week, twelve equal-sized loaves of unleavened bread were to be placed on the Golden Table and remain there until the Sabbath, when they would be eaten by Aaron and his sons. Fresh loaves sprinkled with frankincense would replace the loaves that were eaten until the next Shabbat. The purpose of the Sabbath feast was to *sustain fellowship* and eat this bread that had absorbed the *presence of God* for a week. God doesn't want to simply *save* us, He wants to *dine* with us!

Yeshua shocked the multitudes, and His disciples, when He announced at the Sea of Galilee, "Whoever eats My flesh and drinks My blood remains in Me, and I in him." (John 6:56) Jesus said His words were *spirit.* The *intimate relationship* Yeshua desires with His priests, as we abide in Him, can only be revealed by the Holy Spirit. The entire plan of salvation from the Garden was to bring man back into *communion* with God. Jesus is the Bread of Life. As we identify with Him in His life, as we feed upon the Word, we are nourished and satisfied. "By His stripes, we are healed." (Isaiah 53:5) As we identify with Messiah in His death, who gave His Body (His wholeness) for our brokenness, we are healed.

__The Shewbread, which also means "Bread of His Presence," is a type of Messiah and His identification with the everlasting covenant the Father made with Israel. It is a reminder of the manna from heaven and picture of the coming Messiah, the Bread of Life.__

> *"Hence, also, He is able to*
> *Save forever those who*
> *Draw near to God **through Him**,*
> *Since He always lives*
> *To **make intercession** for them."*
> *(Hebrews 7:25)*

The Menorah also illuminates the *Golden Altar of Incense,* the smallest piece of furniture, standing just before the white linen veil. The *needs of people* are ministered to in the Outer Court and most believers are content to bask in the blessing of *receiving* from God. Those who pursue His Person and Presence at the Golden Altar, deep in the Holy Place, will experience the *highest level of worship* we may offer while possessing this treasure in jars of clay. The Golden Altar ministers to the *needs of God* and is expressed in *prayer, intercession, praise*, and *adoration*. We present ourselves as a living sacrifice, which is our spiritual act of worship, holy and pleasing unto God (Romans 12:1).

__The Golden Altar of Incense is a type of Messiah as the Living Intercessor. The incense, which could only be ignited by a live coal from the Brazen Altar, represents the sweet fragrance of Messiah's intercession and praises before God on our behalf. It's also depicts__ _**our worship and intercession as we co-labor with Him on earth.**_

> _"Therefore, brethren, having **boldness**_
> _To enter the Holiest **by the Blood of Jesus**,_
> _By a new and living way which He_
> _Consecrated for us, through the veil, that is, His flesh,_
> _And having a High Priest over the house of God,_
> _Let us draw near with a true heart_
> _In full assurance of faith,,,"_
> _(Hebrews 10:19-22a)_

A burning desire for intimacy draws us beyond the veil into the Holy of Holies to gaze upon the magnificent _Ark of the Covenant._ We are exceedingly grateful for His blessings and provision, but now we long for _Him_ alone and we enter by the Blood of the Lamb.

**The Holy of Holies represents the Person of Messiah Jesus and the Ark of the Covenant symbolizes His abiding presence with His children.**

The Ark was marched into battle at the head of the army as a symbol of God's _protection_ and _victory_ going before Israel. The Ark was made of wood overlaid with gold. This speaks of the _human_ and _heavenly_ qualities of Messiah. The tablets of the Law were kept in the Ark. Jesus kept the law perfectly and continues to keep it within the Ark of His Person. Only Messiah as _Lawgiver_ is capable of being the perfect _Lawkeeper._ As we abide _in Him,_ we are keeping the Law because He _is_ the Law. If we belong to Yeshua, we are safe in the golden Ark just as the family of Noah was safe in the wooden ark upon the floodwaters.

Under the Old Covenant, access to the Holy of Holies was primarily determined by _ancestry._ When Jesus announced the New Covenant at the Passover Seder in Jerusalem, He was declaring a new way into fellowship with His Father that would be available to _everyone._ The moment we place our _faith_ in Yeshua, we are spiritually _born into_ the priestly family, we are _grafted in_ to the olive tree. The High Priest entered the Holy of Holies only once a year, but Moses was summoned to enter on a regular basis. What an awesome privilege to be invited to enter continually with full assurance as *priests, sons,* and *friends.* The *fearful* approach has been transcended by the *faith-filled* approach to the Throne because the Blood of Messiah and the curtain of His flesh open a new and living way into the Presence of God.

> *"When Jesus therefore had received*
> *The sour wine, He said,*
> *'It is finished!'*
> *And He bowed His head,*
> *And gave up His spirit."*
> *(John 19:30)*

The final article of furniture we encounter in the Holy of Holies is the *Mercy Seat.* The Brazen Altar was positioned in direct alignment to the Mercy Seat and all the other furniture pieces in the Tabernacle point to the ultimate statement of God's heart and eternal plan that it represents. The law is *hidden in Messiah,* so now *grace can flow.*

Tears fill my eyes and praise fills my heart as I write these words because the Mercy Seat represents the finished work of Messiah as the propitiation for our sins. MERCY is the finished work of God in Messiah.

Jesus humbled Himself and came to dwell in a human body, to suffer and die, to be rejected and hated by men so that God could show mercy to *whosoever* shall believe in Him. We will never comprehend the unfathomable love of God and the great cost to the Father to bring this mercy to the House of Israel and to the entire world.

> *"Then He opened their minds*
> *So they could understand the Scriptures."*
> *(Luke 24:45)*

The Ultra-Orthodox love mysteries and secrets and there is a treasure house to be explored in the Tabernacle. Even the disciples' minds needed to be opened so they could fully comprehend who Yeshua was. Pray for a revelation of the mystery of the Person, Provision, and Purposes of Messiah as expressed in the symbols of the Tabernacle. There were three articles of furniture in the Tabernacle that had crowns and each is connected to fellowship with God. They speak of the three offices Messiah would fulfill. The Golden Table foreshadows Messiah as Prophet, the Golden Altar as Priest, and the Ark of the Covenant as King. Pray for a revelation that Messiah Jesus wears all three crowns. Pray for a revelation of the symbolism in the colors used for the curtain hangings and cherubim embroidered upon them that speak of the holiness and righteousness of Messiah. Blue represents His heavenly origin, purple His royalty, and scarlet His suffering for our sins.

Pray for a revelation that Yeshua is the only meeting place between God and man, and the veil, which separated the sacred from the secular, represents Messiah and His righteousness, that now shuts the world OUT and the believer IN with God in the secret place of intimate fellowship. The God of Israel has provided the Way to enter in and draw near by the Body and Blood of Yeshua. Pray for a revelation that Yeshua is the only true tzaddik, the Lawgiver and Lawkeeper. He is the real Ark of the Covenant. He is the only Mediator and Advocate we have with the Father. The law is hidden in Him, so now grace can flow. Pray for a revelation of the profound mercy and grace of God in Messiah symbolized by the Mercy Seat because it is here that we experience the deepest communion with God because of the finished work of Yeshua.

Rolling Away The Reproach

"Whereas you have been forsaken and hated,
With no one passing through,
I will make you an everlasting pride,
A joy from generation to generation.
You will also suck the milk of the nations,
And will suck the breasts of kings;
Then you will know that I,
The Lord, am your Savior, And your Redeemer,
The Mighty One of Jacob.
Instead of bronze I will bring gold,
And instead of iron I will bring silver."
(Isaiah 60:15-17a)

My heart soared with joy when the Lord spoke to me in prayer one day and said, "I am rolling away the reproach of Egypt from My people." For those living in Israel, as the regional conflict escalates and the tourist industry dwindles, the feeling of being *"forsaken and hated, with no one passing through"* is all too real.

The image of Egypt in the Bible is *hard bondage and slavery*. It is *building*, but not *possessing*. It is *giving your strength*, but not *receiving reward*, and *losing* that which God has blessed you with, or giving it over, through disobedience or rebellion. Both *spiritual and natural bondage* hinder us from entering, possessing, and enjoying the fullness of our inheritance. In these last days, God will roll away the reproach of Egypt from His people. The bitter memories of *bronze* and *iron* representing the harshness, atrocities of exile, and seeming silence from heaven, will be washed away by the abundant provision of *gold* (glory) and *silver* (redemption).

**Rolling away the reproach means bringing Israel into the fruitful Land of their inheritance, which is a gift. The Israelites built the cities of Egypt, but inherited cities already built. It is removing the heavy burden, bringing the remnant into their full inheritance, spiritual and earthly, and restoring that which has been captured or relinquished by sin.**

"Then the Lord said to Joshua,
'Today I have rolled away
The reproach of Egypt from you.'
So the name of that place
Is called Gilgal to this day."
(Joshua 5:9)

Forty years of wandering in the wilderness had finally come to an end and the children of Israel had just crossed over the Jordan with the exhilaration of experiencing the miracle parting of the waters. Their feet had touched the soil of the Promised Land, but they hadn't taken any territory yet. First, the _entire army_ was to be _consecrated_ to the Lord through _circumcision_ because they had not been circumcised along the way. God was faithful to bring the next generation across the Jordan according to His promise to Moses (Numbers 14:22-24, 31), but to be assured of His _Presence_ going before them in battle and _victory_ in conquering the nations before them, there first needed to be a _reckoning with past sins of the nation_ and dealing with unsettled issues. There needed to be a _complete break with their history_ associated with Egypt and the _entering in_ to a new beginning. A new chapter was unfolding in the life of Israel. Circumcising the entire army all at once, in fact, _completely weakened_ them and made them most _vulnerable_ to the surrounding nations. Yet, God protected them in their obedience to His command. When the season of healing for this fresh dedication was completed, then the Lord assured that, _today_, the reproach of Egypt had been removed.

**Egypt is a symbol of the seat of idolatry and the land of the harsh taskmaster, of bondage, slavery, and humiliation.**

"But if they confess their iniquity
And the iniquity of their fathers,
With their unfaithfulness in which
They were unfaithful to Me, and
That they also walked contrary to Me,
And that I also have walked
Contrary to them and have brought
Them into the land of their enemies;
If their **uncircumcised hearts** *are humbled,*
And they accept their guilt,
Then I will remember My covenant
With Jacob, and My covenant with Isaac,
And My covenant with Abraham
I will remember; I will remember the land."
(Leviticus 26:40-42)

The State of Israel was miraculously birthed after 2,000 years of wandering in the wilderness of the diaspora. Nevertheless, the children of Israel have yet to take full possession of their inheritance and there is a *mocking* of the nations, as described in Ezekiel 22:4 that plagues Israel and will even increase as the fulfillment of prophecy unfolds and all the nations of the earth come against Jerusalem.

There is a fresh consecration, a circumcision of heart, in the midst of the Land that will take place just as in the days of Joshua, a returning to God that will precede the glorious restoration of Israel's full blessing.

"But arise, and stand on your feet;
For this purpose I have appeared to you,
To appoint you a **minister** *and a* **witness**,
Not only to the things which you have seen,
But also to the things which I will appear to you;
Delivering you from the Jewish people
And from the Gentiles, to whom I am sending you,
To **open their eyes** *so that they*
May turn from darkness to light
And from the dominion of Satan to God,
In order that they may **receive forgiveness** *of sins*

*And **an inheritance** among those who*
Have been sanctified by faith in Me."
(Acts 26:16-18)

When the Apostle Paul was presenting his defense before King Agrippa in Jerusalem and giving his testimony of the dramatic encounter with Jesus he experienced on the Damascus Road, he gives the full revelation he received and the purpose of the Lord appearing to him at that time. Although Saul of Tarsus was a fervent enemy of the believers, God saw his heart and knew he was behaving in ignorance (I Timothy 1:12-14). There was an apostolic calling on Saul's life and God was faithful to fulfill all His purposes for Saul.

We pray for the Ultra-Orthodox because there is a high calling upon them to be ministers and witnesses.

"By faith, Moses, when he had grown up,
Refused to be called the son
Of Pharaoh's daughter; choosing
Rather to endure ill-treatment
With the people of God, than to enjoy
The passing pleasures of sin;
*Considering the **reproach of Messiah***
Greater riches than the treasure of Egypt;
For he was looking to the reward."
(Hebrews 11:24-26)

This high calling to be identified with Messiah is also a call to suffering. The *reproach of Egypt* must be replaced with the *reproach of Messiah* (Hebrews 11:26). We will suffer *persecution* if we follow Yeshua with our whole heart, but in doing so we become *partakers of His sufferings* (I Peter 4:12-13) and through these fiery trials we gradually become conformed to His image. We run the race with endurance because Jesus also suffered reproach from men, enduring the cross and despising the shame *for the joy set before Him* (Hebrews 12:1-3) and there is a great reward in heaven for bearing His reproach. The reproach of Messiah is not the suffering of ruin and exile as the result of sin and subsequent judgment of God. Rather, it is a suffering that refuses the *treasures* of Egypt.

Egypt is also a symbol of all the treasure the world has to offer; the lure of wealth, power, and glory, along with the systems of religion and hidden wisdom whose mysteries do not have their source in God.

We can choose to bear the reproach of Egypt *or* the reproach of Messiah, but we cannot do both. When we suffer for the sake of the gospel, for the Name of Yeshua, the reproach of Egypt will be rolled away.

> *"Therefore let us go forth to Him,*
> ***Outside the camp***,
> *Bearing His reproach.*
> *For here we have no continuing city,*
> *But we seek the one to come."*
> *(Hebrews 11:13-14)*

Jesus suffered outside the camp, bearing the reproach of His brethren and the Romans because He saw the city that was to come. As we serve the Lord with all our hearts, we may be called to *suffer outside the camp.* We may be rejected and misunderstood by *organized religion, the traditional church, or rabbinic institutions and authorities.* We seek the city whose builder and maker is God, the *New Jerusalem* (Hebrews 11:9-10), and this hope and promise strengthens us to share in His sufferings. Speaking of His glorious coming, the prophet Isaiah writes:

> *"He will swallow up death for all time,*
> *And the Lord God will wipe tears*
> *Away from all faces,*
> *And He will remove the reproach of His people*
> *From all the earth;*
> *For the Lord has spoken."*
> *(Isaiah 25:8)*

Gracious Heavenly Father, we pray in the Name of Yeshua, that just as Israel has once again set its feet in the Promised Land after 2,000 years in exile, you would roll away the reproach of Egypt. We pray you would roll away the reproach of the nations, the reproach

of the "holy war" of Islam, the reproach of the religious spirit, the reproach and spiritual bondage of Rabbinic Judaism and the yoke of Torah upon the Ultra-Orthodox, that neither they nor their fathers could bear. In the Name of Yeshua, we place upon them the favor of the nations and the yoke of Messiah — the yoke of love, gentleness and humility, the yoke of grace. We pray that Messiah would be revealed to them and that you would call out those who are appointed to be apostolic ministers and witnesses of the gospel, to suffer for the sake of His Name, and receive their full inheritance both in this life and the life to come. We pray that the anointing that rested upon the Apostle Paul would rest again in even greater measure upon your end-time servants. We pray that the promise of the enduring city will so compel your servants in these last days that considerations of suffering will be as nothing compared to the coming glory of Messiah and His Kingdom.

Father, we also pray, in the name of Yeshua, for inner healing for all Jewish believers, particularly those from an Ultra-Orthodox background, who have been utterly rejected by their parents, friends, and loved one for their faith in Yeshua. We pray that You would lead them through inner healing and deliverance from all the traumatic wounds of persecution as they struggle to understand their identity in Messiah and establish their relationship with Him. We pray for freedom from all fear – fear of man, fear of assimilation, fear of persecution, fear of betraying past generations who have suffered at the hands of those calling themselves Christians. We pray that the FEAR OF GOD would overwhelm and silence every fear hindering them from bearing the reproach of Messiah and entering into the fullness of Your blessings upon them.

The Remnant

"So, too, at the present time
*There is a remnant chosen **by grace**.*
And if by grace, it is no longer by works;
If it were, grace would no longer be grace."
(Romans 11:5)

The theme of the remnant is powerfully threaded throughout Scripture, the image of the faithful few who stay close to God and love Him to the end with all their heart.

Abel offered an acceptable sacrifice, the *Levites* rallied to Moses, *two sons of Aaron* survived the fire of God to serve in the priesthood, *Joshua and Caleb* had a different spirit, the *tribe of Judah* was preserved so that David would always have a lamp for his descendants, God preserved *Elijah and 7,000 souls* from Baal worship, a handful of *exiles* returned to Jerusalem to rebuild the Temple, Jeremiah prophesied that the *good figs* would be restored to the Land, the *Zadokites* were chosen to minister before the Lord.

Ezekiel the prophet was deported to Babylon in 597 B.C. and he prophesied for over twenty years while in exile. His life is a classic image of the remnant that has a personal, intimate relationship with God, even in exile.

"'As I entered into judgment
With your fathers in the wilderness
Of the land of Egypt, so I
Will enter into judgment with you,'

Declares the Lord God.
'And I shall make you pass
Under the rod, and I shall bring
You into the bond of the covenant..."
(Ezekiel 20:36-37)

Ezekiel's heart clung to God in the midst of a godless generation, his heart broke for the rampant idolatry, and His prophecies are ablaze with the call for repentance and the future glory of the remnant in the Messianic age. Ezekiel 20:33-40 promises that God will lead His people into the *wilderness of the nations* where they will *pass under the rod* and be purged of all the rebels. The remnant will serve the Lord on His holy mountains and their sacrifices will again be acceptable. They will no longer profane the name of the Lord among the nations. Romans 11:5 promises that a *remnant of the descendants of Abraham, Isaac, and Jacob*, chosen by grace, will be saved and brought into the fullness of God's purposes. In the end-time gathering, Isaiah 27:12-13 promises a drawing of the remnant from the Euphrates to the brook of Egypt, along with a scattered remnant from the Arab nations that will come and worship the God of Israel, on His holy mountain.

Praying the Scriptures is a powerful strategy of intercession and warfare. Nehemiah and Daniel prayed the promises of God back to Him and entreated the Lord to remember His covenant with His people.

In these last days, Zechariah 12:10-14 depicts a spirit of grace and supplication that will be poured out upon the house of David and inhabitants of Jerusalem, enabling them to repent. This deep repentance releases a fountain that will be opened for the purging of sin, idolatry, and unclean spirits (13:1-2).

Perhaps those who will be repenting most grievously, weeping most bitterly, are the Ultra-Orthodox, for it is they, the modern-day Pharisees, who are *piercing Yeshua* more than any other Jewish group. Just as in the days of Yeshua and the days of the apostles, the Ultra-Orthodox are the fiercest persecutors of the Messianic Body in Israel and around the world. Zechariah13:8-9 is a shining promise that a remnant will survive a terrible devastation in the Land just prior to the return of Jesus. Two-thirds will be destroyed, but *a third* will be brought into the fire and refined.

<u>As we pray for the salvation of the House of Israel, focusing on the Ultra-Orthodox, we are praying for that remnant that will be preserved, tested and come forth as gold.</u>

Along with the Isaiah, Ezekiel, Romans, and Zechariah passages, Isaiah 11 is a glorious chapter to pray, a chapter revealing the promise of a BRANCH that would come forth from the rod of Jesse. It speaks of the coming millennial kingdom and the remnant that the Lord will gather from all the corners of the earth (v.11). Pray these promises to the Lord and call forth the remnant that is chosen by grace.

"Who do people say that
The Son of Man is?"
And Simon Peter answered and said,
"Thou art the Christ (or Anointed One),
The Son of the Living God."
(Matthew 16:13b, 16)

When Peter made this remarkable confession identifying Yeshua as Messiah and Son of God, Jesus was quick to inform him that it was not through his own natural mind that this knowledge came to him, but that His Father *in heaven* had *revealed it to him*. Even though Peter was a disciple of Jesus and had seen Him work countless miracles, He still needed a *revelation* to recognize Him as Messiah and Son of God. So much more today, we need to pray that a revelation of this foundational truth be unveiled to the Ultra-Orthodox.

"...'The man who is called Jesus
*Made clay, and **anointed my eyes**,*
And said to me, 'Go to Siloam, and wash;'
So I went away and washed, and I received sight."
(John 9:11)

**Perhaps the most powerful prayer we could pray for the Ultra-Orthodox is that Yeshua would anoint their eyes that they may see. We are all born spiritually blind even if we have natural sight, but when Jesus touches us, our spiritual eyes are opened.**

The veil over the eyes of the Jewish heart contains many _layers_ and recognizing the Messiah in all His glorious dimensions may be a _process_ for the Ultra-Orthodox. This was confirmed as a major prayer point during a conversation with a secret believer who shared that it is one thing to believe that Yeshua is _Messiah,_ but another thing to believe He is _God._ That is a very difficult concept for Jewish people and she struggles with it all the time. How could God have a Son? Aren't we all sons of God? How is it possible for God to be in a body? Isn't it idolatry to worship a human being? If we are talking about mere mortal man, absolutely! But the _Son of Man_ is altogether different. He is the Word made flesh. Still, there is a need for personal revelation of this truth in her spirit and in her mind.

When Yeshua bowed His head and gave up His spirit to the Father on Calvary, the veil in the Holy of Holies was torn from top to bottom. From that very moment, the restriction that prevented access to the Holy of Holies (with the exception of the High Priest once a year) was forever removed and a _new and living way_ was opened for anyone to come into the presence of God through the Blood of Jesus (Hebrews 10:19-22). Nevertheless, as the _physical veil_ was being torn away from the Temple, a _spiritual veil_ was descending. A partial hardening came over the House of Israel as a judgment on the leadership who persuaded the multitudes to reject Yeshua. The good news is that this is only **partial** and it is **not forever.** There has always been a remnant of Jewish believers throughout the ages and the hardening is only in effect **until** the fullness of the Gentiles comes in.

Amazingly, in the case of Israel, there are two veils to consider.

First, there is a _veil over the hearts of the Jewish people_ that is _God's veil_ (II Corinthians 3:14-16). We cannot rebuke the devil for this veil or bind it away. God Himself put the veil there and only He can take it away in Messiah. Second, there is _Satan's veil,_ the veil that _blinds the minds_ of all the unsaved (II Corinthians 4:3-4). Isaiah 25:7 also speaks of a *veil over the nations*. In the case of Israel, we could say that there is a *double veil*: the veil that God has put *over their hearts* and the veil Satan has put *over their minds*. We pray for God to lift *both*.

Pray that the veil will be lifted from the eyes of the remnant that they may behold Yeshua as Messiah, Son of God, and God the Son. Yeshua took three of His disciples up to a mountain and revealed Himself in all His glory. Moses and Elijah joined Him discussing the work He would accomplish on Calvary. This experience for the disciples, though they would not understand it until much later, revealed Jesus as greater than Moses, greater than Elijah, even greater than angels, as the Book of Hebrews would later confirm. Pray for a revelation that the Name and Person of Yeshua is greater than any other.

> *"Ask of Me, and I will give you*
> *The nations for your inheritance.*
> *And the ends of the earth*
> *For your possession."*
> *(Psalm 2:8)*

King David saw the big picture of the purposes of God when he wrote Psalm 2:6 imploring the only Begotten Son to ask for the nations as an inheritance, but the invitation is also extended to those *in Messiah by adoption as sons*. The calling of God on the nation of Israel is to be a holy people, to confront the idols of the earth with the power and presence of Yahveh, and His Son Yeshua, and to open the eyes of the nation to the God of Israel. They are destined to be *separate in their holiness* (kingdom of priests), but *ambassadors in their proclamation* of the way of salvation. There is a calling yet to be fulfilled by a remnant from Judah and a remnant from the house of Israel (the generations born into the modern state) in these last days.

The full inheritance of God for Israel is, above all, Himself, then a Land and a Kingdom they would possess, and nations they would inherit for His glory.

The calling upon the children of Israel to be a light and witness to the nations was circumvented by the ultimate creation of the religion of Rabbinic Judaism, but we are living in the days of the restoration of all things!

The remnant of Israel will yet fulfill this great calling and commission. Pray that the full remnant of Israel will return to the God of their fathers and to a personal relationship with God, through Yeshua. Pray that their identity will be rooted and grounded only in Messiah Jesus. Pray that this remnant would be freed of every hindrance to fulfill the high calling of God to proclaim Jesus to the nations and possess their full inheritance.

Already, there is a growing Messianic remnant. The fig tree is budding, but it will fully blossom to embrace the destiny prepared for her. Call forth this Messianic remnant and pray they will arise and bring the God of Israel and Yeshua to the nations. Pray that they will lead the nations to discover and embrace their Hebraic roots (in the patriarchs and the prophets). Pray that the fulfillment of their calling will be "life from the dead" and release revival, new oil, and new wine around the world. Pray that they will teach and impart a fresh anointing for intimacy, worship, prayer, prophecy, evangelism, and understanding of the Word of God.

> *"But you, Daniel,*
> *Close up and seal the words*
> *Of the scroll **until the time of the end**."*
> *(Daniel 12:4a)*

There is a thrilling promise in the Book of Daniel that is a key to prayer in these last days. God said that the words of this prophetic book would be *sealed* until the time of the end. The Book of Daniel contains some of the most powerful and revealing Messianic prophecies in all the Bible. As I was praying the first day of a Daniel Fast during the Passover season in 2000, the Lord led me to pray Daniel 9:25-27 prophetically over the Ultra-Orthodox as if I were reading it to them in the Spirit. He then led me to pray Daniel 8:19-25, and Jeremiah 31:31-37. These scriptures speak of the *Messiah*, the *Anti-Christ*, and the *New Covenant*.

I invite you to pray these Scriptures aloud and prophetically over the Ultra-Orthodox and the whole House of Israel. Pray that the Lord will UNSEAL the vital truths of the Book of Daniel, especially those passages that speak of the Ancient of Days, the Messiah, and the Anti-Christ, and that a powerful revelation of the New Covenant will be released in dreams, visions, and personal visitations in these last days.

Glorious Restoration

"For He must remain in heaven
Until the time comes for God
*To **restore everything**,*
As He promised long ago
Through his holy prophets."
(Acts 3:21)

God always fulfills His purposes and promises in the *fullness of time* (Ephesians 1:9-10). Events on His eternal calendar do not just happen randomly. God told Abram that His descendants would be strangers in a country not their own and enslaved 400 years (Genesis 15:13-14), but then they would be freed. God told Moses that an entire generation of Israelites would wander in the desert for 40 years because of their unbelief and none of that generation, except Joshua and Caleb, would enter the Promised Land (Numbers 14:31-34). Daniel 9:24-27 is perhaps the shining example of how precise the prophetic word of God was concerning the timing of the coming of Messiah.

We are living in the days when God is restoring all things in preparation for the return of Messiah. Israel has become a nation after 2,000 years, the exiles are returning to the Land, the desert is blooming, the Hebrew language has been revived, and the fig tree of Jewish believers is growing. Reconciliation walks are taking place across the Land. Restoration and reconciliation are working together as God prepares the Bride to meet the Bridegroom. While these are awesome miracles for which we have cause to rejoice, the restoration of the spiritual heritage of Israel will far exceed anything we have yet seen.

__The works of darkness may rage against God only for a season and that season is coming to an end, Hallelujah!__

The battle will be most furious at the end, because the enemy knows his time is short, but we have the assurance of victory because Yeshua has already won the battle. We can rejoice and be encouraged that our destiny is the Marriage Supper of the Lamb, the New Jerusalem, and eternity ruling and reigning with Jesus, while Satan's destiny is the lake of fire and brimstone forever and ever and ever.

"Stand at the crossroads and look;
*Ask for the **ancient paths**,*
Ask where the good way is,
And walk in it,
And you will find rest for your souls.
But they said,
'We will not walk in it.'"
(Jeremiah 6:16)

In these last days, the God of Israel will restore the ancient pathways leading to eternal life and blessings forevermore.

We will dance on streets that are golden, Amen! Rejoicing is coming for the remnant of Israel and those grafted-in to the olive tree, but first a little *road work*. As history draws to a catastrophic, yet glorious conclusion, as the Lion of Judah is stirring up His zeal to roar from Zion, all humanity is standing at the crossroads. As God is restoring all things to Israel, He will begin with the infrastructure. Building up the highway. Even now, in the spirit realm, the barriers blocking the road for construction are being set in place. God is calling His people Israel back to the *ancient paths*. Isaiah 63:15-16 laments the disappearance of the mighty deeds of God and mourns His restrained heart toward Israel. Perhaps tearfully, Isaiah prophesies of a day when, even though God is their Father, and their Redeemer *from of old*, sadly *Abraham and Israel (Jacob) do not recognize them*. The great prophet sees the day when the personal, living faith of the fathers gradually gives way to academic pursuit, ritual, and formality and God is reduced to a philosophy.

The highway of holiness and the fear of the Lord are ancient paths frequently ignored in our high-tech, instant gratification, self-indulgent world.

"For My people have forgotten Me,
They burn incense to worthless gods
And they have stumbled from their ways,
*From the **ancient paths**,*
*To walk in **bypaths**, not on a highway.*
(Jeremiah 18:15)

Scripture presents two distinct pathways. We are preparing ourselves for eternity depending on which path we choose to walk on in this life. One path leads to intimate knowledge of *God*, revelation from Him, the anointing, and sweet fellowship. *Bypaths* lead to *men*, to human wisdom, striving in the flesh, dead words, and fruitless religious observance. *Ancient paths* are roadways to eternal life and ruling and reigning with the King.

The *highway of holiness* is an ancient path of unreserved consecration, no-compromise holy devotion to the Bridegroom. Isaiah 35 promises that the *unclean* will not travel on this highway, nor any *fools*, or even any *lions*. It is a sacred road and its borders are protected by the glory of His Presence. It is *holy* ground, but not a holier-than-thou-ness of a secluded monastic lifestyle, but rather a way of life separated unto God for His purposes and glory. Only the *redeemed*, the *ransomed of the Lord* may travel on this majestic highway, and they will come with joyful shouting to Zion, Hallelujah!

Bypaths are not even highways. They are unpaved, dirt side roads, a diversion from the freeway of blessing God intends. On bypaths, our hearts become knit to *objects of worship*, rather than to the supreme *Object of worship*. Bypaths may be an interesting adventure in the woods, but they never lead us anywhere spiritually profitable. Ancient paths are the King's Highway to Heaven.

The Bible says that *byways* caused His people Israel to stumble from their ancient ways. In these last days, the overwhelming, magnificent *love of God* will lure His beloved from the *bypaths,* which always cause her to forget God and focus on exalted people and exaggerated issues that distract her from pure devotion to Him. He will mercifully lead her into the wilderness of His grace and back to the ancient pathways. There, He will remove the idols from her midst and forever betroth her to Himself (Hosea 2:14-23).

Restoring the ancient pathway ultimately means restoring the Word of God to its exalted position of authority because the Scriptures themselves are the ROAD MAP to the Kingdom of Heaven.

What happened in the days of King Josiah will again be fulfilled in our day. The *Holy Book* that had been lost and neglected, buried somewhere in the House of the Lord was *discovered* by Hilkiah the priest and *read to the king* (II Chronicles 34:14-10). Just like today, the High Priest and the scribe were not necessarily looking for this Book when they found it. They were bringing out the money that had been collected for the restoration of the Temple and stored in one of its many chambers. You see, they thought the *work on the Temple* was the really important thing and making sure that everyone was paid was the highest priority. But the all-time really important thing to God was *rediscovering His Book*. This Book will again be discovered and the dust blown off its aging cover. Like King Josiah, the remnant of Israel will tear their garments, repent from the heart, and passionately tear down all the altars and idols to restore the House of the Lord.

If we pray anything for the Ultra-Orthodox in these last days, let us plead with God to RESTORE HIS WORD as the ultimate authority of truth, wisdom, and revelation, His precious Word that has been lost and replaced by the Talmud and Kabbalah. Pray that His people will be moved with holy zeal to return to the God of their Fathers with all their heart. Pray that He will bring them to STAND at the crossroads, to recognize the strategic moment in history we are living in. Time is short and the days are evil. Soon and very soon we are going to see the King. Pray that the Lord will move upon them to ASK for the ancient paths, to earnestly seek Him with all their hearts, whatever the cost, for the way back to the faith of the fathers, to WALK in this pleasant way that leads to REST for their souls, along with precious intimacy, pure revelation from heaven, blessings from His generous right hand, and glory in His coming Kingdom.

"Then I will set the key of the
House of David upon his shoulder,

When he opens no one will shut,
When he shuts no one will open,
*And **I will drive him like a peg***
In a firm place, and he will become
A throne of glory in his father's house.
So they will hang on him all the glory
Of his father's house, offspring and
Issue, all the least of vessels, from
Bowls to all jars.
'In that day,' declares the Lord of hosts,
*'**the peg driven in a firm place** will give way;*
It will even break off and fall, and the
Load hanging on it will be cut off,
For the Lord has spoken,'"
(Isaiah 22:22-25)

In this astounding prophecy of the coming Messiah pictured symbolically through the servant Eliakim, God sets the *key of David* upon His shoulders. It is with the *house of David* that God made an eternal covenant promising there would always be a *lamp* and an *descendant* to sit on the throne of David. The Scripture says that David had a heart after God's own heart. This is not to say that David was perfect. The sins of David are well documented, but it is to say that David sought the heart of God. David cultivated an intimate relationship with the Lord those many nights alone with his harp, tending the flock. It was out of the *well* of his personal experience with the Great Shepherd that he could write Psalm 23. The *anointing* upon David's life is unparalleled of all the kings of Judah or Israel.

"In that day, I will raise up
The fallen tabernacle of David,
And wall up its breaches;
I will also raise up its ruins,
*And rebuild it **as in days of old**."*
(Amos 9:11)

Restoring the fallen tent of David is not so much about Davidic dancing and worship as it is restoring the DAVIDIC ANOINTING and heart relationship that David enjoyed with God. David was a

warrior/psalmist/lover of God. The rabbinic spirit, in its essence, is a rejection of the anointing of the House of David. In these last days, God will restore the THRONE OF DAVID and usher the remnant into the fullness of their destiny as worshippers of God, witnesses, ministers of the gospel, and a kingdom of priests.

While there may be much singing about 'David Melech Israel' in Jewish circles, the spirit of rabbinic Judaism is more likened to the *House of Saul*, characterized by living in the flesh, disobedience, idolatry, and witchcraft. Saul disobeyed Samuel's command to wait for him to sacrifice, but Saul, *in a moment of crisis*, offered the burnt offering *to keep the people from scattering* (I Samuel 13:8-14). The seeds of Rabbinic Judaism were birthed in the crisis of the Babylonian captivity and every forward movement was propelled by a further crisis.

The defining feature of Saul's reign is the idolatry of his own power and relentless despising pursuit of David.

There was no fear of God in Saul. Knowing the anointing of kingship was upon David, that he was a loyal servant who would never seize the kingdom by force, Saul's jealously nevertheless raged against David until his death. When Saul sinned, his repentance was not genuine, as he repeatedly attempted to take David's life. Saul sought comfort and counsel through human wisdom and eventually from Samuel through witchcraft (I Samuel 28:3-17). His son Jonathan had a different spirit and his heart was knit to David in covenant friendship, and even his young son Mephibosheth was cared for at the king's table (II Samuel 9:1-7), but God ultimately rejected the House of Saul and destroyed him and all his sons (I Samuel 31).

The *House of David* is characterized by a passionate heart for God, power in battle by the Spirit of God, and obedience. In a crisis, David comforted himself in the Lord (I Samuel 30:1-6). David had the fear of the Lord in that he refused to destroy Saul even when it was in his power to do so. He feared to touch God's anointed (I Samuel 24:1-12, 26:5-21). David's sins were *big*, but his repentance was also deep and genuine (II Samuel 11-12:14, 24:1-14)). Israel's rebellion against the House of David is essentially a rebellion against the *anointing*.

The prophetic passage in Isaiah about *Eliakim* speaks of two *pegs*. God Himself *drives the peg* in a firm place (v.23), giving an image of the *hand of God* in the suffering of His beloved Son on the Cross and also the enduring nature of His Kingdom. All the glory of His Father's throne will hang on this peg. Everything in this kingdom will become holy and sanctified through this peg, every bowl and jar, to the least vessel.

The other peg *is driven in to a firm place (v.25)*. This peg will break, collapse, and give way under the *load* hanging on it. This peg is an image of the *hand of man* in the suffering of the Son of God on Calvary and the burden of the religious system that would spring from it. This peg will be cut off before the return of Messiah Jesus, which may sound harsh, but it is the *mercy of God* to judge and remove the religious system that has become a hindrance to blessing and revival among His people. It may be compared to cutting loose the binding chains from the wrist of a prisoner of war. This is exactly was Jesus said He came to do, to *set the captives free!*

Pray for the restoration of the fallen tabernacle of David, the anointing of David, and the heart relationship of this great patriarch. Pray that the Lord will give the Ultra-Orthodox a revelation of Eliakim as a symbol of Yeshua, both in His suffering, and in His glory. Pray for the raising up of the Tent Peg that will become a throne of glory in His father's house and will cleanse it of all defilement. Pray for the load hanging on the peg that has been firmly set in place by man to give way so that the captives may be set free and the new kingdom, the new wine, and all its blessings may flow unhindered.

> *"You yourselves have seen what I did*
> *To the Egyptians, how I bore you*
> *On eagles wings, and brought you to Myself.*
> *Now then, if you will indeed obey My voice*
> *And keep My covenant, then you shall*
> *Be My own possession among all the peoples,*

For all the earth is Mine;
And you shall be to Me a kingdom of priests
And a holy nation. These are the words
That you shall speak to the sons of Israel."
(Exodus 19:4-6)

These are the *very first words* God spoke to Moses on Mt. Sinai. The giving of the Ten Commandments and the revealing of the pattern and design of the Tabernacle was the not the first thing on God's mind. What God wanted Moses to understand on Mt. Sinai before anything else was the *vision* of His *purpose for creating Israel.* God brought a people out of Egypt on wings of eagles to bring them *to Himself, to be His treasured possession.* God purposed and desired that Israel would be *to Him a kingdom of priests and a holy nation* and this prophetic promise and destiny will yet be fulfilled. The remnant of Israel will be His possession, His holy nation, and a kingdom of priests.

"What are you, O great mountain?
Before Zerubbabel you will
Become a plain;
And he will bring forth the capstone
To shouts of 'Grace, grace to it!"
(Zechariah 4:7)

If we will see the Ultra-Orthodox come into the fullness of God's blessings, then we must witness a deliverance from the Egypt of the religious spirit, the rabbinic spirit, and Kabbalah. We are living in the days for the heads of these spiritual monsters to be crushed.

These spirits may seem like *mighty mountains*, but they will become level ground by the power of the Holy Spirit and the Blood of the Lamb. Every believer will be blessed from Jerusalem in the Messianic Kingdom and it is God's desire that believers everywhere pray for her future blessing. The international network of prayer that is growing for the Ultra-Orthodox will bear fruit. In the fullness of time, the capstone, and Chief Cornerstone, will be revealed and brought forth to shouts of "Grace! Grace!"

_**When the ruling spirits in the Ultra-Orthodox community are
defeated, the priestly office will be restored, the raising up of the
spiritual Zadokites.**_

King Hezekiah and King Josiah beautifully illustrate this spiritual
principle. The first thing Hezekiah did after breaking the pillars,
cutting down the Asherim, and pulling down the high places was to
appoint the priests and Levites to their service (II Chronicles 31:1-2).
Priests minister first to the Lord and then to others. After his holy
rampage to purge Judah and Jerusalem, Josiah celebrated the Passover,
which had become a neglected feast, set the priests in their offices,
and encouraged them in their service (II Chronicles 35:1-2). The
idols must first be removed before the priestly office can be restored
as a pleasing service before God. They cannot co-exist because images
of idolatry defile both the Land and the priesthood.

_**Pray that every idol, every high place, every modern version of the
Asherim, will be passionately torn down. Pray, in the Name of
Yeshua, that the three ruling spirits hindering the gospel from
breaking through to the Ultra-Orthodox (the religious spirit, the
rabbinic spirit, and Kabbalah) will be completely and utterly defeated
and that the Name of Yeshua, the Rock of their salvation, will be
exalted as the Chief Cornerstone. Speak "Grace" to the bringing
forth of this marvelous revelation of the finished work of Messiah
and the grace flowing from the Mercy Seat. Pray for a restoration
of the true priesthood, the spiritual Zadokites, the remnant of
worshippers who draw near to minister to the Lord in the Holy of
Holies. Call forth the highway to Zion, a highway for the holy seed
to come into the Kingdom of God and into His Presence, where
there is fullness of joy.**_

_**As the remnant comes into the fullness of their inheritance, we will
see a restoration of the Father's Name and the Name of His Son.**_

_"Who has ascended into heaven and descended?
Who has gathered the wind in His fists?
Who has wrapped the waters in His garment?_

Who has established all the end of the earth?
*What is **His name** or **His son's name**?*
Surely you know!"
(Proverbs 30:4)

Most of us are familiar with this riddle in the Tenach. The first question is as startling as the last. Who has **ascended** into heaven and **descended**? What is **His name** or **His son's name?** The three middle questions are unmistakable. Who but God Almighty gathers the wind in His fists, wraps the waters in His garment, and establishes the ends of the earth? But what about these mysterious names?

The actual Name of God was stolen from the Jewish people (and consequently from the Church). In these last days, Father God wants to restore *His Name* because it is the key to unlocking the riddle of His Son, whose excellent name has also been stolen from Israel. *Knowing God the Father's Name* is a stepping stone toward *recognizing the Son's Name* and worshipping Him as Messiah *and* God.

"You shall not take the name
Of the Lord your God in vain,
For the Lord will not leave him unpunished
Who takes His name in vain."
(Exodus 20:7)

The people in the Bible spoke the Name of God, the name that He expressly revealed in order that we might *know Him and call upon HIM*. However, because of the command in Exodus, just before the time of Messiah, the rabbis decided it should be forbidden to speak His Name at all, in order to avoid the risk of taking it in vain! They somehow thought they could *protect God's Name* by changing or concealing it. Hence, the title "Adonai" was substituted and subsequently "Lord" or "Sovereign Lord" was placed in English and other translations. In the preface of most English Bibles, you will find a note admitting that, for purposes of Jewish tradition, *Lord* is substituted for *Yahveh*. Indeed, Yahveh calls Himself by many titles: El-Shaddai, El Elyon, Everlasting Father, Ancient of Days, however, *repeatedly* throughout Scripture the Almighty proclaims, "**YAHVEH IS MY NAME.**" But titles are not the same as names. The President of the United States has a name. The Prime Minister of Israel has a name. The Prince of Wales has a name.

> *"Thus you shall say to the sons of Israel,*
> *'Yahveh Elohim of your fathers,*
> *The God of Abraham, the God of Isaac,*
> *And the God of Jacob, has sent me to you.'*
> *This is My name forever, and this is my*
> *Memorial-name to all generations."*
> *(Exodus 3:15)*

Many Christians believe that God's Name is "Jehovah." It is interesting how this word "Jehovah" came about. The vowels in Hebrew are placed under the consonants, and the ancient Scriptures had no vowels at all, until scholars put them in later for easier reading. Ancient Jewish scholars decided to place under YHVH (the Hebrew letters of God's Name) a mixture of vowel points for Elohim and Adonai to prevent people from pronouncing the Name. Christian scholars came along and pronounced it, and thus we get "Yehovah," which then became "Jehovah," as a result of the later introduction of the letter "J" to the English language.

> *"So I will make my **Holy Name known***
> *In the midst of My People Israel,*
> *And I will not let them profane*
> *My Holy Name anymore.*
> *Then the nations shall know*
> *That I am YAHVEH,*
> *The Holy One in Israel."*
> *(Ezekiel 39:7)*

Did Yeshua use the Father's Name in His earthly ministry? Hebrews 2:12 says, "I will declare *Your Name* to my brethren; in the midst of the assembly I will praise you." (from Psalm 22:22) John 17:26 says, "I have declared to them Your Name, and will declare it, that the love with which you loved Me may be in them, and I in them." And John 5:43, "I have come *in My Father's Name* and you do not receive me;

if another comes in his own name, him you will receive." This helps us understand why the Pharisees were so enraged with Jesus. Not only did He speak the forbidden Name, but He was claiming that Yahveh was His father, making Himself equal with God!

Now that we understand how the Father's Name was stolen from the Jewish people, let's see what happened to the Son's Name. Somewhere along the line, in reaction to and in defense against Christianity and the growing persecution against Jews who refused to convert, and also to prevent the Jewish people from connecting the name Yeshua (which means "salvation) with Jesus of Nazareth, they changed His name to Y*eshu,* which is said as a curse and means "*may his name be blotted out and no longer remembered.*" Just for fun, let's re-word this riddle, put it back on the board and see if it's somewhat easier to solve:

> *"What is the name you should never pronounce,*
> *And what is the name you should never remember?*
> *Surely you know!*

Now the mystery is revealed. The Name of the Father is *ineffable* and the Name of the Son is *forgotten.* What a stunning and impressive victory for the enemy. But all that is about to change. It is the promise of God to *make His Holy Name known,* not only to His people, but to all the nations. In His great love and mercy, Yahveh has answered prayers throughout the ages no matter how man addressed Him, but He wants us to know His name and to call upon His name, which is distinct from any other name. He also wants all people everywhere to know that Yeshua, His only begotten Son, is Messiah and Lord and that Yahveh was reconciling Himself to the world *in Yeshua* (II Corinthians 5:19).

I want to be clear that in saying the names of Yahveh and Yeshua are being revealed and restored, I am *not* saying that it is wrong or unscriptural to use the name of Jesus, Lord, or God. There are movements that take an extreme view on this issue. Our Heavenly Father has been answering prayer, healing diseases, and performing extraordinary miracles in the Name of Jesus for centuries. These names are being restored because they are *keys to revealing of the identity of Messiah.* It is crucial for purposes of prayer for the Ultra-

Orthodox that we understand how the process of changing the Names of God occurred.

Pray for a revelation of the Names of God the Father (Yahveh) and God the Son (Yeshua). Pray that the Name of Father God will be restored to the Jewish people and to the Church and be made known to the world. Pray that the curse put on the Name of Yeshua (by changing it to Yeshu) will be broken, that the Name Yeshua (salvation) will be restored and exalted in Israel. Ask Yahveh to give His people a REVELATION that Yeshua is not only Messiah, but Son of God, and God the Son, the Word made flesh. The Word of God says that we shall know the truth and the truth shall set us free (John 8:32). Pray that all fear and hesitation, especially among those who have been raised in Messianic circles, and the lie from Satan that it is virtually sin to speak the Name of God, will be broken and that there will come a freedom to call on His Name. Pray for freedom to pray to the Father in the Name of His Son from the heart, earnestly seeking for truth and intimate fellowship.

> *"And Isaac dug again*
> *The wells of water*
> *Which they had dug*
> *In the days of Abraham his father,*
> *For the Philistines had stopped them up*
> *After the death of Abraham.*
> *He called them by the names*
> *Which his father had called them."*
> *(Genesis 26:18)*

The Lord will also restore ancient wells, places where the calling and purposes of God were clear, but, over time, the well has become hindered or stopped up by the enemy, and the anointing no longer flows freely from that place.

As we pray for the Ultra-Orthodox, particularly for Mea Shearim, we want to move with this flow of God. Isaac, who reaped the hundredfold blessing, also reopened the wells that were dug by his father Abraham. In the case of the Ultra-Orthodox, there are two things that we need to pray because the wellsprings of both the Chasidism and the

197

Mitnagdim were polluted, rather than anointed, from their very inception.

Pray that the wells of Chasidism that were dug by the Father of Lies and flow through the teachings of the Baal Shem Tov (and his later disciples) will be plugged up, sealed off, and forever silenced from their ability to supply any source of power or spiritual fulfillment to the Chasidim. Pray that the wells dug by the Talmudic teachings of the Vilna Gaon will be plugged up, forever dried up, and rendered ineffective in producing spiritual and intellectual fulfillment for the Mitnagdim.

Pray that the wells of Abraham, the father of our faith through a personal relationship with Yahveh, who was called to be a blessing to the nations, who saw Yeshua's day and rejoiced in it, will be reopened. Pray that these wells will begin to flow freely so that the Ultra-Orthodox will be free to return to the God of their fathers, fulfill the calling upon their lives, and bring a personal relationship with God to the nations through Yeshua, the Messiah.

> *"Then I will give her her*
> *Vineyards from there,*
> *And the valley of Achor*
> *As a door of hope.*
> *And she will sing there*
> *As in the days of her youth,*
> *As in the day when she came*
> *Up from the land of Egypt."*
> *(Hosea 2:15)*

In the wilderness of suffering and isolation, God will restore the vineyards of His people.

The vineyard has always been the symbol of Israel in the Bible. In these end times, Israel will be restored to *the intimate, love relationship* with the Messiah that has always been her destiny, and *produce fruit* for the Lord, a *spiritual harvest* for the Kingdom of heaven. They will reap a harvest from among the nations and also bear fruit *that will be enjoyed by the heart of God.* Vineyards are an image of coming prosperity, favor, health, wholeness, and fruitfulness in every aspect of life – all the blessings of Deuteronomy 28 and Isaiah 60.

The Song of Solomon, the passionate allegory of the captivating love of the King for His beloved maiden Israel (also extending to all believers and couples in marriage) ends with the bride *coming up out of the wilderness leaning on her beloved* (Song of Songs 8:4b). The King has wooed her, drawn her, trained and matured her throughout the entire book and finally, in the sweetest expression of bridal love, there is a surrender and abandonment to the Bridegroom as she rests in total dependence upon her divine Spouse. She is completely His. He is a *seal* on her arm and no waters or rivers can overflow this eternal relationship (8:6-7). As the remnant of Israel repents in the wilderness, embraces her Messiah/Bridegroom/King, and comes into the fullness of her destiny, she will be leaning on their Lover God and present to Him a gift of undying love, producing the greatest joy His heart has ever known. This is the climax of the whole story of the Bible. The new Jerusalem is a place where God will dwell with His people forever and ever and ever. A diamond city will descend from heaven as a wedding gift to His bride.

> *"In days to come Jacob*
> *Will take root,*
> *Israel will blossom and sprout;*
> *And they will fill the whole*
> *World with fruit."*
> *(Isaiah 27:6)*

Isaiah 27:2-3 issues an invitation to *sing about the vineyard* God will keep, water, and protect every moment in the day of Israel's deliverance. In the natural, Israel is already producing fruit and flowers in the desert and shipping them around the world. But there is *spiritual fruit* on the horizon, *new wine* from a *new vineyard* that the Lord will jealously guard. This new wine of *revival* will fill the earth with the knowledge of God.

> *"But you will be called the priests of the Lord;*
> *You will be spoken of as ministers of our God.*
> *You will eat the wealth of nations,*

And in their riches you will boast.
Instead of your shame,
*You will have a **double portion**,*
And instead of humiliation they
Will shout for joy over their portion.
Therefore they will possess
A double portion in their land."
(Isaiah 61:6-7)

There is a *restoration of blessing* coming to the remnant of Israel that will far surpass anything that has been recorded in the Bible.

Israel has received double punishment for her iniquities (Jeremiah 16:18). In these last days, the remnant will receive a double portion of blessing and sparkle like jewels in the Land (Zechariah 9:11-17).

Praise the Lord for His faithfulness, goodness, mercy, and lovingkindness. Pray for a double portion of blessing, anointing, healing, revelation, abundance, and fruitfulness in the Kingdom of God for the remnant of Israel. Pray that God will raise up His priests and ministers to the nations, according to His Word. Pray that everything the enemy has stolen from Israel, spiritually and physically, will be miraculously restored. Pray that all the glorious promises of Isaiah 60, 61, 62, Jeremiah 33:6-13, and Joel 2:18-27 will be fulfilled.

Behold the Lamb

"The blood will be a sign for you
On the houses where you are;
*And when I **see the blood**,*
I will pass over you.
No destructive plague will touch you
When I strike Egypt."
(Exodus 12:13)

The greatest spiritual gift God will be restoring to Israel in these last days is the *Lamb of God*. The Passover feast portrays the most profound prophetic image of the work of redemption in Messiah.

Restoring the Lamb means restoring the significance of the Blood.

Today, the traditional Passover seder (service and meal) is a lamb-less and blood-less, festival, completely missing the sacrifice. The focus has become *leading Israel out of the bondage of Egypt*. While this is cause for celebration, the exodus would have been with much sorrow had the Israelites been unprotected on the eve of their departure. On the first Passover, a young, spotless lamb was slain and the blood applied to the lintel and doorposts so the angel of death would "pass over" the Israelites as it moved through Egypt striking every first-born child.

When God struck Egypt with the final and most horrendous plague that would compel Pharaoh to finally let the people go, He also made a way for His people to escape that plague. When He *saw the blood on a household,* that house would be spared from death. God still needs to "see the Blood" so that the penalty of sin and death will not strike us.

Every year, as Passover draws near and the Orthodox are busy purging the house of even the tiniest fragment of leaven (representing sin), the cry of our hearts during prayerwalks has been, "Lord, give them a revelation of the Blood! As they are dusting and searching for leaven, give them dreams and visions of the Passover Lamb whose Blood still needs to be on the doorposts of our lives, the Blood that cleanses, gives us new life, and causes the angel of death to pass over us."

Pray that, as John the Baptist exclaimed when he first saw Jesus, "Behold, the Lamb of God who takes away the sins of the world! "(John 1:29), the eyes of the Ultra-Orthodox will be opened so that this proclamation resounds in their hearts. Pray that even the children will be granted an understanding of the hidden mystery of the Afikoman, a Greek word, meaning "He has come!" The tradition of breaking a pierced matza in half, wrapping it in a white cloth, hiding it away for the children to find, and then bringing it back for "dessert" was likely established by Messianic believers in the first century.

"The fire and the wood are here,"
Isaac said,
"But where is the lamb
For the burnt offering?"
(Genesis 22:7b)

The central theme of the Bible and highest prayer priority for the Ultra-Orthodox is a revelation of the Lamb of God. When Isaac asked Abraham on the ascent up the mountain, "Where is the lamb?," he well understood that a sacrifice was required for worship, that entering into the Presence of God meant the bringing of a burnt offering. Revelation 13:8 says that the Lamb of God was slain from the foundation of the world, which means that *everything begins with the Lamb*. Everything also *ends with the Lamb*. Revelation 22:1 says that the river of the water of life in the New Jerusalem proceeds from the Throne of God and from the Lamb.

For nearly two thousand years, Satan has been able to steal from the Jewish people the power and promise of the Lamb, the key to salvation.

How was the Lamb stolen? When was the river of life diverted from God's people and when did the blood atonement cease to be a central theme in Jewish thought? It appears that sometime after the destruction of the Second Temple, a respected rabbi, named Yochanan ben Zakkai, experienced a visitation (supposedly from God) which forever changed Judaism. He heard the scripture, "I desire mercy, not sacrifice," which is a very good word and one that Yeshua suggested the Pharisees investigate and learn the meaning of. However, instead of recognizing that Yeshua had fulfilled the requirements of the burnt offering, had been sacrificed for sin once for all and that now *His Blood* is our ongoing atonement, Rabbi Zakkai used this scripture to turn the minds of the Jewish community away from the *necessity of a blood sacrifice.* A false substitute (namely, prayer and fasting) became the sufficient means of redemption. Since this cataclysmic change in theology, Israel has been without a sacrifice, or blood covering, and a blindness and darkness has come upon the nation.

> *"Now Isaac sowed in that land,*
> *And reaped in the same year*
> *A hundred-fold.*
> *And the Lord blessed him."*
> *(Genesis 26:12)*

What is most precious for us who pray for Mea Shearim, is that this neighborhood was named after the hundredfold blessing given to Isaac and Isaac was the one who asked the question about the lamb! The story of the testing of Abraham's faith on Mount Moriah is beloved by Jews everywhere and perhaps the most thrilling message of his faith journey is how the son that God did not require Abraham to sacrifice, He would sacrifice for the world with His own Son. Yeshua taught His disciples about reaping a hundredfold blessing in the parable of sowing seed on good soil. He later shared that the one who sows the good seed is the Son of Man, also known as the Lamb of God.

If everything begins and ends with the Lamb, then praying for a revelation of the question asked by Isaac cannot be something that we pray only at Passover. It is KEY to breaking through deception which keeps Yeshua hidden and to the release of the hundredfold blessing that is yet to be realized in Mea Shearim. Pray that the Ultra-Orthodox, who claim to be the most conscientious of God's laws and truths, will realize that they are uncovered without a sacrifice and that they will begin to cry out for the sacrifice and ask "Where is the lamb?" Pray that the Holy Spirit will visit them with a revelation of the greatest gift of mercy ever given to mankind.

ADDENDUM

(Prayer Points Summary)

Treasures of Darkness was written to inspire prayer. This addendum contains a summary of the suggested ways to pray found throughout the book for easier daily use. Please refer back to the chapters where these prayers are located to re acquaint yourself with the details. The chapter titles are underlined with a brief reminder of the subject followed by suggested prayer. As you pray through these chapters, you will see the words "revelation" and "mercy" appear over and again. These are the pillars of all prayer for the Ultra-Orthodox. God must open their eyes, remove the veil, lift the spirit of slumber, and draw them into His gift of mercy in Messiah.

Preparing For Battle

As we pray for the Ultra-Orthodox, our objective is to make intercession on their behalf, entreat the Lord for mercy, and wage war against the principalities and powers coming against them, so that they may be saved.

As intercessors, we stand before God as *priests* who minister first *unto Him* and then *on behalf of others*...Effective intercession prays with *faith* that God hears our prayers and will answer exceedingly, abundantly, beyond what we could ask or think and is fueled by the *power of the Holy Spirit.* The Spirit lifts our prayers to heaven..., gives utterance when we know not how to pray, and imparts discernment and revelation in the midst of prayer.

The dual strategies of prayer for the priestly army can be seen as a double-edged sword: *intercession and spiritual warfare.* Intercession *cultivates a friendship with God* and moves upon His heart, while spiritual warfare *exposes and confronts strongholds*. Generally speaking, intercession is *addressing God* and appealing for mercy on behalf of a person or nation, and spiritual warfare is *addressing the enemy* and taking authority in the Name of Jesus over the works of darkness in the territory where we have been assigned to pray. Both are the privilege of every believer.

As we pray, let us be encouraged that *Jesus is the Ultimate Intercessor and Spiritual Warrior.* He *disarmed* the enemy on Calvary. We fight from a position of victory. However, we must ensure that we are properly dressed in all the armor of God as we go into battle. We must know the enemy and also *know ourselves.* We must be willing to bring any weaknesses, areas of bondage, or ungodly attitudes to the Lord for healing. I invite you to pray the following prayer with me (or something similar) as we prepare to stand in the gap for the Ultra-Orthodox:

Father God, we present ourselves before You. Search us and know us. Cleanse our hearts, renew our minds, and increase our faith as we intercede and confront the forces of darkness on behalf of the Ultra-Orthodox. We humble ourselves before You. Fill our hearts with love, a jealous love for your people, a holy love that tells the truth, a courageous love that risks its life. As intercessors and prayer warriors, we ask you to bind us together and give us one heart as we stand against the wiles of the devil, the real enemy of your people, the serpent who has hated them from the Garden, even from the pronouncement of judgment that, through the Seed of a woman (Yeshua), his head would be crushed (Genesis 3:15). Purify our hearts, O God. We ask you to search us for any trace of replacement theology, Anti-Semitism, or idolatry of Israel. If any of these are hidden in our hearts, we repent before you now and renounce them. We love your people, stand with them in all their trials and afflictions and present ourselves to You as vessels of intercession, but we devote our hearts of worship to You alone. We rejoice with Israel in all the blessings You will pour out according to your prophetic promises. Holy Spirit, cleanse us now from any unholy or unhealthy attitudes or beliefs which may have been imparted to us through our families, churches, friends, school systems, teachings or from any other source. As we pray, we cover ourselves, our families, and all that is near and dear to us with the precious Blood of Jesus. We ask for angelic protection and a fresh wind of your Spirit over our prayers, and we cancel every assignment of hell against us as we co-labor with You to set the captives free. We pray in the Name of Yeshua, Amen.

My Beloved

Once God captures our hearts, then He can give us the mind of Messiah. This is a love relationship first and last. As we pray for the Ultra-Orthodox, our heartcry must be for God to draw them into the intimate bridal relationship that is their spiritual destiny, and to remove their affection for false lovers.

As intercessors and prayer warriors for the Ultra-Orthodox, we stand in the gap, entreat the Lord for mercy, and do battle on their behalf so that the process of blessing, healing, and restoration of intimacy can begin.

Repentance begins in the house of God. When we look at Israel, we are really looking into a mirror. If we are honest, we would have to confess that at some time in our lives we rejected God. Our prayers for Israel need to begin by repenting for any rejection of God in our own lives for who He really is, for creating a comfortable illusion of what we would like Him to be because it's more pleasant to our souls. We also need to repent for any idolatry in our lives. If we ask Him, the Holy Spirit will shine His Light on any hidden areas that need to be cleansed. Since this is a prayer guide specifically for the Ultra-Orthodox, if you are a Jewish believer, I invite you to repent on behalf of the generations of Israel going all the way back to Samuel, who rejected God as Father and King and the grafted-in believers will stand with you in agreement.

Avinu Malkenu, Our Father, Our King. We thank You for Your faithfulness and precious promise to betroth Your people to Yourself once again. O Lord, woo and allure them into the wilderness and speak tenderly to them according to Your word. We pray they would be satisfied and fulfilled by your love and that you would remove the sword, the bow, and war from the Land. Lavish Your affection upon Your beloved who has suffered so tragically and relentlessly at the *hands of the enemy. Father we pray, in the Name of Yeshua, that you would heal the wound in the heart of Your people and restore them to Your love.*

Our Precious Father, how Your heart must break when we reject You for the ways of the nations. We repent for pushing You away in any area of our lives and re-defining you, not according to Your Word, but according to our flesh. We repent of exalting ANYTHING in our lives made with the hands of man. We repent of all generational idolatry and rejection of You by our ancestors going all the way back to Adam who passed down to us man-made religions of any form. We desire only a personal, intimate relationship, a covenant relationship, with the Living God of Israel. We repent for opening the door to the god of this world, for giving him legal access to our various cultures, identities, and social structures, and, in Yeshua's Name, we proclaim that You alone are Father, King, and Husband over our lives and over Israel. We renounce rejection of God and idolatry in all of its manifestations. We declare that ALL our springs are in You. And we repent, along with our Jewish brothers and sisters, for the generational sin of rejecting You as Father and King going all the way back to Egypt, and most particularly to the elders of Israel in the days of Samuel who demanded an earthly king. We renounce man-made political and religious systems, and every Satanic-inspired form of worship.

In the Name of Jesus, we take back all legal ground that was given to the enemy to steal intimacy from Israel, to kill the Jewish people, and destroy the nation of Israel. We re-claim all the blessings the enemy has stolen from Israel, the apple of Your eye, most particularly the bridal relationship. In the Name of Jesus, we bind the spirit of rejection of God and idolatry away from our personal lives, away from our unsaved relatives, and away from the people of Israel. Capture our hearts, O God, and capture the hearts of the Ultra-Orthodox, so that we may take captive every thought to the obedience of Messiah. In Yeshua's Name we pray, Amen.

Who Are the Ultra-Orthodox?

The Ultra-Orthodox are the modern-day Pharisees. The primary reason for focused prayer for the Ultra-Orthodox is that they are a strategic key to the return of Messiah and end-time evangelism. Those in positions of spiritual authority have the *power* to shut the door of the kingdom of heaven to their disciples. They hold in their hands the souls of men. Our purpose for investigating the culture and beliefs of the Ultra-Orthodox is to expose the works of darkness, identify the pillars of deception, and neutralize, through prayer, every high thing that is exalting itself against the knowledge of God. Our supreme joy is to witness the day when the modern-day Pharisees will greet Yeshua with the Messianic welcome, "Baruch haba B'shem Adonai!"

Father God, perhaps the greatest prayer we could pray for the Ultra-Orthodox is that you would cause the words "Blessed is He who comes in the Name of the Lord" to rise from their lips, however you accomplish this miracle. We thank You that You know the beginning from the end and that all things come to pass in the fullness of time. We praise You that in these last days you are preparing the hearts of the Ultra-Orthodox, the ultimate symbol of religious leadership, to greet and welcome You as Messiah King. We present ourselves as priests to intercede on their behalf and we pray you would anoint and give wings to our prayers that they would rise to heaven and accomplish Your purpose for these end times. In the mighty name of Yeshua we pray, Amen.

Mea Shearim

The focus of intercession and spiritual warfare for this prayer guide is Mea Shearim, the Ultra-Orthodox Chasidic stronghold in the heart of Jerusalem. As the conflict over Jerusalem increases, it is timely that we have been praying over the gates and also for specific streets, yeshivas and synagogues. God invites us as co-laborers in prayer to "pass through the gates," to enter, engage the enemy, and take territory for His Kingdom. Capturing this spiritual fortress is to capture the city for Messiah.

I cannot overstress the spiritual heaviness and oppression hovering like a dark cloud over Mea Shearim. The call to pray and the love of God in our hearts compels us into enemy territory. Nevertheless, there is a backlash to every encounter and it is spiritually, emotionally, and physically demanding. It is extremely important to guard our daily walk with the Lord, put on the full armor, and learn how to pray over ourselves so that the enemy will not overcome us.

Father God, I present myself before you today to search me and know me, to reveal any hidden sin in my heart, that I would confess it, repent of it, and receive forgiveness with thanksgiving. I cover myself with the precious Blood of Jesus and ask the Holy Spirit to breathe upon and empower all my prayers. I put on the full armor of God in Ephesians chapter 6 (in word and also in lifestyle). I ask for a hedge of protection and plead the Blood of Yeshua over my family (marriage, children, parents), my health, finances, possessions, and ministry (or profession), and I bind and rebuke any retaliating spirits that would come against me or anyone close to me. Father, I praise you and thank you that you surround me and all who are near and dear to me with your ministering angels. In Jesus' Name I pray, Amen.

Mea Shearim literally means "100 gates," however the better translation would be "one hundredfold" because the name for the community is based on Genesis 26:12 where God blessed the crops of Isaac a hundredfold.

Let us ask God to bless Mea Shearim a hundredfold! Pray that He will draw them into a personal relationship with Himself through Messiah Yeshua, the one and only Gate of blessing. As Mea Shearim literally means "100 gates," pray that every gate in the spirit realm which has been unwittingly opened to the demonic realm will be CLOSED and SEALED OFF by the Blood of Jesus and that YESHUA, the one and only Gate, will be the sole entry point of salvation, knowledge, light, truth, wisdom, revelation, and heavenly secrets. In Jesus' Name, close every gate to the Kingdom of Darkness, and declare the Gate of Salvation to be OPEN to the people of Mea Shearim that they may enter in and find rest for their souls.

The *Yeshiva & Talmud Torah of Mea Shearim* is the root and foundation of the community, established in 1883. It was the first yeshiva built outside of the Old City walls and is located on a tiny street called Yeshuat Ya'akov ("Salvation of Jacob").

Pray that salvation and revival would begin on Yeshuat Ya'akov Street. Pray that the love of God and the convicting power of the Holy Spirit would be poured out in this dark place and that everything the enemy has stolen from the Ultra-Orthodox, through history, loss of life, tradition, religion, deception, and exile would be restored. Pray that the name of Yeshua would leap off the "Yeshua Building" and grab the attention of residents. Praise the Lord that His Name is already high and lifted up and that He is watching over Mea Shearim even if the community is unaware of His presence. Pray for revelation LIGHT to shine upon the face of Messiah Yeshua and draw the remnant to Himself.

As we pray for the gates of Mea Shearim, declare the promise of Isaiah 60 —that violence will no longer be heard in her borders, and that her walls will be called Yeshua (salvation) and her gates Baruch (praise)!

As we enter David's Gate with prayer and thanksgiving, pray for the anointing of David and the restoration of the fallen tabernacle of David in Mea Shearim. Pray that the growing network of intercessors around the world will be for Mea Shearim a flask of oil poured out in prayer, a horn of anointing poured upon the remnant in the midst of their brothers. Pray that when this horn has been emptied upon the heads of the remnant, the Spirit of the Lord will come upon them MIGHTILY from that day forward as it came upon David. Pray that they will walk in power and boldness of faith, declare Yeshua to be the Messiah, and welcome the Son of David to enter the gates of their community.

Pray protection over Sha'ar Lifta (Gate LIfta) and cover it with the Blood of Jesus. Praise the Lord that the darkness over this particular gate has significantly decreased over the last several years. Pray for the oppression to be completely lifted and welcome Yeshua into this gate as the only way to salvation. Although Gate Lifta currently faces a solidly Jewish area, I believe the Lord would also have us pray for the salvation of the Arabs living in Jerusalem as well as for the remnant of Israel. Jesus loves all peoples and died for the salvation of the world. Jerusalem will eventually be a house of prayer for all nations. As the Palestinians cry "Death to Israelis" and the Israelis (even the

Ultra-Orthodox) shout "Death to Arabs" let us proclaim "Life in Messiah!"

Pray over the Mill Gate, and ask for a revelation of Yeshua, the Bread of Life, the Living Manna, and only source of healthy spiritual food for our souls. His Body and His Blood are the New Covenant. It was during a Passover Seder (the "Last Supper") that Jesus proclaimed this New Covenant in fulfillment of Jeremiah 31:31-32. Pray for a visitation of the Messiah upon the Ultra-Orthodox throughout the year, but especially during the Passover season. Pray that the tiny amulet shop would re-open as a flower shop, fruit juice stand, or some other sort of bright, pleasant business, pleasing to the Lord and that He would PROSPER it.

The Jerusalem Gate reminds us that the spiritual destiny of Jerusalem is to be the praise of the earth and a house of prayer for all nations. Pray that this calling will be fulfilled and that the Ultra-Orthodox of Mea Shearim will be transformed into worshippers in Spirit and in truth of the one true God of Israel and His Son Yeshua. Pray they will be freed from the bondage of individual sects to come together in unity in Messiah. We may also pray for the existing Body of Messiah in Jerusalem to be free of sectarianism and come together in love and unity.

What is first sown in the natural produces a spiritual harvest. This is a Kingdom principle. During prayerwalks, an ongoing cry of our hearts has been, "Oh Lord, cleanse the neighborhood, inside and out! Purify the hearts and sweep the debris from the streets. Restore the buildings and crush the spirit of poverty. Defeat the ghetto mentality. You came to give us life and that abundantly."

Pray for a cleansing and purifying of Mea Shearim in the natural and in the Spirit. Praise the Lord for the prayers He is already answering in the neighborhood. Pray that the life of Messiah would be planted in Mea Shearim, along with decorative trees, flowers, and lush green plants that will delights the eye and inspire the soul. Pray that the Ultra-Orthodox will be set free from the spirit of poverty and isolation so that they can be a blessing in Messiah to Israel and to all the nations of the earth.

The vineyard is a symbol of Israel (Isaiah 5:1-7), new wine (Amos 9:13-14), and the intimate bridal relationship with the Lord (Song of Songs 2:15, 7:12, Hosea 2:14-17). It is thrilling to realize that Mea Shearim was built on ground that was originally called *Kerem Kadkod* ("Ruby Vineyard"). The prophetic picture promises that, within these walls, a flourishing vineyard with sweet new wine will come into being!

Pray prophetically into this revelation. Pray and proclaim that the original walled-in city gated community of Mea Shearim will, even now, begin to produce a fruitful harvest, a vineyard of worshippers washed in the Blood of the Lamb. Pray that new wine will be poured into new wineskins. Pray that the Lord will catch and destroy "the little foxes" that would try to spoil the vineyards that are in bloom. Pray that their surrounding walls (battlements) will be protected, in the Spirit, by the Blood of the Lamb, just like the pillar of fire stood between the Israelites and the Egyptians in the wilderness, and that any attempt to hinder or crush the harvest will be shielded by the fire of God.

Pray for the salvation of the rabbis in all the yeshivas in Mea Shearim and all those in positions of leadership that have a tremendous influence in the local community and around the world. There is a remnant chosen by grace. Pray that the God of Abraham, Isaac and Jacob will DRAW them to His Son, Yeshua, the Messiah of Israel. Pray specifically for the salvation of the heads of yeshivas, the heads of synagogues, heads of rabbinical courts, all influential Torah scholars, leaders of the Shas Party, United Torah Judaism, and the United Religious Party, and leaders of Yad L'Achim, the prominent anti-missionary organization and all who engage in anti-missionary activities. Pray for Damascus Road experiences and ask Yeshua to reveal Himself in dreams, visions and personal visitations. Pray that the Lord will lead those who may already be secret believers to other secret believers so they might encourage one another, pray together, and grow in their faith and their desire to courageously declare their beliefs openly.

Pray also for the salvation of the young Ultra-Orthodox man we met. The Lord knows his name. He was unusually friendly in taking the time to show us around. He even took us inside the smaller yeshiva. Pray that he will be used of the Lord to bring the good news of Messiah to Mea Shearim!

Pray for the salvation of the Ultra-Orthodox lady our sister witnessed to who was hungry for more than religion and curious about the gospel. The Lord knows who she is and that she is hurting, searching and very lonely for friends. Pray that He will bring a new believing friend into her life to water the seed that was planted and pray that she will continue searching for the Book of Isaiah until she reads Chapter 53 in her own Bible. Ask the Lord to confirm the truth that was spoken to her and reveal Himself to her. Pray for the salvation of the men who destroyed the flat of the Swiss ladies. Pray also for the protection of these sisters, that they may be permitted to remain in Israel as long as it is the Lord's will for them to be here.

Pray that Yeshua would visit Mea Shearim as a glorious brilliant light, and that the Holy Spirit would come like a mighty rushing wind causing every effort to resist Him to fail, bringing the Chasidim to their knees so that the PEACE OF GOD can shine from their faces. Pray that this wind will blow away the darkness and the deception and that the light will so overpower the darkness that it can have no place in their lives.

Pray that God will commission His chosen vessels, even the most unlikely men (and women) in far-off lands, to accomplish His plans and purposes for the Ultra-Orthodox in these last days.

The Chasidim

The term *Chasid* refers to pious Jews who maintain the highest standard of observing the religious and moral commandments, or who exhibit exemplary behavior in some aspect of life. The word *Chasidim* means "saints" and comes from the Hebrew word *chesed*, meaning *grace*, literally *saints living by grace!*

Let us speak "grace" over the Chasidim. Pray that the Lord will them give a profound revelation of this amazing gift, that He will open their eyes to see what it means to live under grace and to walk in grace. Pray for a revelation of Yeshua, the true Cornerstone, and the Capstone, who came to extend grace to all who would receive this gift by His shed Blood on Calvary.

The founder of Chasidism was Rabbi Israel ben-Eliezer (1700-1760). Rabbi Israel later became known as the Baal Shem Tov ("Master of the Good Name"). Chasidism was birthed after Rabbi Israel experienced an ascent of soul into the upper worlds where he entered the Chamber of Messiah and received revelations. It was later said that the teacher and master who guided him through this experience was the *Prophet Achiya HaShiloni,* who (it is said) was the master of Elijah the Prophet and from whom Moses received the Oral Tradition.

Let us cry out to God to reveal the truth to the Chasidim, however disturbing it may be, that the Ba'al Shem Tov was visited by a demonic spirit posing as the "soul" of Achiya HaShiloni. In the Name of Yeshua, bind the spirit of Achiya HaShiloni and every familiar spirit that would masquerade as the spirit of Elijah (or any other prophet or sage) from visiting, communicating with, imparting knowledge or revelation, or working miracles among the Chasidim. In love for God's people, and even as a warning, we may even pray that the Lord would allow these spirits to reveal themselves as the hateful, grotesque creatures they really are. Pray that the Holy Spirit will unmask these evil spirits so that the Ultra-Orthodox will know they are not hearing from the heavenly realm, but rather from the very depths of hell.

Pray that the Spirit of Revelation and Truth will expose this deception of the enemy and remove the veil from the eyes of the Chasidim to see that Yeshua, the Holy One of Israel is Messiah and also "God with us," whose goings forth are from the days of eternity. Yeshua does not need to learn Torah because HE IS THE TORAH, the Living Torah, the Word made flesh, the Alpha and the Omega, the One "in whom are hidden all the treasures of wisdom and knowledge." (Colossians 2:3) In the Name of Jesus, bind every lying and deceptive spirit attached to this false revelation of Messiah that was given to Rabbi Israel that diminishes His glory and deity. Yeshua fulfilled 100 primary Old Testament prophecies in His first advent 2,000 years ago. Pray that every false messiah will be rejected and that the Chasidim will return to BIBLICAL PROPHECY as the only source of truth revealing who Messiah is. Pray they will repent of accepting mystical experiences as truth over and above the Word of God. Pray they would be freed from distorted interpretations of Messianic prophecies in the Jewish commentaries and would search the Scriptures for themselves to see the fulfillment of these prophecies in Yeshua.

The Baal Shem Tov claimed that he made his ascent of soul using "holy names." The Bible says that Satan *masquerades* as an angel of light (II Corinthians 11:14). He is a created being and, therefore, he cannot create anything original. However, he can *imitate everything that is godly* and, thereby, deceive many.

Pray that this doctrine of demons concerning the holy names of God and the three segulot, this clever imitation of the triune nature of God, will be exposed, uprooted and replaced with the TRUTH of the compound unity of the God of Israel who is Father, Son, and Holy Spirit. Pray for a revelation of the life-giving truth that a Holy Name has been given to all mankind, Jew and Gentile alike, a Name that grants us a new and living way into the very Holy of Holies. Declare to every principality and power, in heaven, in earth and under the earth that Yeshua is the NAME ABOVE ALL NAMES. There is only one Name we have been given, the Name of Jesus. There is salvation in no other Name, healing in no other Name, deliverance in no other Name. Pray that these blessed truths would be revealed to the Ultra-Orthodox. Cry out to the Lord for a spiritual awakening among the Ultra-Orthodox in these last days that will bring them back to the God of Israel and His Word and deliver them from mystical experiences.

According to Chasidic tradition, revealing the "secrets" of Kabbalah to this latter generation prepares the Jewish people for the advent of Messiah.

Pray for a revelation that the secrets of God (as opposed to the secrets of Kabbalah) are shared with only those who are His own (Matthew 13:11) in the Messiah, those who come to Him as little children (Matthew 11:25-26). We need to pray that the eyes of their hearts will be enlightened to understand that the SOURCE of Kabbalah is demonic and that it can never lead them to the true Messiah, only to a counterfeit, as it already has in the case of Rabbi Schneerson. Pray that all hope will be lost in the return of Rabbi Schneerson, that the Lubavitcher Chasidim will turn to Yeshua and not to any other false messiah. Pray that they will know the hope to which the God of Abraham, Isaac and Jacob has called them, the only Messianic hope there is - Yeshua. Pray that the veil will be lifted from their minds to realize what Kabbalah really is and renounce its theology which has superceded study of the Bible, the Word of God. Pray that the Lord will rescue them from the enemy's camp where they have unwittingly built their spiritual houses. Ask the Lord to have mercy on them as He had mercy on us when we were lost in our own form of deception and darkness.

Pray that the Lord would open the spiritual eyes of the Chasidim (just as He opened the eyes of Elisha to see the angelic armies of God) and cause them to SEE and BECOME AWARE of the presence of evil spirits (segulot) in the mystical religion they are practicing, that they would become skeptical, curious, dissatisfied, hungry for the truth and would search the Hebrew Scriptures diligently for themselves.

Tikkun, or self-rectification, is the pursuit of Chasidic thought. The gift of God, purchased with the Blood of Messiah Yeshua, is redemption. Only God can transform our nature, by the power of the Holy Spirit, and conform us to the image of Messiah.

Pray that every deception convincing the Chasidim that "tikkun" is possible in their own strength will be exposed by the light of God's Word. Pray that God will reveal to them the true condition of their soul. Jeremiah 17:9 says that the heart (or the soul) is deceitful above all things and <u>beyond cure</u>. Pray that the Lord will reveal to them His desire is to give them a new heart. Pray the Lord will open their eyes to this basic truth that will set them free and be the beginning of healing and deliverance.

Pray the Lord will open the understanding of the Chasidim to see through the deception that everything has a soul, and that the soul is somehow sacred and should reign supreme. Pray also that the stronghold of relating to God through WORKS rather than faith in the FINISHED WORK of Messiah will be completely shattered. When Yeshua said, "Take my yoke upon you. My yoke is easy and my burden is light (Matthew 29:28-30)," He was referring to His yoke of grace. Daily, the Ultra-Orthodox put on the yoke of Torah (including 613 commandments). As a prophetic act and declaration to all the principalities in the spirit realm, lift off the yoke of Torah (a burden which neither they nor their fathers could bear) and place upon them the yoke of Messiah, the yoke of grace.

Pray that God would reveal to the Chasidim that in the presence of Jehovah there is FULLNESS OF JOY and the ultimate purpose of worship is to usher us into His Presence so that we may adore Him and be changed from glory to glory by His marvelous light, not to achieve oneness with divinity. Pray that God would restore the gift and power of genuine, deep repentance to the Ultra-Orthodox and that out of the ashes of repentance would come a hundredfold blessing and the joy of the Lord as their strength.

The life of the Chasid is intimately connected to the *tzaddik* just as the life of the believer is intimately connected to Jesus. The intermediary role of the tzaddik is KEY to the pervasive control they have over their disciples.

Pray that the Holy Spirit will reveal that Yeshua alone is the mediator between God and man. He has made the way, through His Blood, to intimate communication with God. Heaven wants a personal relationship with the Chasidim. Pray that the tzaddikim, who serve as mediators, would be given a strong revelation of the deception in which they have been partaking and a profound revelation of their own sin in allowing themselves to be exalted to the position of gods in the lives of their disciples. Pray that they would repent, humble themselves before God and release their flock to seek and find a personal relationship with the God of Israel through Jesus the Messiah.

Pray that God would graciously reveal to the Chasidim that Yeshua has made a new and living way for their sin to be removed and for their prayers to reach heaven. Pray that God, according to His promises in Zechariah 13:1-2, would remove the idols and the unclean spirits from Jerusalem and that a spirit of purity and repentance would *be released. Pray that Yeshua, the only pure and true Tzaddik, will be revealed, and that they will adore Him and cleave only to Him.*

The Mitnagdim

For purposes of prayer, it is essential to appreciate that both the Chasidim and the Mitnagdim embrace Kabbalah and consciousness of the serious nature of sin and value of deep repentance as described in the Scriptures has been greatly diminished.

Pray for an outpouring of the love of God and a spirit of true repentance upon the Chasidim and the Mitnagdim. Pray also for a breaking of the spirit of intellectualism and superiority among the Mitnagdim. Pray for deliverance from mysticism for both groups and a return to the Word of God as the highest source of truth.

Pray that the Lord will turn the zeal of the Neturai Karta (which means "Watchman on the Walls" — an extremely zealous fringe group of the Ultra-Ultra Orthodox) toward the gospel just as He did with Saul of Tarsus, who persecuted believers every bit as much as these "watchmen" before he met Yeshua on the Damascus Road. Pray that even one of them will receive a powerful revelation of the Messiah and be turned completely around. Pray that they will fulfill the call to be intercessors on the walls of Jerusalem and witnesses for Messiah.

Kabbalah

Kabbalah, a mystical trend, exploring the "hidden wisdom" of Scripture, has served as an entryway for the occult, false doctrine, and familiar spirits to tamper with the people of God.

Pray that the God of Abraham, Isaac, and Jacob would satisfy the hunger of His precious chosen people for supernatural experiences with a revelation and visitation of Yeshua, the only One who can fulfill the deepest longings of our soul. Pray their eyes would be opened to the verses in Deuteronomy that strictly forbid witchcraft, sorcery, and consulting the dead (even dead sages). Pray the Ultra-Orthodox will come to recognize the dangerous occultic nature of Kabbalah.

Pray for the mercy and compassion of God upon the Ultra-Orthodox. Pray for deep revelation and profound discernment against permitting any "spirit" other than the Holy Spirit of the Living God to "enter their soul." Pray their eyes will be opened to the demonic spirits behind this belief system and that they will close the door of their hearts to any supposed spirit of a past sage. Pray their hunger for spiritual fulfillment, wisdom, and revelation will be found only in a living relationship with Yeshua the Messiah.

Pray for an outpouring of the love of God upon the Ultra-Orthodox that touches their heart and convinces them of God's great love and personal concern for them. In the Name of Jesus, bind every spirit of idolatry that exalts any sage to a level of holiness where his graveside would be worthy as a place of prayer. Pray that the Chasidim will discover Psalm 62 inviting them to pour out their hearts to the God of Israel, who is their refuge in times of trouble. In the Name of Yeshua, bind every lying spirit that would suggest that God is abstract and cannot be touched by or relate to human sorrows - in other words, the sages are really there for us, but God may not be. Pray that the lovingkindness of the Lord will lead them to repentance.

Pray for the salvation of this widow that was tormented by the departed spirit of her husband. Pray for lasting freedom from all demonic oppression through Messiah Yeshua. Pray for the salvation of the rabbi who "ministered" to her that he will receive a genuine gift of discerning spirits. Bind deception and confusion. Pray that the Body of Messiah will not allow emotionalism, or other sentimentalities, to cloud, dilute or compromise the truth of the Word. There is no question that God loves the widow and the rabbi and desires the widow to be free. That is one aspect of the truth. Another aspect of the truth is that ALL OF US are lost until we are found and salvation is found in no other name than the Name of Jesus and deliverance, in the Name of Jesus, is only one of the many blessings of salvation.

Pray that the Lord will give the Body of Messiah wisdom so they will know how to minister the truth to the Jewish people regarding Kabbalah. There is much spiritual confusion in Jerusalem and perhaps around the world. For example, in witnessing to and praying for a secular Israeli woman, I was sharing that God answers prayer, which is simply conversing with the Father in Yeshua's Name, and He will answer her prayers in Yeshua's Name just the same as mine. I have no "special powers." When I pray, it is not "my Kabbalah" as opposed to "someone else's Kabbalah." Please pray that the Lord will give her understanding.

I encourage you to keep Hebrews 7:23-25 close by whenever you pray for the Ultra-Orthodox. Yeshua is *alive* and He ever lives to stand before the Father as our Advocate, Mediator, and Intercessor. His Blood redeems us and turns the wrath of God from us completely.

Pray that these precious truths will be graciously revealed to the Ultra-Orthodox. Pray for the mercy of God to lift the veil so they may know there is protection from evil forces, provided exclusively by the Blood of Yeshua. We have AUTHORITY over the enemy because of the Blood of Messiah. We do not need to depend on "luck." We have been given POWER in the Holy Spirit. Pray that every lie of the enemy, deceiving the Ultra-Orthodox into believing that <u>anyone</u> (man or woman, dead or alive) other than Jesus can stand before the God of Israel as a mediator on their behalf, will be exposed and renounced. Pray that the Lord will deliver the Ultra-Orthodox (and all Judaism) from the system of kabbalistic blessing and cursing and bring them into the Light of Messiah.

Isaiah 9:16 speaks of the *confusion* brought upon the Jewish people by false teachings that lead them astray.

Father, we thank You that you are not the author of confusion. We thank You that the Ultra-Orthodox are hungry for communion with You. You are greater and mightier than any false system of revelation and you knew the devices the enemy would use against your people even before the foundation of the earth. Father, we pray in the Name of Yeshua, that you would unveil the deception of Kabbalah to your Jewish people, particularly the Ultra-Orthodox, that you would unmask the evil spirits behind it, that you would expose every inconsistency of this occultic system with Scripture. We pray for your mercy, grace, and compassion upon every person who has become ensnared and taken captive by the enemy through Kabbalah and we pray, in the Name of Jesus, that you would lead them to freedom. We pray for the convicting work of the Holy Spirit and your lovingkindness to lead to repentance for exalting esoteric teachings above your Word, for entertaining false doctrines, for accepting reincarnation, astrology, using amulets, and seeking spiritual experiences beyond the boundaries of Your revealed Word. We pray for the full restoration of the Word of God to the position of highest, ultimate authority, the final word of truth in their lives. In the Name of Jesus, we bind confusion away from the Ultra-Orthodox and loosen a sound mind upon every genuine seeker to read and understand the intent of Scripture as inspired by the Holy Spirit. We pray for the full restoration of an intimate, personal relationship and fellowship with You through Yeshua, the Messiah, the Holy One of Israel. We pray that every high thing the enemy has planted to lead the Ultra-Orthodox astray will be torn down and that the Kingdom of God will be planted in their midst.

Tzimtzum

The doctrine of *tzimtzum* (a Kabbalistic theory asserting that God *withdrew* or *contracted within Himself* in to create the universe) is the result of *mixing* the truth of Scripture with extra-biblical resources, such as the Zohar. This dangerous practice distorts or perverts the truth and opens the door for demonic activity.

Pray for FREEDOM from all doctrines of demons (such as holy sparks) and an IMPARTATION of discernment to separate truth from error. Pray that the Lord will deliver the Ultra-Orthodox from MIXING the Word of God with any other source, however sacred it may be to Judaism, however many centuries it has been considered precious, however it may depart from unquestioned traditions. Pray that the Lord will untangle the web of deception that surrounds the BASIC APPROACH to Scripture. Nothing is too difficult for Thee! Pray that the Lord will grant revelation knowledge that every angel is not necessarily a "good angel." Pray that the Light of Messiah Yeshua will penetrate the darkness of Kabbalah and draw the Ultra-Orthodox into a personal, intimate relationship with the God of Israel.

Pray for a revelation that, while the glory of God is everywhere present in His glorious creation, the MANIFEST PRESENCE of God does not abide in all places. We can know this for sure because the glory departed from the Temple and even from the Old City of Jerusalem (Ezekiel 11:23) and always departs in the presence of sin, evil, and idolatry. His glory returns whenever there is a returning to God in repentance with all our heart, soul, and mind and approach to Him through the provision of the new and living way of His Son and Mediator, Messiah Jesus.

Pray for a profound revelation of this false gospel being preached to the Ultra-Orthodox through Kabbalah. Pray they would recognize the deception, the demonic source of these doctrines, repent of opening their hearts to it, and turn to the true gospel of salvation in Messiah Yeshua.

Pray for a revelation of the blessed truth that there was ONE TIME when God voluntarily LIMITED HIMSELF, but not by contracting. There was one time when, in miraculous fulfillment of prophecy, God chose to humble Himself by taking on the form of man, even of a baby. God took up space ONE TIME in the sense that if the Messiah was sitting on a chair you could not sit on the same chair He was sitting on, but at the same time, HE CREATED everything composing that chair (the wood, the nails, the elements, every last molecule). If Yeshua would cease to exist for even a moment, that chair would instantly disintegrate because ALL THINGS were created by Him and THROUGH HIM all things consist, literally hold together (Colossians 1:16-17).

Pray that the Ultra-Orthodox would be TRANSFERRED from the Kingdom of Darkness to the Kingdom of Light through the Blood of Messiah Yeshua (Colossians 1:-13-14). Pray they will come to acknowledge that the Son of Man and Son of God came as the Redeemer to REVEAL the Father (John 14:8-10), to be the very image and expression of the invisible God, so that Israel (and subsequently all mankind) could draw near and enter the very Holy of Holies by His Blood. He is the Way to the Father (John 14:6) so that man need not (and truly cannot) ascend through a complex maze of sefirot, redeeming sparks all along the way, to reach the Divine Majesty and secure his own redemption.

The Rabbinic Spirit

Kings, priests, and prophets were the established offices of God in the Bible. The rabbinic spirit has to do with the question of authority. Is the authority of the rabbis from God or from man? Crisis points in Israel's history became the perfect opportunity to create human solutions and systems of worship for self-preservation. Whenever we "make gods" to rescue us (Exodus 32:1), we separate ourselves from the resources of heaven and break covenant with God.

Pray that God will reveal the sin of breaking covenant with Him, of manufacturing our own gods in order to preserve our identity, our nation, our family, our career, or our ministry. I invite you to repent with me for any times in our walk with God where we have "broken covenant" with Him by resorting to our own methods of deliverance in a crisis and failing to depend completely upon Him. Let us repent for the sin of constructing religious substitutes for waiting on God until He comes back down the mountain.

Pray that God will create an insatiable hunger in the hearts of the Ultra-Orthodox for a personal relationship with Him, as the patriarchs had, a hunger that won't take no for an answer, a hunger that desires beyond the outward covenant of circumcision, and ignites a passion in the heart to hear the voice of God and have the assurance of redemption that Yeshua promises to all those who put their faith in Him.

Our identity in Messiah Jesus is the only identity that will ultimately bring us peace, joy, and fulfillment, and glorify our Father in heaven.

Pray that the God of Israel would impart a fresh revelation of the Hebraic roots to the Ultra-Orthodox, even to Messianic believers (and to the Church), and re-direct their focus towards the God of Abraham, Isaac, and Jacob, the Word of God itself, and Yeshua, the promised Messiah. Pray that He will reveal to them their high calling and destiny to bring Jesus, not Judaism, to the nations. Pray for FREEDOM from every false identity defined by man and an EMBRACING of their true identity as a Covenant people of God, an identity that can only be fulfilled and enjoyed in Messiah Yeshua Himself.

Pray for the total collapse of every system of "power and might." As God wrestles with His people to subdue their strength and change them as He did the patriarch Jacob, pray they will yield to Him, resist anger, cynicism, and dependence on worldliness or humanism, and cry out to Yeshua, who is their only salvation. We may want to take a moment to repent for any times in our own lives where we have created life-rafts to help God keep us or something in our lives afloat, where we have mixed together a glue of seeming godliness that results in thwarting His purposes for us and hindering our relationship with Him. Pray the Lord will do a deep work in the hearts of His people (even believers) to come completely out of the bondage of Egypt and into the Kingdom of Light. Pray He will grant discernment to be able to separate the truth of Scriptures from rabbinic conjecture.

The rabbis say that the Written Law (the Holy Scriptures) and the Oral Law are one and cannot be separated. In other words, they are *bound together.* The Word of God says that He has given believers authority to bind and to loose, in Yeshua's Name.

Let us agree in prayer to LOOSE (to sever) the bonds of the Written Law and the Oral Law, to separate them in the spirit realm, to break the unholy and unauthorized connection between the two established by the rabbis (not the Word of God), and BIND (tie, attach) to the hearts and minds of the Ultra-Orthodox (and all Jewish people) only the written, inspired Word of God. Pray that the deception and lie that the Oral Law was given to Moses on Mount Sinai and is equal to or even above the Scriptures would be exposed and rejected.

Pray that every unholy, unhealthy soul tie will be broken between rabbis (and their yeshiva students) and the Talmud, the Zohar, and Kabbalah. Pray also that soul ties between the tzaddikim and their disciples would be severed. Pray that the Holy Spirit will reveal the divine inspiration of Holy Scripture ALONE and create a hunger to return to the pure Word of God in the yeshivas. Pray that the rabbis will repent, for themselves and on behalf of the generations going all the way back to the earliest pairs of ancient teachers, called zugoth, of having used the Oral Law to manipulate and control the lives of their disciples.

Yavneh became the center of rabbinic authority when the Sanhedrin (the Jewish governing body consisting of 70 elders) was transferred from Jerusalem to this coastal city in 70 A.D. At Yavneh, there was a ruling *re-defining who is Jewish.* Based on this decision, Jews who "converted" to Christianity would no longer be considered Jews. This decision would affect future generations of Jews and also created the opportunity for the Church to break from their Hebraic roots. In May 1999, a group of American Messianic Jews, grafted-in believers, Israeli believers, and Messianic pastors traveled to Yavneh to repent, uproot what had been planted in history, and plant, in the spirit, the seeds of healing and restoration.

Praise God for the strategic spiritual warfare He is inspiring in Israel in our day. God is digging down and pulling up the roots that are hindering revival. Pray that the victory experienced in the spirit at Yavneh will be manifested in the natural and that the power of the decision at Yavneh will be BROKEN over the Jewish people. This lie has been a major stumbling block for centuries. The Lord is taking the obstacles out of the way of His people and preparing a highway for His coming! A similar group went to Masada to break the spirit of death, suicide and oppression over that region. Pray that the heaviness over Masada will be lifted and that NEW LIFE will spring forth in the Dead Sea desert.

In the midst of the Bar Kokhba Revolt (132-135 A.D.), Rabbi Akiba ben Joseph declared Simeon ben Kosiba to be the Messiah. Rabbi Akiba changed ben Kosiba's name to *Bar Kokhba* (meaning *"son of the star"*) so that it would give messianic legitimacy based on Numbers 24:17. This declaration enforced the authority of the rabbis and also forced the followers of Yeshua to withdraw from the revolt, causing them to be declared traitors, and effectively cutting them out of the Jewish loop. Rabbi Akiba would become the "father of Judaism" and his interpretations of Scripture affect the Jewish people to the present day.

Repentance precedes revival and revelation. John the Baptist emerged from the wilderness, preaching, "Repent, for the kingdom of God is at hand," and the multitudes came, confessing their sins, and were immersed (baptized) preparing the way for Messiah. Shortly thereafter,

Yeshua was revealed as the "Lamb of God." Repentance begins in the house of God. How we interpret Scripture is an indicator of our maturity and the depth of our relationship with the Living God. It can have a powerful effect, even a "binding" effect, on those we influence.

I entreat each one of us to humbly and honestly come before God and repent of any times we have forced or concocted an interpretation of God's Word to advance our own interests. Repent for any damaging effects our conclusions may have had on others. As the One New Man, let us repent on behalf of the rabbis, going all the way back to Rabbi Akiba (even the sages who influenced him), for distorting God's Word for the purpose of securing power over their disciples and even over the Scriptures themselves, and also repent for faulty interpretations of the Church (such as replacement theology) which have caused it to disconnect from its Hebraic roots.
In Jesus' Name, cancel every effect of these soulish decisions that have "bound" the Jewish people to the decisions of the "majority" and loosen freedom to pursue the pure, undefiled truth of God based solely on the authority of Scripture, even if it means standing alone. Pray that the manipulation of Torah to further the power of the rabbis would be exposed. Pray that the rabbinic SYSTEM of interpretation would be challenged in the yeshivas by those who are hungry for an honest, personal relationship with God and that this system, which is "not in heaven," would crumble. Call forth the Kingdom of Heaven to rise in the hearts of the Ultra-Orthodox.

The Talmud speaks of *erecting a safeguard around* the Torah (Aboth 1:1), which is nowhere commanded by God, so that it would not be willfully trespassed or damaged. In reality, the fence restricted the Jewish people from getting to the heart of the Scriptures, but it didn't restrict the rabbis, who apparently crashed the fence whenever it was deemed *reasonable or necessary*. It is also created a dependence upon the rabbis for instruction. This dependence has created the perfect environment for the *mind-control spirit* to flourish.

In the mighty Name of Yeshua, we tear down the fence in the spirit realm that restricts God's people from His Word and from discovering the Living Torah and we proclaim that access to the Scriptures is now unlimited! We invite God's people to CHARGE towards the Word.

(The image the Lord gave me is similar to when the Berlin Wall came down. People were tearing it down brick by brick with their bare hands, pulling away the barbed wire, and leaping over the wall to freedom.) Let us declare FREEDOM to the captives, liberty to approach the Scriptures and be led by the Spirit to interpret the verses after the heart of God.

In the Name of Yeshua, bind the spirit of mind control from operating in the lives of the Ultra-Orthodox and pray that the rabbis will be freed from the control the kingdom of darkness has over their own minds and the minds of their followers through them. Pray the Ultra-Orthodox will desire to break away from this unhealthy system of bondage and desire to pursue the truth prayerfully through honest personal study of the Scriptures. Pray for a revelation of Yeshua among the rabbis and that they would be blessed with the "mind of Messiah" and the heart of a shepherd after the Lord's own heart. Pray that they would repent, humble themselves before God and release their flock to seek and find a personal relationship with the God of Israel.

Lag B'Omer is celebrated with bonfires in every Ultra-Orthodox neighborhood. It is not a biblical holiday, but occurs between Passover and Pentecost (Shavuot). Lag B'Omer is a day of rejoicing because it commemorates the death of Shimon Bar Yochai (author of the Zohar). When Rabbi Yochai died, a "supernatural fire" suddenly appeared over his grave site. This "miracle" caused people to believe he was a holy sage. The people rejoice because when a sage dies, it is said, his soul "goes to higher levels" and he becomes an "advocate" for the Jewish people. It is believed that fire is a symbol of Torah and the fire of Torah is the Jewish people.

Oh Lord, send YOUR FIRE, the true fire of Pentecost, to the Ultra-Orthodox! Send the fire of the Holy Spirit! Cry out to God that their thirst for the FIRE OF TORAH will be quenched in Yeshua, the Living Torah. Pray that the veil of Rabbinic Judaism, which has blinded the eyes of the Ultra-Orthodox, kept them in bondage to mysticism and the false holiness of the "sages," keeps them distanced from their Heavenly God who loves them and hinders them from discovering the precious Messianic promises in the Scriptures, will be torn away and every deception will be exposed. The Bible says we have an

Advocate with the Father (I John 2:1) who ever lives to intercede for us (Hebrews 7:25) and His name is Yeshua! Pray that they will be delivered from idolatry and the LIE that any person, other than Yeshua, can "intercede" for them in heaven.

The Bible says in Isaiah 5:24 that the root of the tree of His people would become rotten because they rejected the Word of the Holy One of Israel. These are sorrowful words, but it is not the end of the story. We have researched the roots of Rabbinic Judaism because the rabbinic spirit, which hovers like a spiritual canopy over Mea Shearim, is not an obscure nameless, faceless spirit. The sages who laid this foundation have names and their spirits are still very much with us exerting tremendous influence over the modern community. We can rejoice that Isaiah 6:13 promises that when the mighty oak is cut down and consumed, there will be a *holy seed,* a remnant that will remain and be its stump.

Let us first speak prophetically to Mea Shearim (and all Israel) and proclaim that Yeshua is the pure and true Root of their faith and ours (Revelation 22:16). Yeshua is the Lamb that was slain before the foundation of the world, the Offspring of David, the bright Morning Star, and the Branch that will reign in righteousness forever. Let us declare that Jesus is the Solid Rock of Israel, the Firm Foundation, Chief Cornerstone, the Author and Finisher of our faith.

Praise the Lord for the precious promise for the remnant. In the Name of Jesus, we call forth the holy seed, and we come against every name that has been exalted to a position of undisputed authority, even to idolatry, in the history of Israel going all the way back to Egypt. In the Name of Yeshua, we break every soul tie and spirit tie with the founders and sages of Rabbinic Judaism and Chasidism, in particular Rabbi Yohanan ben-Zakkai, Rabbi Akiba ben Joseph, Rabbi Israel ben-Eliezer (the Ba'al Shem Tov), and Rabbi Shimon Bar Yochai. In the Name of Yeshua, we break the power of the rabbinic spirit over the lives of the Ultra-Orthodox. We place upon them the authority of Yeshua and the freedom and liberty of the Holy Spirit. We uproot the OAK of Rabbinic Judaism, the tree of false religion, that the enemy has planted and, in its place, we plant the OLIVE TREE of the patriarchs, the tree of relationship with the God of Israel, and the vineyard of new wine and new life in Messiah Yeshua. Pray for a restoration of the true priesthood, the spiritual Zadokites, who draw near to minister to the Lord. Call forth the remnant and the highway to Zion, a highway for the holy seed to come into the Kingdom of God and into His Presence, where there is fullness of joy.

The Religious Spirit

The religious spirit is the source of all *spiritual pride* and has to do with issues of self-righteousness, seeking to establish your own righteousness before God through works, inevitably leading to pretension and hypocrisy. *Love* is the highest expression of the heart of God in every circumstance and there is no law that love breaks in its kindness and mercy.

Pray for mercy to pour over the Ultra-Orthodox. Pray they would be led by the Spirit and so become sons of God. Pray for a breaking of the yoke of the religious spirit and for freedom from self-righteousness and hypocrisy, the never ending, tormenting cycle of living a lie. Pray for the Holy Spirit to gently and lovingly convict their hearts of sin (original sin and absolute evil, not simply an "evil inclination"), righteousness, and judgment, to convince them that they can never enter the Kingdom of God through good works, that a fountain of grace is open to them in the Messiah. Pray they will be granted a vision of Yeshua, who is the righteousness of God, the One through whom we stand justified and righteous before a Holy God. Pray for a revelation of the GIFT of salvation freely available by FAITH. This gift cost the Heavenly Father everything, even His only Son. Pray for an impartation of the spirit of humility and the power to receive this amazing gift of grace and not disregard it as a "cheap means" of redemption. Pray that they will run to Yeshua in holy desperation and find rest for their souls. Pray for an outpouring of new wine into new wineskins.

Relationship is rooted in *love*. Religion is rooted in *laws*. Relationship is God-initiated, but religion is man-initiated. Everything that God does with Israel is fueled by the passion of this desire: *"You will live in the Land I gave your forefathers; you will be My people, and I will be your God."* (Ezekiel 36:28)

Pray that the Lord will draw Israel back into the intimate, bridal relationship that is her destiny, that the remnant chosen by grace will truly become God's people, and fulfill their calling to be witnesses to the nations. Pray that the heart of stone will soon be replaced by a heart of flesh in fulfillment of His promise in Ezekiel 36.

Pray for a revelation of the precious truth that ONLY GOD can bring us safely into eternal life through the BLOOD OF MESSIAH and no other way. He has made the impossible possible and lifted the heavy yoke. Pray for understanding that the "works of God" are simple – to believe in the Messiah as Redeemer and Lord (John 6:28). Pray for the exposing and renouncing of the religious spirit among the Ultra-Orthodox and a complete deliverance from legalism and spiritual pride. Pray that as they come to faith in Messiah, a fresh anointing to pray, worship, and move in the gifts of the Spirit will be released.

Every year, all over Israel, particularly during the season preceding Yom Kippur, on-going seminars called *Aracheim* ("Values of Life") are presented for the purpose of drawing Jewish people (especially young men) back to God. These seminars are also called *tshuva* (which means "repentance"). On the surface, this sounds great. Of course, these seminars are designed to draw them into Torah Judaism, and the Ultra-Orthodox lifestyle.

Pray that everyone attending these seminars would indeed find the God of Israel and the Moses of the Bible, because Yeshua said, "If you believed Moses, you would believe me." We can boldly pray that they find Moses, because if they TRULY find Moses and believe His words, it will lead them to Yeshua. Pray for FREEDOM from the laws and traditions of men that only create burdens and busyness and hinder intimacy with God. Pray that the strongholds of the mind would be broken, the notion that simply because something has been done for centuries it is necessarily good or godly. Pray especially that the rabbis leading the Tshuva movement would be encountered on the Damascus Road, find the God of Abraham, Isaac & Jacob, AND Moses and that God would bless them and use them to pioneer Messianic repentance seminars leading to salvation!

False Messiahs

There are conflicting views of Messiah in Judaism, ranging from belief that the Messiah will come *when we are worthy* to the broader view that the *messianic potential* is within every soul and the *messianic age* is a state of utopian paradise achieved after centuries of *progressive improvement.* As Judaism moved further from the Biblical prophecies regarding His identity, false messiahs emerged throughout the ages.

Praying for a revelation of Yeshua as Messiah, Son of God, and God the Son, is one of the most powerful prayers we can pray for the Ultra-Orthodox. Flesh and blood cannot reveal Jesus, but only the Father in Heaven (Matthew 16:17). We should also pray for visitations of Yeshua revealing Himself as Lord and King.

Pray for an utter disillusionment with false messiahs and a return to the prophetic Scriptures as the only source of revelation concerning the identity and dual purposes for the Messiah (Suffering Servant/ Redeemer King).

Pray for a breaking of the generational practice of relying on spirit guides, particularly the familiar spirit of Achiya HaShiloni, and the stealing and perverting of the purposes and promises of God through false impersonations and visitations to past sages. Pray that this stronghold, particularly as it relates to revelations regarding the identity of Messiah, will be completely defeated and that the Word of God will be restored as the only guidepost to every issue of life.

The Tabernacle

Some of the most powerful imagery in the Scriptures illustrating the person and purposes of Messiah are seen in the construction of the Tabernacle. Every detail foreshadows some aspect of the life of Messiah and describes how we are ushered into the presence of God.

The Ultra-Orthodox love mysteries and there is a treasure house to be explored in the Tabernacle. Even the disciples needed to have their minds opened to fully comprehend who Yeshua was. Pray for a revelation of the mystery of the Person, Provision, and Purposes of

Messiah as expressed in the symbols of the Tabernacle. There were three articles of furniture in the Tabernacle that had crowns and each is connected to fellowship with God. They speak of the three offices Messiah would fulfill. The Golden Table foreshadows Messiah as Prophet, the Golden Altar as Priest, and the Ark of the Covenant as King. Pray for a revelation that Messiah Jesus wears all three crowns. Pray for a revelation of the symbolism in the colors used for the curtain hangings and cherubim embroidered upon them that speak of the holiness and righteousness of Messiah. Blue represents His heavenly origin, purple His royalty, and scarlet His suffering for our sins.

Pray for a revelation that Yeshua is the only meeting place between God and man, and the veil, which separated the sacred from the secular, represents Messiah and His righteousness that now shuts the world OUT and the believer IN with God in the secret place of intimate fellowship. Pray for a revelation that the God of Israel has provided the Way to enter in and draw near by the Body and Blood of Yeshua. Pray for a revelation that Yeshua is the only true tzaddik, the Lawgiver and Lawkeeper. He is the real Ark of the Covenant. He is the only Mediator and Advocate we have with the Father. The law is hidden in Him, so now grace can flow. Pray for a revelation of the profound mercy and grace of God in Messiah symbolized by the Mercy Seat because it is here that we experience the deepest communion with God because of the finished work of Yeshua.

Pray that the Book of Hebrews (detailing the fascinating shadows and imagery of the Tabernacle) would be discreetly shared with Ultra-Orthodox seekers, along with the Gospel of Matthew (presenting many Messianic prophecies Yeshua fulfilled). Pray that a special booklet combining the Gospel of Matthew and the Book of Hebrews translated into Hebrew and Yiddish would be made available especially for the Ultra-Orthodox. Pray that if this prayer ministry is to be the instrument of preparing this special booklet, that the Lord would provide all the resources to produce it.

Rolling Away The Reproach

Rolling away the reproach is removing the heavy burden, bringing the remnant into their full inheritance, spiritual and earthly, and restoring what has been captured or relinquished by sin. We pray for the Ultra-Orthodox because there is a high calling upon them to be ministers and witnesses that God wants to restore.

Gracious Heavenly Father, we pray in the Name of Yeshua, that just as Israel has once again set its feet in the Promised Land after 2,000 years in exile, you would roll away the reproach of Egypt. We pray you would roll away the reproach of the nations, the reproach of the "holy war" of Islam, the reproach of the religious spirit, the reproach and spiritual bondage of Rabbinic Judaism and the yoke of Torah upon the Ultra-Orthodox, that neither they nor their fathers could bear. In the Name of Yeshua, we place upon them the favor of the nations and the yoke of Messiah — the yoke of love, gentleness and humility, the yoke of grace. We pray that Messiah would be revealed and that You would call out those who are appointed to be apostolic ministers and witnesses of the gospel, to suffer for the sake of His Name, and receive their full inheritance both in this life and the life to come. We pray that the anointing that rested upon the Apostle Paul would rest again in even greater measure upon your end-time servants. We pray that the promise of the enduring city will so compel your servants in these last days that considerations of suffering will be as nothing compared to the coming glory of Messiah and His Kingdom.

Father, we also pray, in the name of Yeshua, for inner healing for all Jewish believers, particularly those from an Ultra-Orthodox background, who have been utterly rejected by their parents, friends, and loved one for their faith in Yeshua. We pray that You would lead them through inner healing and deliverance from all the traumatic wounds of persecution as they struggle to understand their identity in Messiah and establish their relationship with Him. We pray for freedom from all fear – fear of man, fear of assimilation, fear of persecution, fear of betraying past generations who have suffered at the hands of those calling themselves Christians. We pray that the FEAR OF GOD would overwhelm and silence every fear hindering them from bearing the reproach of Messiah and entering into the fullness of Your blessings upon them.

The Remnant

Praying the Scriptures is a powerful strategy of intercession and warfare. Nehemiah and Daniel prayed the promises of God back to Him and entreated Him to remember His covenant with His people. As we pray for the salvation of the House of Israel, focusing on the Ultra-Orthodox, we are praying for that remnant that will be preserved, tested and come forth as gold. There is a remnant chosen by grace (Romans 11:5), even an end-time remnant from the Euphrates to the brook of Egypt (Isaiah 27:12-13). God promises that He will lead His people into the wilderness of the nations where they will pass under the rod and be brought into the bond of the covenant (Ezekiel 20:33-40), and a spirit of grace and supplication that will be poured out over the house of David (Zechariah 12:10-14).

Along with the Isaiah, Ezekiel, Romans, and Zechariah passages, Isaiah 11 is a glorious chapter to pray revealing the promise of a BRANCH that would come from the rod of Jesse. It speaks of the coming millennial kingdom and the remnant the Lord will gather from all the corners of the earth (v.11). Pray these promises to the Lord and call forth the remnant that is chosen by grace.

Perhaps the most powerful prayer we could pray for the remnant of the Ultra-Orthodox is that Yeshua would anoint their eyes that they may see (John 9:11). We are all born spiritually blind even if we have natural sight, but when Jesus touches us, our spiritual eyes are opened.

Pray that the veil will be lifted that they may behold Yeshua as Messiah, Son of God, and God the Son. Yeshua took three of His disciples up to a mountain and revealed Himself in all His glory. Moses and Elijah joined Him discussing the work He would accomplish on Calvary. This experience for the disciples, though they would not understand it until much later, revealed Jesus as greater than Moses, greater than Elijah, even greater than angels, as the Book of Hebrews would later confirm. Pray for a revelation that the Name and Person of Yeshua is greater than any other.

The full inheritance of God for Israel is, above all, Himself, then a Land and a Kingdom they would possess, and nations they would inherit for His glory. The calling upon the children of Israel to be a light and witness to the nations was circumvented by the ultimate creation of Rabbinic Judaism, but we are living in the days of the restoration of all things!

Pray that the full remnant of Israel will return to the God of their fathers and to a personal relationship with God, through Yeshua. Pray that their identity will be rooted and grounded only in Messiah Jesus. Pray that this remnant would be freed of every hindrance to fulfill the high calling of God to proclaim Jesus to the nations and possess their full inheritance.

Call forth the Messianic remnant (that is already growing) and pray they will arise and bring the God of Israel and Yeshua to the nations. Pray they will lead the nations to discover and embrace their Hebraic roots (in the patriarchs and the prophets). Pray that the fulfillment of their calling will be "life from the dead" and release revival, new oil, and new wine around the world. Pray they will teach and impart a fresh anointing for intimacy, worship, prayer, prophecy, evangelism, and understanding of the Word of God.

The Book of Daniel contains some of the most powerful and revealing Messianic prophecies in the Bible. Pray Daniel 9:25-27 prophetically over the Ultra-Orthodox. Pray Daniel 8:19-25 and Jeremiah 31:31-37. These scriptures speak of the Messiah, the Anti-Christ, and the New Covenant. I invite you to pray these Scriptures aloud and prophetically over the Ultra-Orthodox and the whole House of Israel. Pray that the Lord will UNSEAL the vital truths of the Book of Daniel, especially those passages that speak of the Ancient of Days, the Messiah, and the Anti-Christ, and that a powerful revelation of the New Covenant will be released in dreams, visions, and personal visitations in these last days.

Glorious Restoration

The Bible says that Jesus must remain in heaven until the restoration of all things (Acts 3:21). We are living in these glorious days.

If we pray anything for the Ultra-Orthodox in these last days, let us plead with God to RESTORE HIS WORD as the ultimate authority of truth, wisdom, and revelation, His precious Word that has been lost and replaced by the Talmud and Kabbalah. Pray that His people will be moved with holy zeal to return to the God of their Fathers with all their heart. Pray that He will bring them to STAND at the crossroads, to recognize the strategic moment in history we are living in. Time is short and the days are evil. Soon and very soon we are going to see the King. Pray that the Lord will move upon them to ASK for the ancient paths, to earnestly seek Him with all their hearts, whatever the cost, for the way back to the faith of the fathers, to WALK in this pleasant way that leads to REST for their souls, along with precious intimacy, pure revelation from heaven, blessings from His generous right hand, and glory in His coming Kingdom.

Pray for the restoration of the fallen tabernacle of David, the anointing of David, and the heart relationship of this great patriarch. Pray that the Lord will give the Ultra-Orthodox a revelation of Eliakim as a symbol of Yeshua (Isaiah 22:22-25), both in His suffering, and in His glory. Pray for the raising up of the Tent Peg that will become a throne of glory in His father's house and will cleanse it of all defilement. Pray for the load hanging on the peg that has been firmly set in place by man to give way so that the captives may be set free and the new kingdom, the new wine, and all its blessings may flow unhindered.

Pray that every idol, every high place, every modern version of the Asherim, will be passionately torn down as in the days of Josiah. Pray, in the Name of Yeshua, that the three ruling spirits hindering the gospel from breaking through to the Ultra-Orthodox (the religious spirit, the rabbinic spirit, and Kabbalah) will be completely and utterly defeated and that the Name of Yeshua, the Rock of their salvation, will be exalted as the Chief Cornerstone. Speak "Grace" to the bringing forth of this marvelous revelation of the finished work of Messiah and the grace flowing from the Mercy Seat. Call forth the priestly kingdom, the spiritual Zadokites, the remnant of worshippers who will enter the Holy of Holies by the Blood of Messiah and minister to the Lord.

Pray for a revelation and restoration of the Names of God the Father (Yahveh) and God the Son (Yeshua). Pray that the Name of Father God will be restored to the Jewish people and to the Church and be made known to the world. Pray that the curse put on the Name of Yeshua (by changing it to Yeshu) will be broken, that the Name Yeshua ("salvation") will be restored and exalted in Israel. Ask Yahveh to give His people a REVELATION that Yeshua is not only Messiah, but Son of God, and God the Son, the Word made flesh. The Word of God says that we shall know the truth and the truth shall set us free (John 8:32). Pray that all fear and hesitation, especially among those who have been raised in Messianic circles, and the lie from Satan that it is virtually sin to speak the Name of God, will be broken and that there will come a freedom to call on His Name. Pray for freedom to pray to the Father in the Name of His Son from the heart, earnestly seeking for truth and intimate fellowship.

Pray that the wells of Chasidism that were dug by the Father of Lies and flow through the teachings of the Baal Shem Tov (and his later disciples) will be plugged up, sealed off, and forever silenced from their ability to supply any source of power or spiritual fulfillment to the Chasidim. Pray that the wells dug by the Talmudic teachings of the Vilna Gaon will be plugged up, forever dried up, and rendered ineffective in producing spiritual and intellectual fulfillment for the Mitnagdim.

Pray that the wells of Abraham, the father of our faith through a personal relationship with Yahveh, who was called to be a blessing to the nations, who saw Yeshua's day and rejoiced in it, will be reopened and begin to flow freely. Pray that the Ultra-Orthodox will return to the God of their fathers, fulfill the calling upon their lives, and bring a personal relationship with God to the nations through Yeshua, the Messiah.

Praise the Lord for His faithfulness, goodness, mercy, and lovingkindness. Pray for a double portion of blessing (Zechariah 9:11-17), anointing, healing, revelation, abundance, and fruitfulness in the Kingdom of God for the remnant of Israel. Pray that God will raise up His priests and ministers to the nations, according to His Word. Pray that everything the enemy has stolen from Israel, spiritually and physically, will be miraculously restored. Pray that all the glorious promises of Isaiah 60, 61, 62, Jeremiah 33:6-13, and Joel 2:18-27 will be fulfilled.

Behold the Lamb

The greatest spiritual gift that God will be restoring to Israel in these last days is the *Lamb of God*. Restoring the Lamb means restoring the significance of the Blood.

Pray that as John the Baptist exclaimed when he first saw Jesus, "Behold, the Lamb of God who takes away the sins of the world!" (John 1:29), the eyes of the Ultra-Orthodox will be opened so that this proclamation resounds in their hearts. Pray that even the children will be granted an understanding of the hidden mystery of the Afikoman, a Greek word, meaning "He has come!" The tradition of breaking a pierced matza in half, wrapping it in a white cloth, hiding it away for the children to find, and then bringing it back for "dessert" was likely established by Messianic believers in the first century.

If everything begins and ends with the Lamb, then praying for a revelation of the question asked by Isaac cannot be something that we pray only at Passover (Genesis 22:7b). It is key to breaking through the web of deception which keeps Yeshua hidden from their eyes and to the release of the hundredfold blessing that is yet to be realized in Mea Shearim. Pray that the Ultra-Orthodox, who claim to be more conscientious of following God's laws and truths than anyone else, will realize that they are uncovered without a sacrifice and that they will begin to cry out for the sacrifice and ask "Where is the lamb?" Pray that the Holy Spirit will visit them with a revelation of the greatest gift of mercy ever given to mankind.

Sources of Inspiration

The greatest source of inspiration for _Treasures of Darkness_ is the _Holy Scriptures_ (NAS, NKJ, & NIV). The Lord opened the treasures of His Word and subsequently led me to sources that confirmed what He was already speaking to me about the Ultra-Orthodox. My research encompassed books on intercession, Jewish history, Chasidic theology, Kabbalastic theology, and materials ranging from the history of Mea Shearim that were miraculously put in my hands, to articles in newspapers, days at the Israel Museum, as well as conversations and questions asked of residents in the Ultra-Orthodox community.

It is by the grace of God that this prayer guide is in your hands. I never planned to write a book and would have to say that a major source of inspiration was the many intercessors with a burden for the religious community who encouraged me to write (primarily in response to a series of prayer letters sent from Jerusalem). They urged me to share my experiences and insights into the Ultra-Orthodox lifestyle that developed naturally over the years of prayerwalking and getting as close to their world as possible. As I sought the Lord, He stirred up the desire to dig deeper into Chasidic thought so that I could share the key strongholds and diversions from the Word of God. I would caution intercessors against venturing into a study of this sort without the express permission of God, for His defined purpose, and assuring you will have plenty of prayer cover. It is for this reason that I am not giving specific references. If believers embark on a study of Chasidism and the mystical world of Kabbalah, it will not be because this book encourages it.

I am deeply grateful for the many prayers covering this project. The Holy Spirit was daily surrounding me and guarding my heart throughout the birthing process. The spiritual warfare was unspeakable, but I was given fresh strength and encouragement as a constant confirmation of His purposes and I am rejoicing in His victory.

If *Treasures of Darkness* inspires you to pray for the Ultra-Orthodox and creates a passion in your heart for the salvation of Israel, then the Lord will have done exceedingly, abundantly, beyond what I could ask or think with this writing.